Library of
Davidson College

Introducing Social Change

INTRODUCING

SECOND EDITION

SOCIAL CHANGE

A Manual for Community Development

CONRAD M. ARENSBERG
Columbia University

ARTHUR H. NIEHOFF
California State College

ALDINE PUBLISHING COMPANY
New York

Copyright © 1971 by
Conrad M. Arensberg and Arthur H. Niehoff

All rights reserved. No part of this publication may be reproduced or transmitted in any form or by any means, electronic or mechanical, including photocopy, recording, or any information storage and retrieval system, without permission in writing from the publisher.

First published 1971 by
Aldine • Atherton, Inc.
Address all inquiries to
Aldine Publishing Company
200 Saw Mill River Road
Hawthorne, N.Y. 10532

Library of Congress Catalog Number 78-149836
ISBN 202-01072-4

Printed in the United States of America

Second printing, 1974
Third printing, 1977
Fourth printing, 1979

Preface

The first version of this book was produced for technical change advisers working overseas. It was then believed that although much technical expertise was available in assistance programs, there was relatively little social science knowledge being used. Since that original version was quickly distributed, this purpose seems to have been partially fulfilled. To help meet the continuing demand, the first edition of *Introducing Social Change* was published in 1964.

Even before the first version was published, however, a new demand for the book arose. A need was felt for a text or study guide for courses in anthropology, sociology, economics, and communication, especially in reference to guided change in the developing countries. But while this demand has also continued, much new case material and other documentation about the guided change process has become available. We have continued our research in this field and have abstracted some new process variables of particular relevance from case history material. The basic research documents that describe this new material are listed on page 251. For this reason alone, it seemed appropriate to write a second edition.

In 1964, *A Casebook of Social Change,* prepared from some of the most useful case histories in the analysis mentioned above and specifically designed to be a companion volume to *Introducing Social Change,* was published. This new edition of *Introducing Social Change* will add to the usefulness of *A Casebook of Social Change* by describing all the variables.

Developments in the industrial countries, particularly the United States, have also demonstrated the need to revise the text. When the original version was produced, little thought or activity was being given to development efforts among the ethnic minorities of the industrial countries. Development was thought of almost exclusively as an activity relevant to the developing, nonindustrial nations. However, since the mid-1960s it has become apparent that ethnic groups in the industrial nations might also be in need of economic development, and government policies, including funding, have been increasingly pointed in this direction. And as had happened before in overseas programs, it became quickly apparent that sociocultural awareness was needed as well as technical expertise and funding. We have consequently attempted to reflect this new interest in the second edition.

Contents

Preface   v

Chapter

  1. Introduction   1
  2. The Concept of Culture   12
  3. Cultural Change   66
  4. The Change Process   82
  5. Motivation for Change   110
  6. Adaptation Techniques   131
  7. Secondary Strategies   161
  8. The Underdeveloped Areas   176
  9. American Cultural Values   207
10. Field Procedures   232

Recommended Reading   251
References   253
Index   259

1

Introduction

The Challenge

The development of industry in Europe and the United States has resulted in great marvels of production. However, the non-Western nations, with a few exceptions, have not yet shared fully in this productivity, despite the desires of their leaders to do so. Also, there are in the United States, and in other industrial nations, sizeable minority groups which have not been fully assimilated into the productive pattern of the majority. Most live as poverty enclaves within the greater society. This socioeconomic imbalance has contributed to unrest in both the agrarian and industrial nations.

To help create more stability in the world and a greater equality of sharing, the United States and other industrial nations have become involved in efforts to reduce such productivity differences. So far as their technological and financial abilities are concerned, the industrial nations of the twentieth century are in a very favorable position to make such an effort. However, they do have some disabilities, and a particular one is a lack of equally sophisticated social science knowledge.

Many groups of Westerners are involved in the work of technological change. There are government sponsored advisers directly concerned with improving the economic circumstances of poorer communities. Members of philanthropic foundations and other private organizations also are engaged in such work. There are businessmen who, although they may primarily be concerned with making profit, are still involved in assisting poorer communities because they can operate only where there is a fair degree of stability and where people can afford to buy their products. There are missionaries and church leaders who, although they may be primarily interested in disseminating their faith, are also necessarily concerned with assisting the local people in improving their economic lot.

It is true that new ideas and practices have passed from people to people in all ages and in all cultures until many have blanketed the earth. For instance, it is known that some of the plants domesticated by the American Indians, such as corn, tobacco, and potatoes, traveled around the world within three hundred years. Also, firearms spread very rapidly, being adopted by practically all peoples who learned about them and could get them.

In the realm of new ideas we know that democracy, although frequently modified, was adopted by most countries of Asia, Africa, and Latin America. Systems of religion also have traveled far from their countries of origin. Buddhism, which arose in north India, spread to all the countries of South and East Asia before it went into decline in its homeland. From the Middle East, Judaism, Christianity, and Islam were taken to all parts of the world, to hundreds of millions of people of all racial and ethnic types. Thus, if there is any generalization about the nature of man that is absolutely true, it is that he borrows new ideas and ways of doing things from his neighbor, irrespective of the neighbor's race or culture.

There are some differences, however, between the transfer of ideas in former times and those of the present century. Much, if not most, of the transfer of new ways in earlier centuries was not done deliberately. For instance, the American Indians had no intention to spread the seeds and techniques for growing corn and tobacco around the world, even though some of them were willing to show a few local colonists how these things were used. The worldwide spread was initially due to European explorers and travelers who, after learning how to cultivate and consume these products, carried them to Europe, Asia, and Africa. However,

Introduction

even in these regions, most of the spread took place from tribesman to tribesman or villager to villager, when no Europeans were involved. It was thus also with firearms, although the transfer was in the other direction. The Indians recognized the power of the gun by seeing some person or animal killed by it. They then tried to get the new device in every way they could and specifically to use it against the people who then had it, the Euro-Americans.

Social innovations have also spread by accident. Most of the leaders of African and Asian countries which now claim to be democracies picked up this idea of government in European schools. It is doubtful that most of the European powers during the colonial period desired that the idea of democracy, and specifically the concept of self-rule, be spread to the countries they were dominating. Indeed, many Asian and African leaders spent years of their lives in prisons because they proposed that democratic self-government be instituted in their own countries. But new ideas are not stemmed by putting leaders in jail for a few years.

The one set of ideas which Westerners deliberately have tried to give to others in earlier times was Christianity. The Christian missionary has tried to transfer his idea of the supernatural to people of other cultures and religious beliefs since the beginning of the Christian era. But with this exception, there has been no large-scale organized effort by Westerners to give other nations their ideas.

The verb "give" has been deliberately used because *there have been deliberate efforts* by Westerners to change people of other countries or newly absorbed minority groups earlier than the twentieth century. But the process in such instances has depended on force rather than voluntary acceptance. European colonial powers and the United States imposed changes on groups under their domination for a variety of reasons, from genuine desires to assist in the economic improvement of the subject peoples, to out-and-out economic exploitation. Indeed, the modern nation-state continues to try to change its people, whether from minority or majority groups—through legal punishment—every time it develops a new kind of legislation. But regardless of the motives in such instances, the changes are not based on voluntary acceptance.

Since the end of the colonial period and World War II there has been a much greater emphasis on the spread of new ideas and techniques through voluntary cooperation. When working in other countries, the Western technician, whether a government employee, a businessman, or a missionary, cannot enforce his presence or impose his ideas if the local government officials do not want him there. Moreover, even with minority enclaves in industrial countries, voluntary participation is now the rule. Legal enforcement is still used to obtain compliance in general government policies, but cooperative participation is usually relied on in programs to improve the socioeconomic condition of the minority people.

A final difference in contemporary change is the expected time required. Because nonforced change in previous centuries was not undertaken deliberately, it often took long periods of time. Thus, three to four thousand years elapsed before new food growing techniques spread from the Middle East to northern Europe. And even such a basic technique as metallurgy, though known by some peoples by 3000 B.C., had not spread to all peoples of the world by the twentieth century. Today, socioeconomic change is expected to take place rapidly. Planners in the development field think in terms of years or at most in decades—not in centuries. The less developed countries of the world expect new food growing and processing techniques to become effective within their "five-year plans." Although hardly fulfilling the hope, the 1960s were known as the "decade of development." In industrial countries, even community development and other change programs of the inner cities are expected to come to fruition within a year or two; otherwise, government funding usually is cut off.

It might seem that a superior technique of growing a crop, healing the sick, educating the young, or organizing a cooperative would automatically be accepted by those lacking such techniques. If the time required were of no significance, or if the new idea were imposed by law, these practices would probably be accepted in time, although most likely with some modifications. However, if the changes are to be accepted voluntarily in a relatively short time, considerably more effort is required other than merely explaining or demonstrating the new ideas to the potential adopters.

Introduction

One "cause" for this larger requirement is that the transmitters of new ideas—the technical specialists, the community developers, the medical corpsmen, in other words, the change agents—may well have systems of customs and beliefs which differ in significant ways from those of the people they are trying to influence. Such customs and beliefs constitute the culture of each group of people; and *understanding the cultural system of either group can mean the difference between success and failure in introducing new ideas or methods.*

Any sensitive person who has observed development efforts in agrarian (developing) countries, or more recently in poverty pockets of Western countries, can relate instances when technically superior ideas failed to be accepted by local people, primarily because their customs were not understood by the change agent/technicians. Two such instances from Asia will illustrate this type or problem.

A number of years ago an American company drilled several deep wells for the benefit of villagers in Laos. The villagers were well aware of the advantages of a constant source of clear, cool water, and were quite happy to stop using the water holes and intermittent streams which had been their mainstay up to that time. However, within two years almost three-quarters of the newly drilled wells were no longer operable. Most of the villagers were unhappy about the situation but claimed they could not repair the pumps that had been donated. It was later agreed that although the repair job was not very difficult, some source of advice and parts was needed. The well drillers had not concerned themselves with the problem of maintenance, nor had they assigned any responsibility either to individuals or organizations for keeping the wells in repair. The drillers had worked through the traditional headman of each village, but in Laos this office has only limited authority. The headmen had assumed little responsibility for the wells.

By chance, in a couple of villages the wells had been drilled in Buddhist temple grounds. When visited later, it was found that they had been repaired when broken, and even the area around them had been kept clean and neat. The Buddhist monks, who had taken the responsibility in these two instances, probably had far more respect and ability to organize the villagers than did the traditional headmen. If all the wells had been put on Buddhist temple grounds, there might have been far fewer maintenance problems. A respectful attitude for, and a willingness to cooperate with, Buddhist monks is a part of the culture of many Southeast Asian countries; a knowledge of this, combined with a technical improvement (a driven well) might have contributed to project success. The technical improvement alone, except for the two accidental instances, proved to be a failure.

Another example of project failure resulting from a lack of understanding of the customs and beliefs of a people, in this case ideas of ritual purity, is reported from India (Fraser, 1963: 96–98). The American change agents in this instance attempted to introduce a system of sanitary latrines in a rural village complex. To the Americans, latrines would provide a definite improvement in sanitary conditions. However, these technicians were not aware that the concepts of public health on which they had based their project decision were not shared by the Indian villagers. The traditional village beliefs did not include the notion that germs were carried by flies picked up from fecal matter.

Furthermore, the latrines as devised by the Americans were inconvenient. The women had to carry extra water for flushing them and the men needed to return from their fields (a long distance) to use them. The women particularly objected because, according to traditional custom, they went on little expeditions to gathering places of other women each day, for elimination. These trips were highly prized because they enabled the women to relax and gossip, as well as take care of their bodily functions.

Probably most important, however, was the fact that these Indian villagers regarded human excrement and anything that had been in contact with it as very defiling in a ritual sense. Merely washing with soap items that had been thus contaminated would not remove this ritual pollution. They consequently regarded latrines as centers of defilement and were reluctant to have them near their houses.

The change agents had introduced the latrines with the assumptions regarding public health and sanitation that existed in the United States. Failure to get the Indians to accept them was due primarily to lack of knowledge of the villagers' work habits, social interaction, and belief system—all parts of the local culture.

Introduction

These examples of unsuccessful attempts to introduce new ideas have been cited, not because no successes are recorded, but because more learning will occur through the study of failures. There are many change agents who deal successfully with peoples of other cultures, usually by means of good intuitive judgment, but there are probably larger numbers who have not been able to surmount the cultural or subcultural barrier.

It is here suggested that *the insights for crosscultural interaction must be lifted, through study, to a conscious level.* The brain surgeon must use his best judgment for each operation, but this judgment is based on much prior study of the nature of the human body, the characteristics of infection, the uses of various drugs, and all the other aspects of medicine which an M. D. must have apart from his precise technical specialty. In the same manner, the social engineer—government technician, private foundation representative, missionary, or businessman—should study the nature of human society and culture before he begins to administer new ideas, which are the "medicine" of social change.

This book will attempt to assemble the basic cultural factors which should be understood if new ideas or techniques are to be successfully introduced to people of other cultures. It is not presented as a series of exact answers to specific problems, but it is proposed to serve as a guide for thinking out problems of contact and cooperation with peoples of local communities. The ultimate purpose of the book will be to stimulate the change agent to be sensitive to cultural problems.

The change agent requires more than his technical specialty to accomplish the job of guided cultural change successfully. Moreover, although many of his contacts will be officials, either in foreign countries or in poverty programs of the home country, the change agent's main concern must be with the people who he hopes will accept the new ideas—the rural villagers, the poor townsmen, or members of ethnic minorities. *Knowing the elite or government officials is not enough.*

In addition to knowing as much as possible about the culture of the people he hopes to work with, the change agent needs to have an understanding of the nature of culture contact in general: how and why people of different cultures borrow ideas from each other. He should also know something about the processes of industrialization and Westernization, since much of the relations between Western countries and the developing nations of Asia, Africa, and Latin America are products of the forces that were released during the period of colonialism and subsequent industrial urbanization. The ideas of democracy and scientific rationalism in the world today also are legacies of this period.

The sensitivity of the change agent should include the ability to perceive *what is really possible* for the local people. He also needs to become an effective communicator, learning the advantages and disadvantages of the different ways messages can be transmitted and understood. And he needs to understand some basics of motivation—what causes people to want to change their traditional ways of doing things.

To bring about true lasting development, the change agent needs to distinguish between the froth of passing events and the deeper, more persistent habits and patterns which mark a way of life. All peoples have enduring institutional patterns and cultural habits that are often carried through many generations; they can survive modernizations, political upheavals, and the swings of fashion. For instance, the posture that Egyptian farmers assume in cutting grain today is the same as that depicted on the wall painting of ancient Egyptian tombs; and in India an attitude of veneration toward the cow is recognizable in the *Vedas,* the ancient sacred literature of the Hindus. Since those early times, many dynasties and different forms of government have risen and fallen in both countries and now both countries are striving toward industrial modernity. Yet old patterns persist.

If the change agent wishes to introduce a new idea that will permanently fit into the local cultural pattern, he must consider reworking and adapting it to local conditions. In general, a change will be accepted if it provides some real advantage and does not grossly conflict with local cultural norms. But even so, it will need to be cast into a form somewhat different from the original.

Neither this book nor the social sciences on which it is based can give exact directions for solving each specific kind of project problem. There is no complete body of facts about the lives and habits of each of the diverse peoples of the world or of the the thousands of change projects that have taken place. Moreover,

Introduction

socioeconomic change is taking place constantly and in many places quite rapidly; the local customs and ways of thinking of one decade may be out of date the next. Also, the social sciences are rapidly increasing their knowledge in the field of applied sociocultural change. So, what this book can try to do is to instill an approach, a sensitivity, and some general principles for the solution of cultural problems in technical change. Primarily, it can show the change agent how to search out the local customs into which the innovations can best be blended.

The Social Sciences

Knowledge about the different peoples of the world, their ways of living and thinking, and their social institutions, is being gathered, evaluated, and analyzed by several scholarly disciplines. No one of them explains everything about man and his culture, although they tend to complement one another, each explaining a different aspect of man's way. Those most immediately relevant are the following:

1. *Anthropology,* particularly in the division known as *cultural anthropology* in which the varieties of peoples and cultures of the world are studied and compared, and especially the group patterns that constitute total ways of life.
2. *Sociology,* in which the forms and processes of group life and social relationships are studied, particularly through analysis of institutions. Most study of group patterns in sociology has been of Western societies.
3. *Psychology,* particularly in the division of *social psychology* in which the nature, role, and learning process of humans are studied, together with the effects in behavior and attitude resulting from the individual's group membership. Like sociology, social psychology has traditionally been most concerned with Western man's behavior.

Although the social sciences above are very important for an understanding of the cultural characteristics of different peoples, they are not the only disciplines concerned with the study of man.

Such fields as *economics, political science,* and *history* are concerned with specific kinds of human behavior or study man in particular contexts. However, these areas of study are much more likely to be covered in traditional training programs. There is little doubt that he who wishes to understand human affairs needs to know something of the history, economics, and political events of the poorer countries, and the ethnic minorities of the industrial countries. Unfortunately, the usual curriculum in these subjects today is inadequate for providing information that will facilitate introducing new ideas to poor communities. There is thus a definite need for the cultural, interactional, social sciences.

Anthropology was chosen as the discipline around which this manual was organized because it has concerned itself more than have the other disciplines with the study of non-Western or minority peoples and with an understanding of the whole way of life of a people. This broadness of approach perhaps enables anthropology to be more helpful in organizing the relevant data supplied by other disciplines and in providing a comparative outlook. The field procedures of anthropology were primarily developed for discovering and describing non-Western ways of life as quickly and directly as possible; and the concepts of the discipline were developed to provide an understanding of these diverse ways.

Organization of the Manual

The manual is divided into ten chapters, as follows:

1. An introduction to the cultural problems of change in general.
2. A description of the concept of culture, man's unique achievement which was responsible for his dominance over all other animal species and enabled him to expand to all regions of the earth. This includes the effects of race, language, and environment on cultural development, as well as the main components of which a cultural system is constituted.
3. A discussion of cultural change in its various forms, both directed and undirected, and whether it has depended on coercion or voluntary participation.
4. An introduction to the process of directed change, and one

Introduction 11

of its most critical requirements, effective communication techniques.

5. A discussion of the motivation necessary to bring about change, including both direct and indirect advantages.

6. A treatment of the method of adapting an innovation to existing ideas and customs, such as patterns of leadership, social organization, economics and beliefs.

7. The change process is discussed further, treating such secondary strategies as obtaining participation, being flexible in project implementation, utilizing timing effectively, following though continuously, and establishing means for maintaining a new practice.

8. A profile of the primary characteristics of most agrarian (developing) nations.

9. The main characteristics and cultural values of America as a sample urban, industrial culture, primarily to encourage the change agent to develop some sensitivity of his built-in biases.

10. Field problems of the change agent, and in particular those methods from anthropology that can be modified for his use.

2
The Concept of Culture

Biological Drives

Man, like all other animals, has certain biological requirements. In former years a great deal of man's behavior was attributed to "instincts," or biological drives. Certainly, like other animals, man does have a biological make-up which includes a number of "drives." But it has been widely recognized in the last several decades that the specific behavior of man, although beginning with these biological needs, is very strongly altered by each social group through the training of its young. To consider man's behavior as a simple product of instincts is an oversimplification and denies *the very essence of man-ness,* which is *patterned behavior produced by learning.*

There are still widespread ideas based on this old way of thinking. A common one is that a given people is "naturally" lazy. In recent decades many middle class Euro-Americans have regarded the Amerindians as lazy because they did not take the initiative to improve the land or homes on their reservations, or to better themselves in the usual middle class way. However, such an opinion ignores the fact that American Indians worked strenuously and intelligently in the labors that were necessary for survival in their pre-Colombian cultural patterns. It also ignores the fact that the reservation Indian usually does not have the training or opportunity to get the kinds of jobs available to the middle class American in modern society. And perhaps finally it should be stressed

The Concept of Culture

that the modern Indian probably does not have the same goals as are general in the Euro-American population. The "laziness" that does occur is more probably a result of the Indian having lost his original cultural values without substituting the Euro-American ones. But the situation is a product of cultural change (military defeat and economic exploitation), not any instinctive or "natural" quality.

The same is true of other characteristics often attributed to people of other cultures when they are claimed to be instinctively (or more commonly nowadays, "naturally") religious, or aggressive, or peaceful, or hard-working, or overly sexual, or other. Aggressiveness, leading to warfare, has sometimes been claimed to be a natural characteristic of man. It is impossible to deny or affirm such an instinct as a primary "cause" for warfare. Almost all animals have some aggressive tendencies, particularly in relation to sexual activities, and one could safely assume that man does also. However, some human societies approve of warfare while others approve only of peace, and children are consciously and unconsciously trained to admire the warrior or peace lover. For toys they can be given either guns and tanks, or tractors and derricks. Anthropologists have thus concluded that the specific degree and kind of aggressiveness or religiosity or sexuality of a people is a product of cultural training and thus is subject to change.

In sum, since man is an animal he shares certain needs with them. Those accepted by most anthropologists are quite basic and limited in number. Such "drives," common to all animals, must be satisfied by all societies. They are the need for food and water, for protection from the elements, for rest, sexual relations, social recognition, and perhaps for territory.

The ways different cultural systems can exploit and control these drives are numerous, but some way must be found. Thus, the sexual drive is related to perpetuation of the group and a whole society must permit it in some form, although it is clear that no society permits complete freedom of action in the activity. Part-societies, such as religious orders which prohibit sexual relations of their members, can exist only because the greater society of which each is a segment, permits sexual activities and continues to provide recruits.

But for all the biological drives there are wide ranges of possibilities. For example, take the need for social recognition. In a relatively rich industrial culture such as that of the United States, a man will work hard in order to buy a series of large, expensive cars which he will use not only for transportation but also as symbols of status. A man of a hill tribe in Southeast Asia, not being familiar with nor able to afford such an expensive item, will nevertheless try to save enough from his meager resources to buy a pair of ivory ear plugs. He will pay the equivalent of thirty to forty dollars for them, which will show others that he too is successful in terms of his own culture. Social recognition can come from having been on an important religious pilgrimage (the *hajj* for Muslims); or, until the extensive influence of Western feminism, in many societies it could come from having several wives; or from being a dedicated party member in a Communist country.

Although procreation, the need to reproduce young, must be fulfilled by all cultures, the basic act which causes it, sexual intercourse, can be and usually is controlled in a variety of ways. There are cultures that permit considerable freedom of sexual conduct for women as well as men, especially before marriage. The island cultures of the Western pacific had sexual codes of this sort. Some of the modern Israeli kibbutzim also permit considerable sexual freedom. Other cultures, such as those of the Middle East and South Asia, tend to be very restrictive in their codes about women's behavior. Even such a sexual taboo as incest is by no means constant. In some cultures certain kinds of first cousins are the most desirable marital partners while other kinds are absolutely forbidden. Nevertheless, despite the different rules in different societies, all cultures recognize the need for the male-female union and arrangements are always made to permit this activity and even to reward it socially.

Man's Unique Achievement

Homo sapiens begins on an animal base and certainly shares the basic drives with other animals, but he has achieved an entirely different manner of adapting to life. Physical evolution has permitted all animals to develop specializations of great variety and

The Concept of Culture

has enabled the different species to adapt to a great diversity of environments and natural conditions. They have developed fins with which to swim, wings with which to fly, fangs and claws with which to kill, and long, slender legs with which to run swiftly. Different species have been able to adapt themselves to life at the bottom of the sea, near the tops of mountains, in lush rain forests, and in arid deserts.

The changes in animal form have been physical specializations, inherited through the genes. They have fitted particular kinds of animals to particular kinds of conditions. This has enabled each species to survive well under those particular conditions; but there has also been a disadvantage to such physical, genetic change: each animal has been required to follow the kind of life its body was built for. A lion does not have the capacity to convert itself into a vegetarian. Neither its claws nor teeth are suitable for gathering grass or chewing it. The deer is not capable of becoming a meat eater because it has no way to kill other animals efficiently or teeth to tear meat apart with. Man, on the other hand, can change his diet from vegetarian to meat-eating or vice versa with no bodily change whatsoever.

How does man have this capacity of nongenetic change that other animals lack? First, it must be emphasized that man did pass through evolutionary physical changes, just as did the other animals, and probably still continues to do so. We know that he went through several million years of changes until, in his modern physical form as Homo sapiens, he inherited the earth. This is the physical creature we know today, an animal with an unspecialized body, standing erect, with hands free, specialized eyes, and a very large brain in proportion to the body. It is believed that these particular physical changes, working together, permitted man to develop a new kind of adaptation to living, one that at least during the last one million years seems to be more advantageous than the physical specializations that the other animals continue to depend on. With his accurate eyes and efficient hands, man has been able to make tools in place of the specialized body parts of the other animals. He has learned to fight and kill without fangs or claws, to race over land without being swift-running, to fly without wings, and to cross great bodies of water without fins. Moreover, he has learned to speak and, with the words he has invented, to communicate his ideas freely. Man became a tool-making animal with the ability to communicate his ideas and thus to build from one invention to the next. He became a knowledge accumulator, the inheritor of experiences from all past generations. Man's unique achievement was the development of learned patterns of behavior which in the broadest use of the term is what we call *culture.*

Learning Culture

Culture is the sum total of what individuals learn in common with other members of the group to which they belong. Basically, it is what an individual has learned from the people who reared him, most of which they learned from their elders. Cultural knowledge also includes what the individual learns from his fellows and from his teachers when they formally or informally pass on group knowledge. And although tool-making is the most specifically human behavior, culture includes much more. All kinds of group learning and behavior are included, such as the customs men have developed for living in groups harmoniously, the ideas they have of deities and the supernatural, and the beliefs they have of what is noble and good.

An example of learned behavior is the custom of shaking hands to establish a relationship of friendliness. This is a part of Western cultural patterns which seems "natural" to an American or European. To most South and East Asians it is not natural at all because they were taught to bow at the waist or to hold their palms together near the face while bowing the head slightly. Such customs are so deeply ingrained in the individual that often he is not aware that they have significance only in his own culture. Europeans and Americans have taught the educated class all over the world that handshaking is the proper way to establish cordial relationships, despite what particular practice may have already existed to serve that function. The official symbol used to mark American aid overseas is a pair of clasped hands painted on the side of a jeep or on a crate containing donated American equipment. Undoubtedly, the American who devised this insignia in-

The Concept of Culture

tended it to symbolize brotherly friendship. However, to most Asians, clasped hands must have strong associations with European or American dominance. The habit was learned from colonial masters in these countries. The majority of Asians, the rural villagers will use their own forms of greeting when at home or among themselves.

Beliefs about the supernatural are a part of culture. The devout Westerner tends to believe that religions are exclusive patterns of ideas. His culture has subdivided the supernatural world into "religion" and "superstition," the latter being ideas of occurrences beyond the normal that the "religious" person does not believe. There is no idea that many kinds of supernatural beliefs could be held at the same time or by the same person. To most Buddhists, Hindus, and followers of other Far Eastern religions, there is not this idea of exclusiveness. There is room for all kinds of deities and spirits in the belief system. But this too is a cultural difference, imparted to the Asian and Euro-American respectively in their learning process.

Specific cultural behavior and ideas are learned and passed on from one generation to the next. This idea is essential to understanding the concept of culture. Other animals learn individually from experience and can pass on a portion of what they have learned to their young, but only by demonstration or in an immediate situation. For instance, meat eating animals teach their young some hunting techniques. Mother foxes are known to bring animals they have caught to their dens where the cubs learn to kill the crippled animals. Later, the adults will take the young out on hunts where they can learn the parents' techniques through observation. Dr. Goodall, in her recent study of chimpanzees in the wild, indicates how the young watch their parents insert blades of grass into anthills to withdraw the termites which are hanging on. The young try to imitate the older animals but are very inefficient. Eventually they learn, however (Miss Goodall, 16 mm film). The point, in regard to both the foxes and chimpanzees, is that learning is very inefficient—primarily because these animals cannot explain anything. They do not have symbolic languages.

Man is the single species which can pass on information about situations before they are encountered. If foxes had symbolic languages, with words that stood for things and ideas, they could explain to the young cubs where to go and what to do to find and catch gophers, instead of compelling them to go along on hunts. With a similar system, the adult chimpanzees could gather the young in a circle and explain in detail what variety, length, and stage of maturity of grass blade to be used before the young started the trial-and-error process of learning. Only man can simplify and organize the experimentation of his young with the world. He can pass on information from persons whom he has never seen and information that was gathered through time when he did not live; and the stream of information he will pass on will go to persons in the future that he will never know. Man is the "time-binder." Unlike other animals, he has, through his culture, the experience of the past and even the ability to project to the future through scientific predictions and religious prophecy.

It is generally believed that most human behavior is learned in the process we call enculturation. In simplest terms, this process is the transmission of the cultural group's customs and beliefs by means of reward and punishment. Each infant is subjected to such influence into early adulthood. The language, the way of eating, the kinds of foods, the value system, all are transmitted to the young in the growing-up process. A child of Euro-American parents who spent his infancy and childhood with a Chinese family would grow up to be culturally Chinese. In language, ideals, preferences, even in the way he walked and held himself, he would be Chinese, a product of the thought and behavior of those who had reared him.

During the frontier wars with the North American Indians, a number of Euro-American women and children were taken captive. The Indians treated them like other Indians, thus enculturating them into their way of life. American soldiers and settlers made strenuous efforts to "liberate" such "captives" on many occasions, but were often amazed to find that the Indian enculturated "whites" regarded themselves as Indians and felt little sympathy for the way of life of their liberators. The biological background of these people was of little consequence when weighed against the enculturation process.

And though it became fashionable in the 1960s to stress the

The Concept of Culture

racial integrity and uniqueness of ethnic minorities in the United States, the reality of enculturation applies to them also. The American Negro may resemble the forest villagers of the Congo or Nigeria, who are part of his biological ancestry, but he has relatively little in common with them except his appearance and a desire to re-establish cultural contact. In living in the Americas, individuals of Negro ancestry have gone through an enculturation process, through many generations, in which their African culture was replaced for the most part by the Euro-American tradition. If, by a different set of historical events, Euro-Americans had been taken to Africa as slaves and several generations had been enculturated there, their ancestors would today be culturally Africans. The American melting pot is indeed one of the most convincing kinds of evidence of the power of learned behavior. People from all races have been absorbed into the "great tradition" irrespective of their cultural backgrounds.

Culture and Race

In the most basic physical sense it is true that *all men are alike and that differences between groups do not exist.* What this means in biological terms is that all men presently living and the great majority of those who have lived for the past 40,000 years have belonged to a single species, Homo sapiens. Men from any group can interbreed freely with women from any other and produce fertile offspring—one of the main criteria for establishing a single species.

Yet despite this oneness, any observant person knows that groups of people do differ in appearance in different parts of the world and often even in the same region. Most of us feel sure we can identify a "Negro" or an "Oriental" or a "White." It is probably not as easy as we think, particularly when we get into the area of mixed ancestry. For instance, it is well known that considerable numbers of people with some African ancestry have "passed" as "Whites" by getting their hair straightened and having other cosmetic treatment when this was a desirable kind of social action. Now, when American "Blacks" are more concerned with stressing their African ancestry, they face the opposite problem. Many of them have such light skins, due to the Caucasoid part of their ancestry, that they would find it difficult to "pass" as Afro-Americans were it not for their hair. The genetic dominance of kinkiness in hair evidently remains long after skin color changes due to racial mixture. So the emphasis on the "Afro" hair style is seen, in which kinky bushiness is frequently the only physical characteristic which indicates African ancestry. The phrase, "Black is beautiful," refers to an ideal much more than to an actual skin color.

And yet there is a difference between people, especially when they are in large population blocks in different continental areas. If a person boarded a plane in New York City, and landed first in Accra, Ghana, and later in Taipei, Taiwan, he would surely notice basic physical differences distinguishing the people who were milling about in the two airports, and that they would also look different from most of the people in the New York airport.

Men have long been aware of variations in physical appearance between different groups; so it was probably inevitable that when the Western sciences of anatomy and physical anthropology developed in the nineteenth century, there would be efforts to subdivide the peoples of the world on the basis of their physical appearance. In the classifications that were developed, a great variety of traits were used to describe the different groups of men, of which the most common were stature, body, head and nose shape, hair texture and color, and skin and eye color.

The idea of "race" was first applied to the large look-alike groups of people who were relatively easy to distinguish from comparable groups, each being native to a particular region of the world. Thus there were the Caucasoids of Europe, the Negroids of sub-Saharan Africa, and the Mongoloids of East Asia. However, there were still large numbers of people who did not fit these categories well; also, there were considerable distinctions within some of the groups. Thus, the people of India were more like Europeans than any other people except that they were not very "white."

The term "white" is, incidentally, one of the least accurate descriptive terms existing in the popular vocabulary. Physical anthropologists have long abandoned it because it is so imprecise. The only individuals who have truly "white" skin color are al-

The Concept of Culture

binos, and they can come from any group of people, including those of African ancestry. What is popularly called "white" is a combination of pink and tan. There is no single word in English which clearly describes this color. Cosmeticians use the term "flesh" or "skin color," meaning simply the color of nonsunburned Caucasoid skin. However, the term "white" has been taught to so many people all over the world, that even African and Asian people accept and use the term to refer to light tan skinned people of European ancestry. That is what they learned either from their schoolmasters or in popular conversations in their own ethnic groups. The terms "yellow" and "black" for racial distinctions also were abandoned long ago by scientists because of their inaccuracy. What are popularly thought of as members of the "yellow race" are also truly tan or light brown colored people with ancestors from East and Southeast Asia. Even "blacks," particularly Afro-Americans, tend as a group to be more dark brown or tan than black. A "black" mayor in one Los Angeles suburb has very light skin and blue eyes!

In the popular mind, Negroes are thought to be characteristic of Africa, but a large number of people who are very similar physically, the Melanesians, live in the Southwest Pacific. Also, there are very tall Negroes in East Africa (the Nilotic peoples), and extremely short ones (the Pygmies and Negritos) in Central Africa, the Philippines and Malaysia. Moreover, the Caucasoids of northern Europe, such as the Swedes, are different in appearance from southern Europeans, such as Italians and Spaniards. Because of these variations within the "continental races," the smaller groups have been classified by some anthropologists as "subraces" with such names as Nordics, Alpines, Mediterraneans, Pygmies, and Forest Negroes.

Because of the difficulties in classifying varieties of men, many anthropologists in the last twenty years have abandoned the effort to establish clear-cut types based on physical appearance. Such scientists now prefer to talk about gene pools where a population group statistically shares some physical characteristics which are highly impervious to environmental influence. Needless to say, most of the old criteria for racial classification does not fit this requirement. One of the most popular genetic traits now used is blood type. In this area too, the various blood type groups parallel those with different physical appearances in only a vague way.

Concentration on genetic characteristics also serves to prevent misunderstanding the phenomenon of bodily change occurring in response to socioeconomic changes, such as diet. In the old classification system, body build and head shape were used for racial traits. However, it has since been found that these characteristics will radically change in one generation if the diet of the population is improved.

What does this mean? It means that so far as physical characteristics are concerned, the idea of "race" as a clear-cut, unchanging, observable type is no longer popular in anthropology. There is considerable argument as to how a racial group is to be defined. However, the main "continental races" of the past are still generally accepted, as are many of the subgroups. The terms Negroid, Caucasoid, Mongoloid will be used where applicable in this book, but referring strictly to the observable physical characteristics. The popular terms based on skin color—white, black, red, yellow, brown—will not be used. Where there are groups of indeterminate or ambiguous racial background, but who have some kind of cultural base in common, the ethnic term of origin or residence will be used, such as Afro-American, Euro-American, Asian, Brazilian, Thai.

Interest in the physical differences of human groups grew in the eighteenth and nineteenth centuries when the tropics were colonized and an international slave trade became established. The people who were colonized, enslaved, or exploited economically were of a wide variety of physical types, but the majority of them were darker than most of the Europeans that were doing the exploiting. But it is hard to understand the interest in physical differences by these Europeans unless we consider another of their characteristics: their need to moralize. Christianity, the dominant religion of Europe, insists that the actions of its followers be morally just. Moreover, it fairly clearly implies that men are equal—at least "under God." So, Europeans who were intent on exploiting darker skinned peoples economically felt the necessity for providing a moralistic explanation. What was simpler than biological or "racial" inferiority? Explanation was offered that the darker skinned people were not equal to the lighter skinned people and therefore their different treatment was to be considered morally justifiable.

Slavery was, of course, not invented by Europeans. Men have been exploiting other men, often through slavery, since the earliest of civilizations; but racial differences were not always used as a justification for such treatment. The early civilizations came closer than do modern cultures to recognizing that differences between groups of men are primarily cultural. They tended to divide people into categories of "citizens" and "barbarians." Barbarians were usually people who did not know the "civilized" way of doing things, rather than those who had different physical characteristics.

The idea of racial inferiority was first used to justify European domination of dark skinned people in colonial possessions, including those in bondage. Americans, having a European cultural legacy, continued the idea. And although slavery did not become established in Europe, the idea of racial quality remained there also and partially contributed to the onset of World War II in the Nazi theory of the Aryan "master race."

It seemed that ideas of racial inferiority or superiority would have been abandoned as potentially dangerous, and yet they have remained among many significant world groups. Certainly not all Euro-Americans have abandoned "racist" concepts, although this way of thinking seems to be much weaker than it was thirty years ago in this ethnic group.

What is more disturbing is that a reverse tendency of "racism" has appeared and seems to be growing. The darker skinned peoples who were once accused of being inferior racially by "white racists" are now claiming that their ancestors have achieved great things because of their race. They are using the same kind of argument the "white racists" used but merely turning it around. For instance, in the teaching of the Nazis, all great achievements of mankind came from the Aryan master race. Now, one hears much about the achievements of the "Black race" or peoples of other kinds of skin color.

In a recent proposal for a Black studies program it was claimed that there were such things as White history and Black history, as if the skin color of peoples was the primary determining characteristic for their behavior. This thinking ignores the influence of culture and cultural change. The Nazis argued that a person of German ancestry would be permanently stamped as a German and would be loyal to the ancestral land no matter where he migrated. The most significant disproof of this idea was in the hundreds of thousands of young American men of German ancestry who willingly fought in the American army and contributed to the destruction of the Nazi empire in World War II. Their ancestry had practically nothing to do with their attitude toward Germany, since they were Americans by culture. The Japanese-Americans too had committed themselves to American culture even though Euro-Americans put many into relocation camps.

So when darker skinned people claim to have a black or brown or red racial integrity, they are ignoring the effect of cultural change and implying that there is something special about darkness, just as the Nazis claimed that blondness and fair skin were associated with superior attributes. There is little evidence to be derived from anthropology to support either claim.

Groups of men do differ in a general way in appearance. East Indians can usually be distinguished from northern Chinese, and most Swedes can be separated from most central African Negroes. However, these physical differences are merely a means of distinguishing groups visually and would have little significance except for the addition of the idea that the mental ability of the different groups also is different. The crux of the older racist theories was that darker skinned people were inferior in mental ability.

Most of the "scientific" information which purported to prove this inferiority has been derived from intelligence tests in the United States. The greatest body of this information was intelligence tests given to soldiers newly inducted into the army. As a group, Afro-Americans made lower scores than did Euro-Americans. It was later shown, however, that Afro-Americans from northern cities had higher scores than those from the rural South and even rural southern Euro-Americans. More recently, studies of Afro-American children have shown that those born in northern cities do better on IQ tests than those born in southern rural en-

The Concept of Culture

vironments. Despite the early conclusions about the lower mental ability of Afro-Americans, later information has seemed to show that environment is at least equally important. Few would disagree that these people as a group have had poorer schooling and poorer opportunities for advancement than have Euro-Americans as a group. Thus, it has been concluded by most social scientists in the last twenty years that intelligence tests do not really measure innate ability any more than what the individuals have learned. Another problem with such tests is that they tend to favor the group which devised them; that is, they measure the kind of knowledge that is valued in the culture of the test designers. Therefore, people of other cultures or subcultures, who may have other kinds of knowledge or skills, will come out second best because their kind is not included in the tests.

The general conclusion that has been arrived at through anthropological research is that *there is no evidence to prove that any group of people differs systematically from any other in mental endowment.* Within all groups there seems to be about the same range of human abilities. That the majority of great men have appeared among Euro-Americans in recent centuries can be explained more easily on the basis of opportunity rather than racial background. The potentially great have had more chances to fulfill themselves if they grew up in a Euro-American country than if they matured in an African or Asian land. If we consider why no African Columbus discovered America, a simple explanation is that no African culture then had ships capable of making such a trip.

Not only have anthropologists concluded that no differences in mental endowment among groups have been proved, they also think it is unlikely that hard evidence will be produced to prove this idea in the near future. The fact is that inborn intelligence is so deeply entangled with the effects of education, opportunity, and social environment, that separating them by psychological testing would be extremely difficult.

One of the best arguments against the idea of innate superiority of one group over others is provided by a brief look at man's cultural history. In the past 400 years Europeans have been in the ascendancy in technical and political developments, mainly as a result of the industrial revolution and the expansion of Europeans to other parts of the world. However, before that time, civilization had been advanced by people of other racial or subracial backgrounds. The Sumerians (who lived in the area today called Iraq), Egyptians, Hindus, Persians, Chinese, and Arabs developed mighty civilizations and contributed significantly to the base on which Europe's industrial revolution was built. There is a long list of achievements and inventions from these peoples which we use today. Some of the more important are the domestication of animals and plants; the wheel; the smelting of copper, iron, and steel; the solar calendar; the zero and the place numeral system; irrigation systems; gunpowder; the magnetic compass; writing systems; and printing.

The American Indians, who in earlier times were considered too often as "uncivilized savages," also have contributed a great deal to world culture. Their main achievement was in the discovery of useful plants. A large share of the world's crop production is of plants originally domesticated by the Indians, the most important of which are corn, beans, cotton, tobacco, potatoes, cocoa, and cassava (tapioca).

Sub-Saharan Africa has often been cited as the continent where little in the development of man took place. Although in recent centuries this area has not been a center of civilization, it now seems probable that the first faltering steps toward "man-ness" took place there some two million years ago. The South African "ape-men" (*Australopithecus*) now seem to have been the first creatures to develop the bases for culture, tools, and a symbolic language. In sum, the differences in cultural development throughout the world appear to have been influenced very little by the physical characteristics of the people.

Even though the subdivisions of the continental stocks are difficult to characterize by physical appearance, and even though no mental inferiority has ever been proved, a notion of "race" continues to exist in the world. In fact, the concept has even been reinforced recently by certain groups. Over the centuries most old, inbred populations have developed recognizable types that can be associated with a common culture. "Look-alike" types have emerged, sometimes of several varieties. For example, in Ireland,

The Concept of Culture

where florid redheads, swarthy "black Irishmen," and blue-eyed, fair brunettes (the "colleen" type) are common, a black African, a tan, black-haired Punjabi, or a Mongoloid Japanese would look different and "un-Irish." Also, certain racial mixtures, along with some kind of cultural or subcultural pattern, can create a racial type in the popular mind. Thus what today are referred to as "Blacks," or Afro-Americans, are mainly a mixture of Negroid and Caucasoid physical stock which has a common history of slavery and economic exploitation, along with some few African cultural survivals. It must be reiterated that there is no necessary relationship between the physical appearance and behavior of different groups, even though this idea has continued in the popular mind. Thus, it is not more "natural" for Irishmen to eat potatoes and believe in a universe dominated by an exclusive god (Christianity) than for Japanese to eat rice and profess belief in a system which claims no deity (Buddhism). What these people do is a product of their cultural history, not what they look like.

There seems to have been a tendency recently to stress physical differences or similarities for political or social advantage. Thus, politicians in India and the Middle East have stressed their racial brotherhood with sub-Saharan Africans, although physically both are of Caucasoid physical stock. But it was of advantage to use skin color and ignore other physical differences, to promote cooperation in the Afro-Asian bloc. Although Asiatic Indians have little in common with Africans except their recent history (both groups were colonized by Europeans) and their present economic status (agrarian rather than industrial), the twentieth century political tie has been of some usefulness.

On the other hand, on the island of Trinidad in the West Indies, where Africans were first brought as slaves and Indians were later brought as indentured laborers, there has been a considerable amount of economic and social friction between the two groups; thus, they stress differences in physical characteristics. In other words, people of the same racial ancestry can have entirely different attitudes toward people of another racial ancestry where the economic and social conditions are different.

Racial feeling enters a society when some members isolate themselves from others with distinguishable physical characteristics and assign social rank on this basis. Such racial attitudes are learned in some cultures and never learned in others. In New Zealand the native Maori were subjugated by British colonizers but are now treated as full citizens with little prejudice by the majority. Hawaii has often been noted as the "melting pot of the Pacific," where people of European, Japanese, Filipino, Chinese and Hawaiian ancestry live together with relatively little ranking of superior or inferior groups. On the other hand, we know that ancestors of the British and Dutch who settled in South Africa established a very formal system of racial ranking in their policy of "apartheid." Also, Euro-Americans in the continental United States continued some ideas of racial ranking from the slave period. In sum, racial bars still exist in the world but they appear to be steadily less significant since the end of the colonial period and as the Western concept of "inalienable rights irrespective of race, creed, and color" spreads.

Attitudes toward other groups of people vary from country to country and, although they may be related to physical characteristics, the bases for distinction are usually economic or social. The change agent will have to learn the bases of distinction in the social group where he is working. Thus, in the countries of Southeast Asia—Laos, Thailand, Burma—the population is usually of two types: the hill tribes and the dominant people of the valleys. There are also significant numbers of more recent immigrants, particularly East Indians and Chinese, who live in the cities or lowlands. The majority population of these countries may note some physical differences between the groups (Chinese with the lightest skins and mountain tribesmen with the darkest), but the primary distinction in their minds will be based on customs and language. Thus the Thai, Chinese, and hill tribes of Thailand all have languages of their own, their religious beliefs are distinct, and many of their social customs are unique to their people.

In other countries, the distinctions have no racial basis and may even lack language differences. Thus, the Muslims and Hindus of north India cannot be distinguished by physical appearance and they speak the same basic language, even though two names (Urdu and Hindi) are used. Basically, they are distinguished from

The Concept of Culture

one another only by their writing systems (Arabic and Devanagari) and their religious beliefs.

In Latin America, there are people of African, Amerindian, and European ancestry; and there are some physical differences distinguishing these groups, even though there has been much intermixture. However, people in these countries are most often divided into groups according to their social and economic position rather than their physical characteristics. In general, people of European ancestry are in the most favored classes; however, when individuals of Amerindian or African ancestry achieve the same education and wealth, they tend to be accepted as equals by the Euro-Americans. This is particularly true in Brazil (Wagley, 1952). Thus, even when the terms *indio* and *negro* are used, they tend to signify the social status of the individual more than his ancestry.

There is no logical correlation between race, language, nationality, or culture except that people who live near one another over long periods of time tend to interbreed (racial mixing) and learn one another's languages and customs (cultural mixing), particularly if they become part of one national unit. Thus, two groups of distinct racial stocks—Negroids and Caucasoids— after living in one national unit—the United States—for five to eight generations, can end up by sharing the same language and culture, even though in slightly different forms. Afro-Americans with poor, rural backgrounds, tend to have a dialectic form of English which, although it may make then sound different, does not keep other Americans from understanding them.

However, if social barriers are kept high, different racial stocks in the same nation can retain their distinctiveness, both racially and culturally. This is true of the Bantu and Euro-Africans in the Union of South Africa. A people can be of the same race and even share the same nationality and language, while being separated from another group by not much more than religious beliefs (as with the Hindus and Muslims of India and Pakistan). All combinations are possible and occur in one part of the world or another.

It is culture, not physical differences, that ultimately defines social status. The change agent should be prepared to recognize, understand, and work within a framework of some kind of group distinctions, since these are the norm for mankind despite the Western philosophy of egalitarianism. Some such distinctions and subordination are usually present; it must be learned on its own terms.

Environment

All animal species except man have managed to cope with their environment primarily by means of physical specialization. To move to new surroundings, such as from the temperate zone to the Arctic, has demanded of the species the growth of dense fur, thick down, or blubber. Such change in an animal type can occur only through genetic mutation—an irreversible process that requires a long period of time. This kind of adaptation, though it may well be suited to specific conditions, by its very success reduces the possibility of other kinds of change. An animal that is well adapted to Arctic conditions (for example, a polar bear or a walrus) is completely incapable of surviving in a desert or tropic forest.

In contrast, the human animal, man, has developed a completely different method of responding to his environment—a method that is neither one-way nor dependent on genetic mutations. The development of *culture* has been the unique human way of adapting to different environments. This body of learned behavior provides man with many alternative solutions to the problems of survival which are teachable in a single generation to any creature capable of speech and tool manipulation. There is no requirement for genetic change in the human body for adapting to a new environment.

Thus, in moving to the Arctic, man too must solve the problem of cold temperatures; but the solutions will vary according to the cultural knowledge available to the different groups. Man's answer to cold weather has been warm clothing, closed structures, and various heating devices—all a part of his technological knowledge, not his physical constitution. The Eskimo, the Chukchi of Siberia, the preindustrial Scandinavians, and industrial Euro-

The Concept of Culture

Americans have successfully met this challenge in different ways. The Eskimo invented snow-block and semisubterranean houses, the Chukchi drawstring felt bags to be used as tents, the Norwegians moss-chinked log cabins with iron stoves, and modern Americans concrete and steel structures heated by furnaces.

Such kinds of cultural adaptation are cumulative. Each generation can build on the knowledge of the previous generation, or can borrow ideas and techniques from neighbors. This knowledge is not transmitted through man's genes but through his learning abilities, his eyes, his ears, and his touch. The possibilities of adaptation have increased so much through the development of culture that man has been able to cover the earth regardless of climatic conditions—an achievement matched by no other species except a few parasites to man himself, such as the mouse and rat. By the twentieth century the only regions of the world that had not been claimed as habitations by man were the Antarctic, the tops of the highest mountains, and the depths of the seas. In all three of these remaining regions, man is working strenuously to develop adaptation technologies. But his most impressive recent effort to develop adaptation techniques has been for survival in space. Just as the once tropical animal, man, took his tropic environment to the Arctic, now the earth animal, man, takes his earth environment to other solar bodies.

Man not only adapts to specific environments, he changes them. While animals may change their environment to a limited degree, their effects have been insignificant compared to those of man. Man has burned the vegetation of the prairies, denuded forests on a continental scale, deliberately changed the course of rivers, created large lakes, turned fertile land into deserts, turned deserts into fertile land, produced artificial rainfall, and even created great clouds of gas over his largest settlement areas, the cities.

And although we often think that man's influence on the environment is only recent, there is indirect evidence that he has been affecting it a long time. There are places in Asia which have been under cultivation so long and so intensively that botanists cannot specify the original wild vegetation. Also, it is believed that man literally cut out the forests of Europe with stone and iron axes 4,000 to 5,000 years ago, and the Sahara desert appears to have been greatly enlarged by men who allowed their goats to eat the vegetation on its margins.

Man's ability to cope with environmental variation has been very successful compared to that of other animals, although he has not been able to divorce himself from environmental limitations. If the technological level is simple, the environment limits possibilities greatly. Thus, in a harsh climate, such as that of the Arctic or the Kalahari desert of South Africa, people with simple technologies have been able to work out specialized hunting techniques which permit survival. However, such a dependence on gathering wild foods does restrict the possibilities of further cultural elaboration and practically precludes a civilized, urban way of life.

Although the environment of a given area may impose limitations, it does not determine a particular level of development. The possibilities of adaptation increase as the technological level becomes more complex. In the Kalahari desert the Bushman barely manages to eke out an existence hunting wild animals and gathering wild plants; yet the same land could be made fertile with an adequate irrigation system. The Eskimo of Alaska managed to survive by hunting sea mammals and caribou; today the industrial technology of the Euro-Americans has permitted the construction of cities, an increase in population, and the exploitation of natural resources, such as minerals, fish, and timber, much more fully than was possible with the Eskimo's level of technology. It seems now that Alaska and the adjacent area of Arctic Canada will become one of the major oil producers of the world, bringing to the surface a mineral which the Eskimo hardly knew existed, much less having the technological capacity to use it.

Similarly, in Southeast Asian countries, such as Thailand and Burma, the lowland people, who have a technology and social organization which permit them to dig drainage and irrigation canals, can exploit the rich river valleys. The tribal people in the hills of the same countries eke out a much poorer existence, cutting down forest patches to grow dry rice which is much less productive than the lowland's wet rice.

There are, of course, serious disadvantages in the unlimited elaboration of technologies and exploitation of the natural envi-

The Concept of Culture

ronment, as those in the industrial countries are now too painfully aware. Man's technology can be such a powerful force that without control it might even make the environment uninhabitable. But although pollution is an extremely serious problem, it does not negate the real achievements of man's cultural exploitation of the environment. However serious the air pollution in New York and Los Angeles, few people would prefer the precarious existence of tribesmen such as the Kalahari Bushmen or other hunters.

The same environment can support a variety of cultures and economies, depending on the technoligical knowledge of the people. In the semiarid plateaus of Arizona one finds five different subcultures side by side: Navajo shepherds, Hopi gardeners, Spanish-American villagers, Mormon farmers, and Anglo ranchers. These different groups exploit the same environment in different ways. Conversely, a relatively uniform culture, especially its technological system, may cover both mountains and plains, many countries, and a variety of languages, as in western Europe. Thus, we can state that *environment limits culture but does not determine it.*

In the southern part of the world there are countries dominated by mountains, forests, oceans (island areas), savannas, and deserts. In different ways, according to their level of technical knowledge, local peoples have adapted to the local conditions sufficiently for survival. But since their technological knowledge is less than that in the industrial countries, their patterns of adaptation contain more environmental limitations. However, Euro-Americans who go to tropical countries from their own cooler climates can easily read more influence into environmental limitations than is justified. They often feel less energetic and frequently attribute this to the effect of the heat and/or humidity. Also, the ordinary citizens of tropical countries may appear to work less than similar people in European or American countries. It is thus easy to conclude that the climate is affecting them negatively and has retarded cultural development.

Moreover, if one maps the developed regions of the world (industrial nations) except for one, Hawaii, all are found in mid-latitudes (Shannon, 1957: 2–11). This might seem to be a good argument that the climate (at least, the temperature) is directly responsible for lack of development. However, it is necessary to investigate other possible explanations. It can be argued that people in the nonindustrial countries work less because the economies are relatively poor and there is not so much advantage in working strenuously. This view is supported by the fact that people with opportunities for advancement in such countries—business and professional people—very often work as hard as similar Americans.

Also, it should be realized that different work rhythms are possible. There may be some different arrangement of time for labor and rest which are better suited to the tropics. There is no reason to believe that the pattern worked out in the cooler latitudes will naturally be best in all regions. Farmers in the tropical countries usually work quite hard during the growing season. They tend to start with the earliest light, work until late morning, eat and rest until mid-afternoon, and then work again until near-darkness. The mid-day rest period is probably quite sensible; the early and late afternoon are much cooler and many Americans and Europeans have learned the usefulness of the mid-day siesta. The European or American who has an air-conditioned office in Bangkok, New Delhi, or Lagos cannot honestly compare his working habits with those of the Thai, Indian, or Nigerian who works in the hot sun or in a very hot, closed shop in the local bazaar.

Thus, there may indeed be a real need for some adaptation to tropical conditions by the northerner, especially in change of work habits, because he is not only in a different physical climate, he is also working (at least to some degree) in a different cultural climate. He may attribute some of his frustrations to climatic conditions. But it must be remembered that Americans and Europeans who have lived for many years in the tropics find no more difficulty to work there than do their counterparts at home. They have adapted to both the physical and cultural climate.

The question still remains as to why the nonindustrial countries are almost all in the warm zones while the industrial ones are in the cooler regions. To gain perspective on this question we need to look back into geographic history. The Renaissance, European expansion to the tropical world, and industrialization are events of the last 500 years only. Thus, those countries which are now

The Concept of Culture

called developed, except Japan, are places where the majority of the population is of European ancestry or where European colonists remained as permanent settlers to establish the dominant technical and social life patterns. In Canada and the United States the native Indians constitute only a fraction of the population, and even the Afro-Americans make up less than ten percent in the two countries. The three countries of South America which are classified as developed according to their standard of living and participation in the world economy (Argentina, Chile, and Uruguay) have populations of predominantly European ancestry; the Indian population has long been eliminated or absorbed. In those sub-Saharan countries of Africa which are classified as developed (South Africa and Rhodesia), the majority is non-Caucasoid; however, it is the minority of European ancestry who came to these countries as permanent settlers and established the economic systems, with a dual standard of living, the highest for themselves.

In the Pacific region Hawaii, New Zealand, Australia, and Japan are classified as developed. However, modern Hawaii, although it has a widely diverse population, was developed by continental Americans and its pattern of technological and political life was integrated into that of the United States. New Zealand and Australia, like the United States and Canada, are countries where European immigrants came and established economic and political systems similar to those in their homelands. The pre-European populations were absorbed. This leaves only one country—Japan —which was developed (industrialized) by non-Europeans; and it is in one of the cool regions of Asia.

It can be argued that this distribution of developed countries signifies that Europeans who resettled chose areas of the world which were similar to their native countries. The Japanese have proved only that race is irrelevant. It is possible that if the industrial revolution had taken place in India or the Middle East, the developed areas of the world today might be in the warm zones, with a technology suited to these regions.

The popular view of development is a short-range one, that of the last 500 years. Anthropologists have been looking at man's cultural history with a much longer view and they have learned that most of civilized life during the past 7,000 years was centered in the warmer regions of the earth, if not in the full tropics—in the Middle East, India, Southeast Asia, China, and subtropical areas of the Americas. The basic inventions which were listed earlier, produced by darker-skinned people, occurred in these areas. Northern Europe achieved very little of technological significance until the close of the Middle Ages. And even the achievements that did take place in the industrial revolution were based on developments from the warmer zones of the previous 7,500 years—the wheel, domestic animals and plants, the solar calendar, decimal mathematics, writing systems, printing, the compass, etc.

In sum, it is probable that the difference between the poorer and richer nations is no more a matter of climatic differences than of race. It is rather a product of cultural development, which is largely independent of either physical differences or climate.

Language

Spoken language is inseparable from the total cultural pattern of a people. Intelligent beings might have invented some other basic form of communication but man has devised only this one. And it is so essential to his way of dealing with the universe of natural events and other people that it is difficult to conceive of the most primitive form of human existence without it. The facts of ethnography support this idea in that no group of people has been found anywhere in the world who did not have a spoken language.

Most simply defined, a language is a system of sounds in which each vocal unit represents an idea. Thus, the concept of "horse" may be indicated by the sounds *cheval, caballo, ghoraa, maa,* or "horse." And the marvelous nature of the system is that however arbitrary the particular sounds are, anyone who speaks the same language can use that particular set for discussing this creature without even being in its presence. It is a completely different sort of communication from that of other animals.

Since man transmits almost all his ideas through his particular language, each generation gets its knowledge in these terms. Thus, the continuity and growth of any cultural system are directly de-

The Concept of Culture

pendent on its language. Even cultural change requires this communication vehicle before it can permanently be made a part of a system. In order for new ideas to spread within a cultural system, or from one to another, they must be verbalized, which means incorporating them into the language. Such highly specialized, rapidly changing professional activities as modern medicine are very directly dependent on the evolution of a new vocabulary. Without the printed books (frozen vocal messages) and verbal explanations of the senior surgeon, the young intern would never be able to absorb the knowledge necessary to perform the delicate operation himself. Simply watching the older man would never provide enough knowledge.

A language is inextricably linked to all aspects of a culture. Probably nothing more clearly distinguishes one culture from another. In fact, a separate branch of linguistics has been developed to provide analysis based on this idea. It is called ethnolinguistics and attempts to describe a cultural system primarily on how the universe is described in the individual language. The proponents claim that a culture can be described primarily as a system of word classifications.

Writing systems are frequently confused with spoken languages, although from the linguist's point of view writing is strictly secondary. However, the writing form can make a common language seem completely different. So far as the spoken language is concerned, Hindustani and Urdu of north India and Pakistan are merely separate dialects. Visitors from India in Karachi can speak Hindustani to local Pakistani merchants and be understood with no difficulty. However, these same Indians could read the language only in its Hindi version, a writing system derived from Sanscrit; the Pakistani merchants, on the other hand, read their version of the language in Urdu, an Arabic derived script. The same distinction exists with Bengali in the Indian province of Bengal and East Pakistan.

Spoken forms of languages represent what is actually happening in the culture much more closely than do written forms. Unless a writing system is changed periodically, it tends to become conservative and reflect spoken forms of a previous age. There are in English, and in many other European languages, silent letters which actually were once pronounced; although the spoken language has changed and these sounds dropped, they remain in the written form. Also, languages change through the use of slang (spoken form) but it usually takes some time before slang terms are permitted in the written form. However primary the spoken form of a language may be, the written form is very important in modern life, particularly because it enables men to keep ideas in an unchanging medium and expedites the process of cultural information transfer (education). The growth of the scientific method and the development of highly trained specialists have depended largely on the development of writing systems.

However, people in literate societies have been subjected to the written form so early in their lives that they sometimes tend to overemphasize its importance. *A system of writing is merely a technique applied to a spoken language in order to give it a visual form.* It does not in itself make that language superior to one which is not written. A culture which does not have a written language or in which the majority of people are illiterate does not suffer because the language is inferior but because communication is much more difficult. It simply takes more energy to contact the same number of people by the spoken word than by the written word.

Language has sometimes been singled out as an explanation for the backwardness of certain cultures. It has been implied or stated by such popular theorists that some languages are incapable of transmitting the ideas necessary for modern, industrial life. However, based on the research of the last eighty years, linguists and anthropologists have concluded that the potential of communicating all ideas exists in all languages. In a less technically developed society there may be difficulty in expressing many technical ideas because of a paucity of vocabulary which in turn is the result of there not having been need for such words. Languages appear to become elaborate when there is a cultural need for such elaboration. When such Oriental languages as Japanese and Chinese were used for expressing ideas developed in industrial cultures, there were some initial difficulties. Now, however, after borrowing heavily and changing their forms to a minor extent, they serve as perfectly adequate vehicles for modern industrial-technical culture.

The Concept of Culture

It has been said that generalizations were not possible in "primitive" languages. However, the consensus among anthropologists is that the specific kind of generalization made in a language is really a reflection of what parts of the universe it selects to be general about and what parts to be specific about. And in this sense, one language seems to generalize as much as another, although in different areas of occurrence. For instance, the Eskimo language has been described as having a large number of specific terms to describe snow rather than one general term as in English. This characteristic makes sense when it is realized that the different forms of snow affect the lives of the Eskimo much more specifically than they do an American. A blizzard spelling deprivation or isolation, a precipitation indicating warmer air and the beginning of spring, travel by dog sled, travel by snowshoes, building houses, and various forms of hunting—each is associated with a different kind of snow. It is important to be able to specify these in words to the visiting hunter or the family members planning the next day's activity.

For devices which they may see but which are not intimately associated with their lives, hunting people may have but a single term, while the language where the item has been developed may have many specific terms. Thus, Eskimo hunters may have but a single word for an airplane, while an American will be aware of the large number in his language, both for the different kinds and parts of the machine. But to the American snow is indicated by only one word.

What this means is that each language reflects that which is important in the culture and can change rapidly either by the invention of new words or by borrowing them outright from other cultures. Thus, machine terminology will enter the Eskimo language when the Eskimos start using snowmobiles extensively.

There is one very popular topic of conversation about languages, particularly by those who have tried or who are planning to try to learn a new one; and that is, whether some languages are intrinsically more difficult to learn than others. This can be best answered in two ways. First, it should be stressed that all languages are learned by all normal children with reasonable proficiency by the time they are six years old. Moreover, this accomplishment has nothing to do with the child's ancestry. Although a child born and raised in China usually learns a Chinese language first, and a child born in north India usually learns Hindi first, this is only by coincidence. The Indian child would learn Mandarin just as easily as Hindi if that were the language he heard when he grew up.

The second observation to make about the relative difficulty of different languages is that one with a great similarity to the speaker's original language should be easier to learn than one less similar. If a person's original language is tonal, he should be able to grasp a new set of tones more easily than someone whose original language ignored tonality. However, none are insuperable. Some people do learn languages easier than others, but the difference in amount learned is more often due to a different degree of application than to a lack of "ear." Anyone who doubts this view need only look to the overseas Christian missionaries or the more recent young political missionaries, the Peace Corps volunteers. They assume from the beginning that they will learn the local language—and, except for those who stay in the cities or with English speaking peoples, they do.

In sum, language is undoubtedly the most important key for understanding another cultural system, and primarily in its spoken form. Also, being able to speak the local language or dialect to some extent provides a very important means of getting along with the local people, who feel well disposed toward someone who has taken the trouble to learn the core of their communication system.

Technology

The technology of a people is their major means of adjusting to the environment. In fact, language and technology are the two most basic characteristics of human culture. Which came first is still being debated and will never be known for certain. It probably does not matter very much. Most believe that the first attempts to make crude tools occurred at about the same time as the first attempts to create words. It is fairly clear that tool making without language communication would hardly allow for the development of tool traditions and thus accumulation of techno-

The Concept of Culture 41

logical knowledge. Too much of the knowledge gained would die out with the death of the inventor if he had no efficient means to transfer it to other people. Language provides that means.

Despite the problems created by uncontrolled development (pollution, population expansion), the one clear indication of man's success as a species has been in technology. Different religious beliefs, value systems, ways of organizing human relationships, and systems of production have been developed by men during their two-million-year history and it is possible that there has been some progressive change in these parts of culture. But it is next to impossible to prove the superiority of one religious belief or one economic system over another, which is why we can spend so much time and energy arguing the issues of "communism vs. capitalism" or "arranged marriages vs. free choice of spouses." Such arguments make no sense in the field of technology, and they are not heard. It is not possible to argue the merits of a stone axe as compared to one of steel for cutting down trees, or of a bow and arrow as compared to a firearm for killing animals or men. The steel axe and the gun obviously do the job better and the simplest demonstration will prove this.

There are no people in the world who do not recognize the advantage of improved technological methods or devices. The same people who will resist a new system of political organization (communism, capitalism) or a new religious belief (Christianity, Islam) will be much less likely to show resistance to the new technological device (the outboard motor, the bus, the firearm). In a few instances a superior technology may be rejected due to conflicts with other customs in the culture. But the more usual reason for lack of adoption of advantageous new ideas is simply lack of understanding of their value or lack of means to acquire them. American farmers were reluctant to adopt hybrid corn when it was first introduced in the 1930s. It did not look as impressive as the old varieties and required the adoption of several new practices to be successful. However, there were a few early innovators in each community whose success quickly demonstrated the value of the new kind; within about ten years the hybrid varieties had replaced the nonhybrid forms almost everywhere.

The same has been true of such items as metal pots and pans

and guns throughout the tribal and peasant cultures of the world. They were adopted whenever people learned about them and had chances to get them. Outsiders may admire the beautiful artistry of the native pottery, but the local people know too well how easily it is broken compared to the pot of cast iron or aluminum. And the primary reasons that villagers in Asia, Africa, and Latin America do not have more guns is that they cannot afford to buy them or the government restricts their ownership. The cost of a gun to a villager is so great in parts of Africa that muzzle loaders (Dane guns) are still being made and used. It is not that these villagers do not recognize the superiority of the high velocity factory-made rifle or shotgun, but the cost of this device and shells for it are simply beyond their financial resources.

In a few recorded instances, tribal people adopted technical devices superior to those they had before but which were ultimately detrimental to the whole cultural system. The adopters were too impressed with the technical advantages to assess the other influences. The Maori of New Zealand are reported to have decimated their own people in intertribal warfare once they obtained guns, which they sought most eagerly (Lizitsky, 1956: 206–207). In Australia a tribe of aboriginals is described as falling apart because the members adopted steel axes to replace those made of stone. Steel axes became available through Christian missionaries and the urge to replace the stone ones was too strong to resist; those tribespeople who had the opportunity acquired the steel axes. From their immediate point of view, they obtained a superior implement for cutting wood. Unfortunately, the stone axes had functions which the steel ones did not have. They were an integral part of ritual life; they were the most valued possession and principal manufacture of the older men; and they were a very important trade item with other tribes. When they were replaced by steel axes, which could be obtained and possessed by anyone, which were not included in the myths and ritual life, and which were obtained from missionaries instead of through trade with other tribes, much of the old way was lost. In fact, people began to doubt their rituals, women and young people ceased to respect older men, and intertribal trade fairs went into decline. It was suggested by the anthropologist who studied these people that the culture disintegrated so rapidly because the social and religious life of the people became so weakened (Sharp, 1952: 69–81).

Of course, there are some new ideas of a political or religious nature that ultimately cause a culture to perish, but the cause and effect is usually more difficult to prove. Also, conflicting social or supernatural ideas may be quickly rejected because people are more emotional about them, which in turn may be a result of the fact that their advantages or disadvantages cannot be clearly proved. Although the Maori, the Amerindians, and practically all other tribal people quickly adopted the guns of the Europeans, they were by no means so interested in the donors' political ideas. In fact, the Maoris, the Amerindians, Zulu, and numerous other tribal peoples used this newly acquired technological device against other tribal peoples first, and later against the suppliers of guns, the Europeans.

The same divided reaction existed among most Western social reformer/critics in the 1960s. They attacked ideological and social systems without being able or willing to do without the technology of industrialization. Systems of social control (police) were attacked, but without any suggestion of doing away with guns or weapons. Dissidents adopted the technological devices that formerly were the province of those in power: the microphone, loudspeaker, electronic bullhorn, newspaper, and television. But they were ostensibly using the technical devices produced by the industrial society to bring it down or to change it. And even while they accused "the establishment" of producing pollution and overcrowding, they traveled with relative freedom on the freeways and in the vehicles which produced the noxious gases of the urban complex. It is easy to reject the social and ideological aspects of the industrial state, but it is much more difficult to do without its technical products.

Because technology is so basic to the survival of a culture, it is the kind of activity in which men show the most "rational" behavior. Rational, objective knowledge is necessary for even the most basic kinds of technical efforts. In order to grow a grain crop, a peasant farmer must know a series of techniques. He must know when to plant the crop, how to prepare the fields, which fields to use, what kind of seed grain to plant, how to irrigate, and when and how to harvest the ripe grains. This is not to say that he will not also use religious beliefs to help bring the rains or to drive away the insect pests. His ideas of the supernatural will temper and complicate his "rationality." But his technology will be practical and based on his observation of nature. It was indeed this practicality that enabled him as an inheritor of his cultural system to work out the successful adaptation to the region's environment.

Economic Organization

With the exception of a few marginal types, man is everywhere a social animal. There is leeway for some hermits or religious ascetics in every society, but only in small numbers. If they were abundant, the society would not reproduce itself.

In order for groups of people to live together without constant friction, some rules, arrangements, moral and ethical codes to govern the dealings of one person with another are necessary. One of the most important kinds of social convention that man in all stages of culture has been required to develop is what is called an economic system. Most simply stated, it is a set of beliefs and rules which makes possible the production, distribution, and consumption of the things produced with the technological knowledge of the culture.

The complexity of a given society, which is based largely on the level of technology, will primarily determine the complexity of its economy. A people with a simple hunting and gathering technology will produce little surplus or variety of goods, which will minimize the need for much trade. In addition, because of their limited type of production, they will have little need for individual ownership of land, specialized workers, true money, markets, and a host of other economic features that those in industrial economies take for granted. Even in peasant societies, where the majority are agricultural producers, a number of features that exist in urban, industrial economies may be lacking. Such peasants will have pronounced attitudes of landownership, even holding on to land which is noneconomic. There will be some specialized

The Concept of Culture

workers and most products will be available through money purchase. However, the bulk of goods produced will be for direct subsistence rather than for the market. The concept of an hourly wage scale for labor given may be lacking; the direct profit motive may be weakly developed; and many economic relationships may be based on kinship and social cliques. These differences, however, are relative rather than absolute.

Much of the economic behavior of people who are not in the mainstream of industrial societies may not appear rational to Westerners because no clear-cut profit motive is obvious. People buy gaudy, expensive clothes which they "cannot afford," or give lavish feasts or parties to neighbors, or build "monuments" to make their small countries distinctive. Within the total social system, such behavior may be more "rational" than it first appears. Better understanding might be obtained if the idea of reward—and even more specifically, social reward—is substituted for the idea of immediate profit. The individual everywhere has a need for food, clothing, housing, and sexual gratification. However, these needs do not have to be immediately or individually satisfied. Immediate, individual satisfaction may well destroy the possibilities of long-term security, which is a need most peoples also recognize.

For instance, hunting and gathering peoples try to emphasize generosity and even conspicuous giving, which seems to make considerable sense for groups with such primitive technologies. Peoples such as the Bushmen of South Africa and the Semang of Malaya tend to share the products of the chase with one another. Since they do not have good methods of storage or of accumulating capital that can be liquidated in time of need, their economic insurance is the goodwill of their neighbors and relatives. Each individual may be primarily concerned with his own family, but the long-term insurance for that family will come through generosity within the group. And not only can the giver depend on future benefits of a material nature (a share of the receiver's catch), he can also obtain prestige and be considered a generous man—a comodity that also can be cashed in.

Many tribal peoples, such as the Maori of New Zealand, the New Guinea highland tribes, or the northwest coast Indians of

Canada, formerly indulged in elaborate feasts for social benefit, both to the individual and the group. The New Guinea tribesmen slaughtered many pigs and roasted great piles of yams, while the Indian groups gave away and destroyed large quantities of fish oil. To the outsider, the feast may have appeared to be wasteful, but the feast givers knew they were gaining prestige and followers. This kind of behavior differs only in degree from that of the politician in an Asian or African country who gives a big meal to peasant farmers if they will come to town to vote, or to the American businessman who gives a case of Scotch whiskey to his clients at Christmas.

The peasant communities of the world often depend on kinship relations as their form of economic insurance. They usually do not trust banks and other financial institutions controlled by city dwellers. A man is expected to stand behind his family and relatives, who are usually more numerous than those which compose an urban family in an industrial society. Young men are helped by older men in financial affairs, but their loyalty is expected in return. Also, the men of middle years are expected to help their younger brothers and sisters as well as more distant relatives. The family will thus stand, rise, or fall as a unit. It is in its way an insurance corporation based on kinship. This social unit has proved of great value to the individual and the whole society on a peasant-agrarian level, although it may create problems when Western ideas of economy are introduced. In particular, an individual profit motive will cause difficulties. The individual is not particularly stimulated to change his ways in such a system, particularly if it means more work, because added wealth will only mean more relatives to support.

It is almost inevitable also that where kinship is strong, people will expend a considerable amount of their wealth on family ceremonies, particularly for marriages. It is no accident that people in the societies of Asia, Africa, and Latin America will spend considerable amounts of energy and money on marriage, while Americans and northern Europeans will spend less. To Americans and northern Europeans, kinship relations are really not very important. But to the Asian or African, such relationships are quite important and thus the binding together of different families

The Concept of Culture

through marriage is vital; consequently, the ceremonial and financial aspects of the institution must be treated seriously. Thus, the extended relationship unit becomes an insurance corporation of considerable importance.

Even persons in the industrial nations are not psychologically at ease to work for nothing more than immediate profit. In the socialist-oriented industrial countries, the state provides many forms of security in jobs, health, and for old age. In the capitalist-oriented countries, such as the United States, there also has been a growth of state security provisions, but in addition there has been a tremendous growth of commercial insurance buying. An insurance policy is mainly designed to provide the security that immediate profits cannot guarantee.

Another important form of human endeavor which is not purely "economic" is found in ritual and religious efforts. In Latin America, the Buddhist countries of Southeast Asia, and the Hindu and Muslim world of South Asia and the Middle East, people expend considerable amounts of effort and money on fiestas, fêtes, *bouns,* pilgrimages, and religious fairs. In Laos the easiest way to motivate the working class people to community effort is through religious festivals. Westerners, with their ideas of efficiency and separation of work and play, tend to be critical of such affairs. However, more understanding will be obtained if in evaluating such "uneconomic" activities in nonindustrial societies, the function of the behavior in the total culture is considered as well as any possible alternatives. Because a fiesta has the elements of a county fair where everyone has a good time, it has considerable social significance in places where entertainment facilities are limited. Furthermore, since people are working and spending money for religious ends, they are receiving another kind of reward, the psychological satisfaction of believing that they are establishing good relationships with their gods or saints. This is a need which most Westerners will not deny even though they tend to consider religious and secular affairs as separate kinds of activity. But there has never been any proof that the separation of church and state has really increased the productivity of Westerners, much less their personal life satisfaction.

In sum, the economic behavior of other peoples differs in certain ways, and barriers to understanding will be created if such behavior is simply measured against Western industrial standards. In particular, caution should be maintained against classifying others' behavior as "irrational" until its function is known in the total cultural context.

Social Organization

Apart from subsystems which regulate economic behavior, men have come upon at least three other principles for organizing social relationships. Their emphases vary according to the technological advancement of the cultures, but some elements of these kinds of social organization are found in all societies.

First and most important is the principle of *kinship* which the technologically primitive people depend upon the most and urban, industrial people depend upon the least. This is the pattern of responsibilities toward, and rights expected from, relatives. The whole idea is derived from the basic human institution of marriage, the uniting of two unrelated people to produce a third. So far as is known, marriage and a family system has been almost universal, and two of the most basic functions seem to have been to bind together large numbers of people (the in-laws) and to rear children into the cultural system.

In the nonindustrial societies of the world, the importance of parents, brothers and sisters, uncles and aunts, nieces and nephews, cousins, in-laws, clan and caste members—all people who are believed to be related to one another through some common ancestor—is still a powerful force. They face the world together for many purposes: rituals, mutual protection, enculturating children, and providing psychological support. Such ties are weakening in many parts of the world as urbanization and industrialization increase and as peasant peoples become more deeply involved in international trade; but kinship relations still remain significant in agrarian societies.

Common territory is the basis for a second kind of social institution. This means that people who share the same area and also have some cultural ties tend to cooperate in certain ways, at least enough to protect the area from outsiders. Some kinds of terri-

The Concept of Culture 49

torial organizations are primitive hunting bands, village communities, neighborhoods, cities, and nations. Normally there are customs or rules which members of such territorial units are expected to follow, and the units usually have names with which members identify themselves when among strangers. Most territorial units are in some degree of competition with neighboring ones. The city neighborhood tries to get the best school system from a limited total city budget; the village community tries to get a paved road from a limited provincial budget; the hunting band in a semiarid region protects its water holes from indiscriminate use by other bands.

The territorial unit seems to have expanded both in size and power in human history—and usually at the expense of kinship relationships. The development of the early city-state seems to have been the crucial step in the transfer of power and authority away from kinship control. This has continued right up to the development of the industrial state, where family control is always sacrificed to state control.

In the agrarian nations of the world, however, the nation-state has not yet become so efficient or powerful; thus, people will settle disputes through their relationship units or at the very least thwart the efforts of the state representatives to intervene. In Somalia, a country with a high percentage of nomads, the central government is weak and murders are usually settled through blood payments or feuds, the lineage (extended relationship unit) taking the responsibility (Mahony, 1962: 11–15). Once a state becomes strong enough to assume control through its police officials (as in India and Pakistan) it will not permit a matter as serious as murder to be handled by kinship groups.

The third kind of institution which men have devised to organize their relationship with others is the *special interest group*. This is a group organized solely because of some mutual concern of the members apart from common territory or kinship—ritualistic, occupational, recreational, or other. Those in urban industrial society are quite familiar with groups of this kind because most belong to some: trade unions, professional societies, church groups, recreational clubs, academic associations, and others. In an Asian country, such as India, a village man may belong to several also: a religious group (Hindu or Muslim), an occupational caste, and perhaps also a brotherhood of athletes and a political party.

All societies except those on the lowest technological level have some such groups. In general, the special interest group also has become more common at the expense of kinship relationships. This seems largely to be a result of the increased complexity found in societies that are technologically more advanced with a natural increase in division of labor. A man who embraces Christianity while his brother staunchly adheres to Hinduism, the traditional family religion, consequently weakens family relationships. In fact, a Hindu family in India probably would completely ostracize a Christian member. Political party membership can cause the same kind of separatism, although perhaps of a less emotional nature.

Besides these formally organized social groups, there are kinds of social relationships of which most people are aware but which are not so specific. Once such is *rank* or *class difference*. There are practically no cultures of the world in which all men (or women) are treated as equals, and there are relatively few cultural traditions in which equality of treatment is even kept as an ideal. Most cultures assume that some groups of people should be treated differently than others, and have mechanisms to accomplish this end. The idea of treating people exclusively according to their individual worth is probably very unusual in world cultures and in a sense denies the meaning of social organization, in which group membership is the deciding criteria for judgment. In most cultures individuals and groups are ranked by means of traditional systems based on ethnic, linguistic, educational, occupational, and economic differences. The student of culture must not allow his cultural bias to influence his understanding of the basis of such ranking in the culture being studied.

Sometimes traditionally ranked groups are fairly rigidly arranged, as with the castes of India; sometimes the distinctions are more fluid, as with those between people of Spanish and Indian ancestry in most of Latin America. Almost everywhere in the non-industrial countries there is a clear distinction between the upper, urban class, who have political and administrative control of the country, and the relatively underprivileged, rural peasant class.

The Concept of Culture

The industrial countries also have group distinctions based on ethnic background and economic and educational qualifications, although in general these seem to be less pronounced than in the agrarian nations. The change agent will have to learn the particular distinctions of the culture in which he is working before he will be able to decide whether he is going to oppose the local system or accept it as another legitimate way of organizing human relationships.

The need to know the class or caste differences in the local culture is tied closely with the need to know the *power structure;* that is, who controls or influences the main body of citizens. Except for the very simply organized societies (hunters and gatherers), all societies have patterns of leadership and power control. Individual men have been seeking throughout history to achieve a state in which absolute freedom was a birthright of all, but in fact, once the simple hunting band level of society was passed, this condition seems to have been lost for all time. There are probably some good reasons for this historical development, even though each individual would like to have no control exerted over him by others.

The main reason for the existence of power structures seems to be the very complexity of the society. This idea can perhaps be most clearly illustrated by comparing the simple band society with the one depending on irrigation farming. The hunting band seems to have no more elaborate power structure than that represented by the man who is most knowledgeable and capable of finding and capturing wild game. He is more likely to get other hunters to go with him than is the unsuccessful hunter; and to a minor extent his word will be listened to in other affairs. But this man's power is limited only by his ability in word and deed to convince others to cooperate. If they choose not to go on a hunting party or to abandon one after having started, the hunting "chief" has no way of bringing them back. This arrangement is adequate for that techno-economic system; getting game by any small group of men is not crucial to the band's survival. Furthermore, the arrangement is somewhat self-correcting since the lack of prowess of a poor hunter-leader will very quickly become apparent to all.

On the other hand, the society depending for its survival on irrigation farming has a very complicated power structure with explicit rules and methods of social control to force people to use water in exact amounts and at exact times. This too makes sense because the very essence of irrigation is to distribute a scarce resource in a manner which will cause the group to be most productive. If the system were not highly organized, some people would get too much water and others would get too little. This is what actually happens when irrigation systems are developing. More shootings took place in the far West of the United States over water control than over cattle rustling. But since an irrigation system is complicated and the people who control its users have specialized knowledge, there will be a natural tendency for them to take special privilege. In general, modern governments and bureaucracies are like the systems to control irrigation use rather than the free, democratic systems of uncomplicated hunting bands.

Apart from the formal means of *social control* exerted through the power structure which we think of immediately—laws, police, prisons—there are other effective mechanisms more commonly used in local communities. One is the implantation of guilt complexes in the enculturation process so that if someone violates a formal or informal rule of the society, he feels that he did something wrong. This is probably a very effective mechanism, but it depends on the efficiency of the enculturation. Fear of supernatural punishment, or that one will become sick or suffer in some other way if he violates a social norm also can be an effective control. Obviously, this works only in cultures where there is deep belief in local deities or other supernatural agencies. But perhaps the most common and effective kind of local social control that exists in all kinds of societies is that which depends on shame or ridicule. The person who commits a deviant act is laughed at or held up to shame—a very effective mechanism for preventing him from doing that again. Social laughter is an excruciating punishment which only the very self-reliant are able to ignore.

The Supernatural

When it concerns the vital activities of life, men of most cultures are not content to rely solely upon practical knowledge

The Concept of Culture

based on observation of the natural world. To be "rational" and "scientific" may be a laudable goal in a few cultures (but probably not for the majority of people even in them), but the fact is that these ways of thinking do not explain or control the universe in entirety; and evidently most men need complete "explanations," if not complete control, of the world. Thus, there is an important function for belief in the supernatural.

A people with a culture that embraced no other technique than prayer to grow rice would not survive a generation. And yet, despite all the practical knowledge and techniques obtained through rational observation, there are many things that can occur to the farmer to prevent him from reaping a good harvest. The rain may come too late or too early, or it may begin at the right time but stop just when the young plants need it the most. An insect plague may descend on the growing plants or a disease may attack them. The farmer may become ill just at harvest time.

Such events are unpredictable "accidents." But the world is full of specific events, usually harmful, which people cannot predict. What does the individual rice farmer do? Does he fold his hands and say, "It is fate, or *kismet,* or *karma,* or 'God's Will,' and cannot be helped." Not if he is a normal, secular human being, which the majority of the people of the world are! Using the knowledge that his culture has provided him, the individual will try to remedy the situation as best he can in trying to get supernatural assistance. He will pray, or make ritual offerings to the field spirits, or perform some magic act to bring the rains or drive away the insects.

To the Southeast Asian rice farmer, as to the American corn farmer, the world is a place where certain happenings are more predictable than others. He is fairly certain that if he plants a seed in moist ground, a plant will come up; he is far less certain that the rains will come in sufficient quantity at the right time. The only real difference between the thinking of the rice farmer and the American farmer is that a lot more things about the world are predictable to the latter. But even for the American there are vast areas of existence that are not predictable, and for many of these he also will turn to the supernatural for answers or control. He may try some "scientific" methods of obtaining rain, such as cloud seeding; but before turning to ritual, the Southeast Asian farmer also would have tried to solve the water shortage by using water from catchment basins or wells.

The American may pray for such mundane assistance as financial well-being just as the Plains Indian used to ask his Guardian Spirit for ability to capture horses and become a great warrior. The great advances in science-based medicine have made much human sickness more predictable and controllable to the American than to the tribesman or the Asian peasant farmer; nevertheless, when confronted with a grave illness for which there is still no certain cure, the American too will pray. Even in connection with such highly scientific efforts as space exploration, modern industrial man will sometimes turn to the supernatural for assistance. On one of the early American-manned space shots, an astronaut had been successfully launched and had completed his orbits, but unaccountably disappeared when entering the earth's atmosphere for the re-entry. Tension mounted to such a point after several minutes of no contact that the television announcer informed the viewers that "some prayers would not be out of place."

And though Western industrial man may have narrowed the area regarding the universe about which he gives supernatural explanations, there is one area in which he knows no more than does "nonscientific" man; that is, what happens after death. He must either admit that there is no evidence of any further existence for the individual when the life processes cease, or depend on some kind of supernatural (religious) explanation. And though there may be a few who are willing to accept the "no further existence" explanation, this is evidently insufficient for the majority, even in urban industrial society.

The point is that men in industrial, urban cultures do not think in a different way from people in tribal and agrarian societies; it is simply that the former rely less on supernatural explanations and methods of control because there is a greater amount of practical knowledge available. It is sometimes popular to contrast "scientific" with "nonscientific" thinking. But if scientific thinking is that based on objective observation of natural events, then all cultures possess it. In this sense, the first men who learned to utilize fire and chip stone spear points had the first scientific knowledge; they were applied physical scientists.

Village people in agrarian societies may sometimes use premises

The Concept of Culture

which have not been validated in the scientific tradition; for example, Latin American villagers will attribute illness to such "non-rational" causes as bad air, bad body humors, or fright. But it must be remembered that the germ theory of disease is less than a hundred years old in Western Europe and America, and that well up into the twentieth century Americans suffering from malaria believed it was caused by "bad swamp air."

If a cultural system lacked much Western scientific knowledge, some quite different beliefs about natural phenomena would be quite logical. Lao villagers have very little of the meteorological knowledge available within the Western scientific tradition, such as the earth's rotation, the movement of air currents, or the basic land forms of Greater Asia. They can, therefore, logically interpret the coming of the monsoon rains as an answer to a rain-making ceremony. One such, tied to the Buddhist calendar, is performed annually in Laos. It takes place in April or May, when the earth is dry and parched and the time for rice planting draws near. The coming of the rains is vital and a ritual exists to help ensure this to happen. Furthermore, there is evidence of the ceremony's efficacy each year in the fact that within two or three weeks, the rains do come. This ritual was witnessed one year when a downpour followed on the same day. Cause and effect had been "proven." The only way to "prove" that this ceremony had nothing to do with the rains would be to deliberately not hold it for several years and note the results. While this would be a most appropriate procedure for a group of Western scientists, it could hardly be expected of a village society with different cultural assumptions, at least before they had some understanding of Western meteorological ideas. Otherwise, the risk would be too great from their point of view.

On the other hand, if there are obviously advantageous results from a Western innovation, village people will rarely pass it by to remain dependent on supernatural help alone. Sulfa drugs and penicillin have entered into the pharmaceutical knowledge of village people all over the world simply because they produce clearly observable benefits. The curing of yaws, an unpleasant skin disase found in the tropics, provides a dramatic example, it being effected within weeks and months in one place after another with penicillin. Under the U.S. Point Four Program in Colombia and Ecuador, a campaign to cure this ailment was instituted among the Negro villagers of the coastal areas. They had previously depended on herbal medicines and native curers; and although these treatments had not been very effective, they still had no faith in the new medicine. However, despite their fears, some submitted to the penicillin injections. The results were so dramatic that within a couple of years everyone accepted the new treatment, convinced that this was one disease the medical doctors could cure. They continued to treat other ailments with their own medicines (Erasmus, 1961: 26–27). Almost exactly the same occurrence was described by a young Ibo schoolteacher as having happened throughout his region of Nigeria. He claimed no one had yaws any longer, and if a case were reported, it would be immediately treated with penicillin (Niehoff: field information).

In all cultures, people have their own sets of beliefs about the natural environment, the human body, how to grow crops, make tools, and how to get along with other people. Furthermore, though there are always some skeptics, the majority of each culture accepts the beliefs which explain the creation of the universe, the causes of disease, death, and the afterlife. Some of what other people believe may be demonstrably true, some may be false according to Western scientific thought, and most will probably be unprovable. Some of these beliefs may strike us as myth or legend (the religious history of another people) or merely popular religious faith. Some such beliefs may be firm and difficult to dislodge—rocks of faith upon which the religion and entire way of life of the people have been built. The central theologies of the world religions are of this kind. Other beliefs, especially those not concerned with the supernatural, may not be so vital that they cannot be replaced by equally satisfactory ones. The belief that malaria was caused by bad swamp air was replaced by the idea that it was carried by mosquitoes. In either event, merely refuting traditional beliefs with Western scientific argument will rarely cause other people to give them up.

Values

Although less obvious than other beliefs, another kind are those which constitute the value system. The popular American connotation of the word "value" is the financial worth of a thing. When

The Concept of Culture 57

one asks "What's its value?" he usually wants to know what a thing is worth in dollars and cents. This indicates the centralism of economic considerations in American thinking.

However, in using the term for crosscultural understanding, anthropologists will use a much more comprehensive definition, such as "broad beliefs of central importance to which a moral or emotional worth is attached." As might be guessed, supernatural or religious concepts can be part of a value system although they might not be central nor the only ones. It depends on the cultural system whether religion is singled out as the central theme or whether it is merely another guiding principle for action. Examples of central values that have been described by anthropologists are piety in Southeast Asian Buddhist countries, aggressive masculinity among males in Latin American (Wagley, 1951: 7), personal self-control among Pueblo Indians (Benedict, 1946: 66), and personal achievement, usually economic, among contemporary North Americans.

There can even be negative beliefs of central interest; that is, ideas which promote fears and tension in the cultural system. Such negative interests frequently stem from religious idea systems and, surprisingly, they can even have some positive effects. The fear of an all-powerful deity in Judeo-Christian-Islamic theology has undoubtedly inspired much effort and is accountable to a considerable extent for the artistic achievements of the cultures dominated by these religions. There can be a central interest in controlling the body and the senses, to keep the biological drives in strict check. The "Christian ethic" of Europe and America was a negative interest of this sort. Anthropologists report that among Greek peasants, firmness and self-discipline are still the central virtues, which sounds like a variation of the "Christian ethic" (Mead, 1961: 63).

It has been said that the Navajo Indians have an inordinate interest, based on fear, in ghosts and witches and that they spend a great deal of time and thought trying to counteract the influence of these creatures. Archeologists in Arizona and New Mexico have reported difficulties in persuading Navajos to work as laborers on excavation sites because they fear the ghosts of the dead people whose remains might be disturbed. Although the Pueblo Indians of the same area also believe in ghosts, these beings do not appear to be so central in the peoples' thinking. In any event, the Pueblos would willingly work on any site if the pay were adequate. This difference is also reflected in the varying practices of disposing of the dead. While the Navajos take great pains to dispose of the body and to see that the spirit of the dead person is properly placated, the Pueblos dispose of their dead with little ceremony. In fact, in the old days many of the Pueblo dead were simply buried in village trash heaps.

Anything in human experience can come to have an emotional significance. When certain ideas from such experience are adopted by the group, when the emotions become standardized, and when elaborate ways of seeking or avoiding the experiences are developed, then we are dealing with a cultural value. The adults in the system attempt to pass these values on to their children and try to force some degree of conformity on all members by setting up systems of reward and punishment.

Cultural values tend to be conservative, probably because their validity is very difficult to prove or disprove. If two cultures are obviously viable but entertain opposite values (aggressive masculinity in one, gentle calmness in the other), who can say which is correct? Thus, changes in cultural values tend to be resisted much more than changes in other areas of culture, and specifically in technology and economic relations. The East Indians of Trinidad came from a culture which highly valued a large kinship unit and the personalized relationships which are characteristic of kin-based systems. In Trinidad, however, the rural people became financially able to buy cars, and this increased mobility weakened kinship relations. But still the people of Indian descent were trying to maintain as much of the greater family system as possible. The most important ceremony they engaged in was for marriage, for which considerable sums of money were spent. And although young men could travel about visiting and having affairs with girls of other ethnic backgrounds, dating with girls of Indian ancestry was strictly frowned upon. Also, a "decent" marriage was still one arranged by the parents. Thus, changes have taken place in the economics of the Indian family and ultimately they will take place in the family system. But so far, the "value" on kinship relations has served as a conservative force.

The Concept of Culture

Not all individuals feel the same degree of emotion toward a given value but very few are permitted to violate them with impunity. A culture rewards and punishes individuals in proportion to the significance it places on the value. In the first instance it attempts to build in feelings of "ought" or "ought not" toward behaviors concerning the values. But it also constructs patterns of social rewards and punishments if the person's conscience does not control him sufficiently. Thus, the man in India, and to a lesser extent in Trinidad, who shirks his family responsibilities may get little financial assistance from his relatives when he needs it, and when he wants to get married he will get the poorest choice of bride. So too will the American be penalized if he ignores the value of personal achievement. Not only will he not get the best job, he also will not get the socially most desirable woman as his wife, nor the respect of his children or other community members. This last generalization applies, of course, to the mainstream of American society, not to ethnic minorities with different values or to deviant subgroups, such as "hippy" communes. However, these other groups will have values of their own for which they will have techniques of reward and punishment. The commune will have a positive value on cooperative behavior and the sharing of goods; and the individual who wants to keep significant amounts of private property will be ridiculed, shunned, and probably ultimately rejected from the community.

Thus, he who will understand the way of life of another people will need to have more than merely a list of customs and "hard facts." Although they are not so easily learned, the values of a people and the emotional intensity which back them must be understood to some extent. The technical, social, and supernatural customs of another people do not need to stand the test of utility, efficiency, or truth in the Westerner's sense. They may be the objects of so much emotional and moral value that no one wishes or dares to test them. Some such concepts may appear to the outsider as merely alternatives, others as ridiculous, and still others as sacred or glorious. To the degree that emotional intensity is attached, they are a vital part of that culture and cannot be understood simply on the basis of Western values. Furthermore, their very pervasiveness makes knowing them essential.

Customs

Some special characteristics of man's way are worth singling out for brief discussion. One is the fact that each custom can, and usually does, have both an obvious function (*overt*) which the local people can themselves describe, and also a function which will only be clear to a social-analyst (*covert*).

Thus, most peoples have developed special ceremonies to mark the important stages of man's life, such as christenings, confirmations, weddings, and funerals. In some societies great expenses are entailed for the proper fulfillment of such rites. However, these are not insignificant or arbitrary events where wealth is uselessly wasted. They are methods that have been arrived at by trial-and-error for preserving individual mental health and group stability through the necessary but difficult transitions in human lives. They prepare individuals for their new roles and allay the shock of change that might threaten social order and continuity.

Even minor customs that may seem to be mere petty manners or play appear in a new light in this sense. Children's games are often play-acting of adult roles which inculcate the values and customs of the culture in a way that formal schooling might neglect. Of course, such games have the overt function of providing recreation, but covertly the culture is instilling its values. This is graphically illustrated by the games played in three cultures studied by anthropologists. One culture is that of the Kung Bushmen of South Africa, a people with a hunting and gathering economy ("The Hunters," 16 mm film). The games young boys play are tailored toward their adult role. They practice using hunting weapons on insects, small animals, and birds. In contrast are the Dani people of the New Guinea highlands who have a cultural system greatly given to warfare (Matthiessen, 1962). Their boys play with weapons also, but significantly they throw the play spears at one another rather than at small animals. They are preparing for their adult role as manhunters. The third culture is that of the contemporary United States, where in recent years there has been a significant change in the types of toys produced for children, particularly for boys. It appears that a fair number of people have became aware of the covert function of these items. Although peace has been an ostensible goal of the United

The Concept of Culture 61

States since its inception, periodic warfare also has seemed to be necessary to most people. The soldier has been treated as a heroic figure and a very high proportion of boys' playthings has represented the machinery of warfare. Now there appears to have been a shift among many people toward peace as the only possible goal. The American soldier receives sympathy rather than respect for his military role. It is significant, therefore, that the war toy has greatly diminished in variety, and many toy manufacturers are deliberately reducing or eliminating this line.

The covert function of a custom is not always easy to detect, but to learn it is worth the effort. In order to do so, the student of culture will need to step outside the biases of his own culture. This principle was apparent to the hospital personnel who permitted Navajo grandmothers to camp alongside pregnant mothers in government hospitals. Although this practice complicated the sanitary provisions, the administration was willing to put up with it for the covert functions of the grandmothers' presence. The grandmothers were transmitting much traditional child lore as well as comforting the mother in a strange environment. Covertly the grandmothers were establishing an atmosphere of stability which was a reason for the younger mothers to stay.

Another distinction regarding customs is that they have a *real* and an *ideal* aspect; that is, each system attempts to establish a goal to be achieved in the practice of each custom, and children are taught this in the enculturation process. As a matter of fact, the ideal is probably unreachable, as perhaps ideals are supposed to be. There is instead a real, normal behavior which is typical of most people. There has been, for instance, an ideal in American society that heterosexual activities will be undertaken by young adults only within the confines of a social institution, marriage. This undoubtedly never was fully reflected in real behavior, but presumably the discrepancy between the ideal and real has increased in recent decades. However, the ideal still exists, although for how long is not certain.

An ideal can be so demanding that a culture provides a way for individuals to take alternative roles. The Plains Indians had an ideal that men should be aggressive warriors and young boys were trained to go in this direction. Most did, although many must have had to suppress real fears to go on the raiding missions that were required. However, some young men just could not bring themselves to such dangers and chose to become transvestites, men who took on women's clothes and behavior. Although this was considered to be a secondary role for males, it was an accepted one, and having it permitted the tribes to retain their primary ideal.

It appears likely that these two aspects of customs constitute a necessary logic in that if there were no difference between ideal and real patterns, the social group could have no goal other than to just continue existing in unchanged form. It would be cultural perfection and there would be no logic or possibility for change or improvement. However, a great deal of the youthful dissidence in recent years seems to stem from an unwillingness to accept any discrepancy between real and ideal patterns in Western industrial culture, and particularly in the United States. If the older generation teaches to do one thing—in religious ethics, social inequalities, war-peace—but does less, this is regarded as hypocrisy and is condemned. The clearest example seems to be in regard to egalitarianism—racial, ethnic, sexual, etc. The American ideal seems to stress equality of treatment of humans in all respects except perhaps age (now below eighteen) and perhaps physiological sanity. And although it is clear that this ideal has never been achieved, it does seem that at least since the Civil War there has been a steady movement toward less discrimination on these criteria. No person of African ancestry can be bought or sold and there are explicit laws to prohibit discrimination on the basis of race in all kinds of civil service jobs although there is discrimination against Afro-Americans in real estate negotiations; also, although people of Jewish ancestry can go to almost any college or university in the country, there are still vacation resorts and country clubs which keep them out unofficially; and finally, although women now have the vote for all public elections and are in all universities (including the former all-male schools), there still has not been a female president nor are there many women airline pilots. In sum, although the ideal in egalitarianism has not been reached, there has been a decrease in the discrepancy between it and real behavior in the United States. Moreover, it is inconceivable that the ideal pattern will ever be achieved in en-

The Concept of Culture

tirety. And so far as understanding a culture is concerned, efforts should be made to learn both the covert functions and real behavior of customs as well as the more obvious overt functions and ideal behavior.

Functional Patterns

Up to now, cultural behavior and beliefs have been treated in separate categories—language, technology, economy, social organization, supernatural beliefs, values—as if they existed in isolation. And although it is useful to subdivide culture in this way for description, anthropologists know there are no such sharp divisions in the actual processes of a culture. If a rice farmer is asked what is necessary to ensure a good crop, he will likely give a description of the planting techniques, plus mentioning that if the gods are willing to accept his prayers or ritual offering, and send him sufficient rains at the right time, and keep the insects out of his fields, he will be successful. To the farmer the ritual as well as the planting techniques are part of the same process. The Westerner, with his penchant for subdividing, would probably consider these activities as separate—one supernatural (religious) and the other technical.

In fact, this kind of thinking has created some serious problems for Western industrial man. To a large extent the failure to consider interrelationships rather than the separate occurrences has created the pollution crises of the mid-twentieth century. The fact that there was a direct relationship between profit-making (economics) and the air they were exposed to (health) was rarely thought of until people's eyes started to burn. Also, the relation between sanitation (health) in elaborate sewage systems and loss of recreation areas in stream pollution was not well understood until recently. The expansion of the field of ecology, which concerns itself with these relationships rather than the individual occurrences, is a sign of this new way of thinking.

Anthropologists have long believed that the many subsections of culture are interrelated to make up functional patterns. Very often economic activities are intimately interrelated with social customs and religious beliefs. Many tribes of South and East

Africa have traditionally depended on cattle as their primary source of food. But cattle also have social meanings. To obtain a wife, cattle must be exchanged between families of the bride and groom, which is a guarantee of good faith and good behavior on both sides. Also, in certain groups, such as the Zulu, an ox must be sacrificed periodically for the spirit of the deceased head of the family; the whole kinship group must then feed on it in a specified way. To neglect such a ritual responsibility would cause the displeased ancestral spirit to neglect the living members' fortunes (Cassel, 1955: 37). As a result of these and other interconnections, the Zulu cattle herder develops a special attitude toward his animals.

It is worthwhile to make a comparison with the American cattle rancher whose life is also affected in many ways by animals, but indirectly rather than in the intimate and direct way of the Zulu. To the American, cattle are a means of making a profit; they have a cash value. If raising some other kind of animal—sheep, pigs, horses—were more profitable, the rancher would probably change. However, the American rancher does have most of the same needs as the Zulu and his animals help to fulfill them, although indirectly, through the cash they bring. Successfully raising cattle will enable the Euro-American rancher to live comfortably, to acquire prestige, to have a better wife choice than the poor rancher, and even to gain merit in supernatural affairs (the successful rancher will be able to donate more to the church). The point is that there are functional interrelationships between several aspects of culture for both the tribal herder and the industrial rancher. Marriage, religion, and personal position in the community would be affected in both instances if cattle were taken away. The principal difference between the two lifeways is in the directness of benefit. To the Zulu the cattle themselves are the end product, while to the rancher they are only the means.

Many instances could be cited to show how different forms of behavior are, to more or less degree, *functionally integrated* into a total pattern and tend to reinforce one another in fulfilling the personal needs of the individuals and in maintaining social cohesion. In a mature, well integrated culture, customs show close

The Concept of Culture

consistency, congruence, and mutual support. There are a few instances on record in which customs were functionally integrated to such a high degree that a comparatively simple change helped to cause the collapse of the whole system. The introduction of steel axes among one group of Australian aboriginals, cited earlier, appeared to have caused the dissolution of the prestige of older men, a loss of trading partnerships between tribes (which had depended on the exchange of stone axes for other items), and the destruction of tribal myths which had been central in explaining the peoples' place in the universe. Very few cultures are this highly integrated, but all have points of vulnerability.

One might imagine the consequences of a disclosure that the Christian Bible was a hoax which had been deliberately written several hundred years ago to deceive people. The basis of morality in Christian countries would be taken away and people would be forced to generate an entire new set of morals or find some other kind of justification for the ones which are now accepted. "Equality under God" would no longer exist nor would there be any moral justification for not taking another person's property, wife, or life. Moreover, the great networks of property built up by church organizations would be shaken and probably ultimately liquidated. There would be no more reason to believe in life after death, and all of the funeral businesses would have to be eliminated or changed. (These are, of course, only a few of the consequences.)

Most changes that occur in a culture are not so drastic as either of the above, nor are all customs so critically integrated into the total pattern. However, it is difficult to conceive of any change so particular that it would affect only one custom or form of behavior in a cultural system.

A culture in its entirety does not just consist of technological, social, supernatural, and value aspects. These customs are functionally linked in an intricate structure that contains emotionally toned interconnections. This is one of the main discoveries of anthropology: that no culture can logically be divided into separate parts and be truly understood. It makes up a functional pattern.

3
Cultural Change

Conservatism

To many Westerners traveling to the tropical, nonindustrial countries for the first time, it will seem that remarkably little has changed during the past hundreds, or even thousands, of years. In the agrarian countries men can be seen employing the same implements that were in use at the time of Christ or before. Asian villagers can be found using a type of potter's wheel in use four thousand years ago, or tilling the fields with oxen, harness, and plow dating from the same period.

Romanticists describe the villager's life as going on unchanged generation after generation. Therefore, it might seem that any ideas of change are out of place, and that these people do not want to change. There is an element of truth to this idea. A definite conservatism does exist in all cultures, and probably necessarily so. In general, there is a need for continuity; otherwise, the cumulation of knowledge that is the essence of culture would be lost and each generation would have to start afresh with nothing more than its biological heritage. In order to insure this continuity, people are enculturated when quite young to believe that their system is the "right" one. This attitude, which anthropologists have labeled "ethnocentrism," is engraved on the minds of most people in most cultures. It simply means they are taught that their culture and group is of central importance, irrespective of actual achievements. The main consequence of this process is to

Cultural Change

make the majority of people in a cultural system into conservatives. One does not change frivolously if he believes his way is "the correct way." Such persons are the culture carriers, and without them the continuity of the system would be lost.

If culture is looked at as a system, it must be accepted that each is a workable means of adaptation to a given environment; and within its own terms each does have the minimum mechanisms for giving individuals the satisfactions they require. Moreover, by means of the enculturation process, all individuals have been given specific patterns of behavior which are predictable to others. Change would upset this. The system, through its carriers, will hardly be favorably inclined toward change for its own sake. In fact, any particular culture will attempt to perpetuate itself as much as possible, regardless of the odds of success and irrespective of the actual level of technological development. Almost all the tribal people of the world have tried to hold back or resist the force of the agrarian and industrial cultures to maintain their own way, even though an outside observer would have to admit that much success in this effort was not probable. It has already been mentioned that one of the main forces for adopting the technology of Europeans and Americans by tribal people, particularly their weapons, was to preserve their own way of life.

Competition

Despite the conservatism existing in all cultures, a certain measure of which is certainly necessary, change is constant. The view that life is as it was hundreds or thousands of years ago anywhere in the world is based on superficial observations and the ethnocentrism of the viewers. It is true that in a village of India one may still see an oxcart similar to a type used at the time of Christ, but not far from the village there will be a railroad track or a paved road where the villagers can board a train or bus to the nearest town or city. And though the villagers may use pottery vessels made on the local wheel, they will also use aluminum pots and pans made in Indian factories. A large share of their clothing also will come from factories, either Indian-made or from industrial countries outside India.

Why, if the majority of people in a culture tend to be conservative and the system seems to favor continuity, will change take place in all cultures? If each system were absolutely isolated from others, there would be relatively little force for change, even as there is relatively little force for genetic change in animal species that live isolated on islands or on remote continents. Australia is full of marsupials, most varieties of which have changed or disappeared in other parts of the world, and the only place where giant tortoises still survive are on the remote Galapagos Islands. So also are there still a few hunting and horticultural peoples in isolated corners of the world. A few tribal people still live at the headwaters of the Amazon, but they are under intense pressure by modern Brazilians. Another region where tribal people can be found is the central plateau of New Guinea. In fact, one of the most graphic descriptions of a tribal way of life is of a New Guinea horticultural group, the Dani, who still live a relatively untouched way of life because they were on the most remote part of the plateau, protected by a great "mountain wall" (Mathiassen, 1962).

However, even the lack of change among such groups is a relative matter. They simply have not changed as much as others. But a significant fact about most cultures is that they have changed quite a lot because they have not been so isolated as the Dani of New Guinea or the Yanomamo of Brazil. And not only have they been in contact with other cultures more extensively, they have been in competition with them, and mainly to retain their territory. During man's history, the people who have been able to survive and perpetuate their culture (with self-selected changes) have been those who could maintain their territory despite outside pressure. And those who have been able to keep their territory have had the most efficient cultural systems, mainly in technology but also in economic patterns and political organization.

Irrespective of the morality of taking other peoples' lands, the cultures that have developed techniques superior to those of their neighbors have ultimately absorbed or conquered those neighbors. And basically the cultures that have done the absorbing are the ones that have changed most. The main patterns of the aboriginal Amerindian cultures were destroyed by the incoming Europeans

Cultural Change

who had a superior technology and organizational ability. During the previous two hundred years European culture had been changing rapidly. When the Amerindians were forced to deal with the territorial pressure of the Europeans, they did not have time to make the changes necessary to keep from being absorbed.

The cultures of the Amerindians when Europeans arrived had in most places replaced other, less rapidly changing Amerindian cultures. Thus, we know that the Inca Empire of South America and the Aztec confederacy of Mexico had achieved their preeminence only one hundred to two hundred years before the arrival of the Spanish conquerors. In both cases these governments had been built by a local tribe that had developed the organizational ability to expand and absorb the tribes around it.

The competition of cultures is most dramatic when the differences between them are greatest. Thus, the pressure exerted on tribal peoples in the last four hundred years by industrial, European powers has created dramatic conflicts all over the world. One of the most intriguing developments, in which the tribal people recognized the competition and tried to solve the problem through ritual means, is known as the "cargo cult." Tribesmen, primarily in the South Pacific and Africa, became aware of the great power and amount of goods possessed by the "white man." Mythologies were developed to explain that the goods (cargo) actually belonged to the local tribal people, and ritual procedures were developed to obtain them. These cults reached their most elaborate development in New Guinea where the idea was generated that ships first, and airplanes later, were actually being manned by the ancestors of the tribesmen and that they were being improperly diverted by Europeans. By performing the proper rituals, which included ceasing to produce traditional foodstuffs, the tribesmen could force the ships to dock and the airplanes to land in their area and disgorge the goods. Many tribes followed through to the point of killing their pigs and throwing their yams out to sea. Australian government authorities then had to feed such cult tribes while attempting to discount the idea of the "cargo" so they would go back to producing their own food again.

This competition between cultures is probably the main basis for the drive toward "modernization" and industrialization by the agrarian nations of the world. After obtaining independence from the European powers, most of these countries soon realized that their competitive position in the world was really quite poor and that they would be dominated economically or reabsorbed by some other power if they did not improve their condition. The competition also was reflected in individuals who learned about and wished to have much of the equipment that was possessed by people in European and other industrial countries—autos, refrigerators, sanitary plumbing, electric lights, etc. And despite a few ideological dissenters, the great majority of leaders in these countries soon came to believe that industrialization and science-based technology was the only sound way to become so modernized.

Although the competiton of national cultures is readily recognized as the main stimulus for widespread change, this tendency exists with any size of group or even with individuals. Two political parties in the same culture are in competition for the public offices; two neighborhoods in a city are in competition for a larger share of the school budget; and two individuals trying for the same job or trying to pass a college examination which is graded on a curve are in competition with one another. And if there is a standard kind of behavior for each situation, but one individual or group changes in a significant way, he or it will be more likely to win the competition.

All such competition does not mean that one group will conquer or absorb another; but if competition continues over a long period of time and one group wins consistently, the other group will probably dissolve or be altered significantly in some manner. Thus, a political party that never wins will be replaced by another, and the neighborhood which always gets the smallest share of the budget will probably lose its social cohesion or be reorganized.

Also, such competition does not mean that human societies constitute a jungle of devouring beasts with never any effort in common. On the contrary, the words "group," "society," "institution" really mean cooperative aggregates of men with some common behavior and goals, and engaging in common effort to achieve them. Thus, although there may be some competition

Cultural Change

within a social group (the struggle for leadership), the basis of its viability is cooperative behavior. The individuals of a national culture work together in competition with other nations; the political party members work together to defeat the other political party; and the members of a neighborhood development council work out strategies to get as much of the city budget as possible. Thus, cooperation is the key to group existence, and if there were no other groups existing there seemingly would be little stimulus for change. The single group would continue with its old ways which would never be shaken by any pressure from outside.

There are at least three significant attitudinal and behavioral mechanisms that stimulate change. First there is cultural *conservatism,* the tendency for each culture to have self-perpetuating mechanisms, reflected in the average man who acts as a culture carrier. The positive effect of conservatism is transmission of the cumulated knowledge from one generation to the next. Then there is *cooperation,* the normal tendency for the individuals of the group to work together to achieve some common goal. This also assists in the cultural transmission process since the knowledge comes to be shared by a larger number of people. And finally, there is intergroup *competition,* the tendency for the different groups to compete with one another for the resources available. This competition paves the way for change since any group which changes its behavior in a significant way immediately gains an advantage over those which are simply perpetuating the previous pattersn. So, *continuity through conservatism* and *change through competition* act as complementary rather than contradictory forces.

Diffusion

There is only one way to achieve something absolutely new in human culture, which is by invention. This process can take place in any culture, although obviously a new idea can only be built on ideas already in existence. No one would expect a tribal group with a hunting technology to invent an airplane which could fly, but an individual in that society might invent an improvement on a bow, arrow, or canoe paddle.

As a matter of fact, most of the developments we call inventions are really just recombinations or improvements of existing processes. Cultural systems rarely seem to produce people with the capability of taking giant steps without antecedents. Thus, a hunting group with no boating tradition would not produce an individual who would simultaneously invent an elaborate dugout canoe, carved wood paddles, and sails. Instead there would be a series of steps beginning with log use, followed by raft construction, followed by pole pushing, then paddle wielding, and much later in the history of the device would come canoe building and sail installation. The same is true of cultures with highly developed technologies. The airplane began with the joining of a bicycle to a primitive gasoline engine, and adding wind foils. And although once started, airplane development took place at a relatively rapid speed, there still were a series of steps required to produce the supersonic jet and space rocket. Only in fiction could people produce a rocket capable of going to the moon or Mars even before powered aircraft were in existence.

And although we give a great deal of attention to inventions and inventors, the bulk of growth in any one culture occurs through the borrowing of ideas and processes from other groups or cultures. Even the way we commonly use the word "invention" is a matter of borrowing or diffusion. The new idea or technique may well be invented or discovered by one person in a culture, but it becomes culturally significant (and individuals get to know of it) only when it becomes widely accepted within the culture. In other words, *it has diffused throughout the culture.*

The really advantageous invention will spread throughout its culture of origin and then pass on to other cultures. There is actual archeological evidence of this happening to certain items. Specific plants, such as corn (maize), tobacco, potatoes, and cassava, were domesticated by the Amerindians, and the approximate time and area where they first appeared is known, although the specific inventors or discoverers are not. But it is known that after 1492 they spread around the world in about three hundred years. There is a similar history for the invention and spread of iron smelting and the alphabet from their point of origin in the Middle East.

Cultural Change

Cultural borrowing is primarily a matter of economy of effort. It is much easier to take over someone else's idea or discovery, whether a neighbor in one's own culture or someone from another culture, than to invent the item anew. Individuals in any culture are limited by background and time. They can get new ideas with far less effort by borrowing them; and chances are that the person from whom they borrowed the new ideas had already borrowed them from someone else, possibly from another culture.

The chief means, then, for bringing about change is the diffusion of ideas from one culture to another. The occasions for such diffusion are many: exposure to new peoples and ideas in wars and military occupations, through trade, missionary activity, immigration, intermarriage, improved transportation, and any other method by which people learn the ways of others. Whenever different people are brought together, they tend to adopt each other's ideas. This process has been so constant in man's history that it is possible to trace the growth of a culture primarily in terms of what has been borrowed from other cultures.

Most cultural diffusion that has occurred in man's history has not been directed; that is, ideas or techniques have passed from one people to another without any overall deliberate plan either by the donor or the recipient group. A trader or missionary has visited a country with something new, say a domesticated plant. He has shown several people how to grow and use it, or perhaps just told them about it, and then took no further interest in it. If someone had become intrigued enough to try it and it proved useful, the plant would probably then be passed from neighbor to neighbor, village to village, tribe to tribe, across continents and seas, and ultimately it would be found in the most remote corners of the world.

Significant diffusion has taken place merely because one group observed some new practice in another and saw an advantage to themselves. It is believed that the Indians of the American Plains observed the domesticated horse with all its trappings as being used by the Spaniards and decided that this animal would be useful to their way of life. They then captured horses and copied the saddlery of the Spanish, ultimately to transform their way of life in using the horse for buffalo (bison) hunting.

Earlier the diffusion of domesticated plants from the Amerindians was mentioned. Indeed, their travels have been dramatic. Within three hundred years there was hardly any place in the world where these plants had not been adopted if they would grow well. The history of these plants alone indicates the willingness of people in all cultures to accept change if it is clearly beneficial.

Borrowing new ideas or practices is obviously dependent on access to them. Certain cultures may be isolated and the members will have relatively little opportunity to learn of new ways. They may acquire some more obvious innovations, such as tobacco and corn, the knowledge of which can be carried from neighbor to neighbor and tribe to tribe without involving specialists. On the other hand, an innovation which is more specialized but which may bestow just as much or more benefit in the long run may never get to these people. An example of such an innovation is a writing system. All over the world, band and tribal people failed to get writing systems until they were dominated or absorbed by urbanized cultures. Thus, an alphabet was carried eastward from India almost two thousand years ago, primarily by Buddhist and Hindu missionaries. This writing system was modified to fit the local languages of the valley people in Burma, Thailand, Laos, and Cambodia. These were the people who came into contact with the missionaries. The people in the hills in those countries had practically no direct contact with the foreign visitors and so did not learn to write their languages. There are still many of the Mon-Khmer languages of the hill region of Laos for which no writing systems have been produced. Also, as a consequence of this isolation, many other new ideas that the lowland people learned from the Indians were missed by the hill tribes.

Apart from access to new ideas, there is a matter of cultural willingness to adopt them. Some cultures have patterns which favor the borrowing of new ideas, while others attempt to rely on the existing system without getting anything from outside. The values around the old customs may be so strong that people are afraid of the threat of modification or replacement which the new can always cause. The Pueblo Indians of New Mexico and Arizona were so strongly committed to their own religious beliefs and

Cultural Change 75

communal way of life that for almost four hundred years they have steadfastly rejected many new ideas of the Spaniards, Mexicans, and Anglo-Americans. On the other hand, the Indians of California generally adopted Christianity, mission life, and Spanish overlordship from the earliest days.

A cultural system can change in respect to borrowing when the members come to believe that the adoption of new ideas is more advantageous than maintaining old customs exclusively. Several Asian countries at first attempted to defend themselves against the industrial European powers by keeping the new ideas out, later they reversed their decision. Japan was one of the earliest to decide to close itself off from the encroaching West, but it changed policy in the nineteenth century and embarked on a deliberate program of getting Western ideas, particularly those of a technical nature. Until World War II there was a stereotype of the Japanese visitor as a man with large eyeglasses (presumably from reading so much) and a camera (for taking pictures of the new objects). As a matter of fact, the Japanese were industrializing themselves through this process to the extent that they became able to compete aggressively with the source cultures, both in military and trade activities. This is a pattern which the Turks also followed and they even adopted many Western social customs. Kemal Ataturk attempted to liberate women in a Western way and to adopt the Western alphabet as a substitute for the Arabic one. Although at a somewhat later date, China too has gone through this kind of transformation by adopting social ideas of Eastern Europe.

It is a part of ethnocentrism that cultural diffusion is a one-way process, from the dominant cultures to the "lesser breeds," from the industrial to the tribal or agrarian cultures. The people of dominant cultures tend to think of such cultural borrowing as the "spread of civilization." Although it is true that most borrowing goes in this direction, the process practically always goes both ways. World history has shown time and again that conquerors take over some of the ways of the conquered and that colonizers learn from the tribal people over whom they impose control. In the history of China before the period of Western influence, nomadic invaders came from the steppes of Central Asia time after time to impose their own dynasties. In each instance they became absorbed by the Chinese they conquered. The last such was the Manchu dynasty. The Pilgrims of New England would have starved if they had not borrowed the Indian techniques of growing corn, beans, and squash. The Norman conquerors of England learned much from the Saxons, as did the Portuguese and Spaniards from the Indians and Africans they enslaved.

When change is not forced on a people, they are much more apt to borrow ideas of a technological nature than those of social organization or the supernatural. The kinds of things that have been universally borrowed are all of a technical nature. This probably occurs because the advantages of technical practices are most easily demonstrated. The usefulness of domesticated plants (such as corn, wheat, and rice) or animals (such as cattle, pigs and chickens) or metallurgy or pottery can be quickly recognized. An even more recent example is motorized transport on land, sea, and air. A man who has been paddling a canoe can easily be convinced that an outboard engine is superior; and the two-hour trip in an airplane as contrasted to the two days necessary on dusty roads provides a convincing demonstration.

On the other hand, ideas of democracy and representative government have been carried to many parts of the world by Europeans and Americans, as well as Euro-American ideas of family relationships. But the nonindustrial nations have by no means adopted such ideas and customs as wholeheartedly as they have welcomed outboard motors and airplanes. Although Turkey in its effort to modernize adopted several social ideas from the West (such as liberation of women), this movement generally has been slow to spread to Islamic countries. In the meantime, there has been absolutely no resistance in these countries to airplane transport.

Firearms and religious beliefs provide another example. Although firearms and Christianity became available to most non-European people at the same time, firearms were adopted by all cultures to replace earlier weapons, while Christianity failed to become more than a minority religion in most of Asia, the Middle East, and Africa. Christianity did become the predominant religion of Latin America (although the Indians of Mexico, Guatemala, Peru, Ecuador, and Bolivia had little choice in the matter,

Cultural Change

and the remaining Latin American countries were settled by European Christians).

Social groups do not borrow indiscriminately; they borrow what will best fit the pattern of their own culture or will disturb that pattern least. And once a new idea or technique is borrowed, it is reworked and reinterpreted so it can be integrated into the old pattern. Earlier the reinterpretation of goods and means of transportation into the "cargo cults" of the South Pacific was described. Among other things, the dark skinned Melanesians interpreted the "white" skins of the airplane pilots and ship crews as being the skins of ghosts and thus their own ancestors. They believed that the pilots of the "cargo" vehicles were really the Melanesians' own people and needed only to be redirected through ritual means back to their own villages; then the living tribespeople would get the cargo.

The North American Indians borrowed elements of Christianity, the psychedelic Mexican cactus button, *peyote,* in combination with certain Indian beliefs to make up the Native American Church. They took the *peyote* button in religious group ritual in the same way that Catholics and Episcopalians take their holy communion, but of course the Indians obtained supersensory effects which the wafer of bread in the Christian ritual would never provide. But the Indians did pray to Jesus. There were all manners of reinterpretations and modifications to make up the "new" institution.

The people of Western European countries also modify and reinterpret what they borrow from others. The "pajama" was borrowed from India where it is an outdoor garment. It was reinterpreted by the British to be sleepwear. The Euro-Americans borrowed the basic human foodstuffs of the Indians, maize, modified it in certain ways (hybridization), altered the techniques of cultivation, and made it primarily into animal feed. They also used it to make a distilled liquor, bourbon, replacing the barley their ancestors had used in the Old World.

Anthropologists have long believed that cultural borrowing is a healthy process for a given culture and for the cultures of the world generally. The ones that borrow most freely are the most viable. The great borrower of Asia was Japan. In its heydey, England was the great borrower of Europe, and in more recent times the United States has been an indefatigable borrower of ideas, and people with ideas, from all over the world. The results have been dramatically described in a famous passage by Dr. Ralph Linton:

> Our solid American citizen awakens in a bed built on a pattern which originated in the Near East but which was modified in Northern Europe before it was transmitted to America. He throws back covers made from cotton, domesticated in India, or linen, domesticated in the Near East, or silk, the use of which was discovered in China. All of these materials have been spun and woven by processes invented in the Near East. He slips into his moccasins, invented by the Indians of the Eastern woodlands, and goes to the bathroom, whose fixtures are a mixture of European and American inventions, both of recent date. He takes off his pajamas, a garment invented in India, and washes with soap invented by ancient Gauls. He then shaves, a masochistic rite which seems to have been derived from either Sumer or Ancient Egypt.
>
> Returning to the bedroom, he removes his clothes from a chair of southern European type and proceeds to dress. He puts on garments whose form originally derived from the skin clothing of the nomads of the Asiatic steppes, puts on shoes made from skins tanned in a process invented in Ancient Egypt and cut to a pattern derived from the classical civilizations of the Mediterranean, and ties around his neck a strip of bright-colored cloth which is a vestigial survival of the shoulder shawls worn by the seventeenth century Croatians. Before going out for breakfast, he glances through the window, made of glass invented in Egypt, and if it is raining, puts on overshoes made of rubber, discovered by the Central American Indians, and takes an umbrella, invented in Southeastern Asia. Upon his head he puts a hat made of felt, a material invented in the Asiatic steppes. [1936:326-327]

In short, the United States as well as the countries of Western Europe borrowed very heavily to achieve the technological and economic leadership of the nineteenth and twentieth centuries. It is suggested that any countries now in an agrarian stage of technology will be required to borrow some of the more recent developments of the industrial countries if they are to approach the productivity of the industrial nations.

Cultural Change

Planned Change

Probably most cultural change in history has taken place by accident; that is, new ideas or techniques have been passed from one group to another without any deliberate, conscious effort. However, there has been, at least since 4000 B.C., the time the first city-states were developed, a process of change dependent on group coercion. The most common type has been change imposed on subject people by a conquering state. A well known example has been the pattern of imposing levies and ultimately taxes. Throughout history, newly dominated people have been forced to give over a portion of their production to the central authorities. But even after the newly incorporated group was given citizen or semi-citizen status, the system of taking a portion of their production would continue in the form of taxation. Basically, a system of taxation implies a hierarchy and governing body which needs wealth both to support itself and to administer the larger body politic; furthermore, such a system implies a punishing or controlling force (police) which can apply coercion to those who do not comply.

This kind of change continues right up to the present with all societies which contain hierarchical organized leadership. It has become fashionable to regard changes presented to the body politic by law as "democratic" or the "will of the people." If this were absolutely so, there would be no need for coercive power through police enforcement to bring about the changes. Thus, the graduated income tax was a change originally devised by specialists in government, economists primarily, and which was not only originally imposed by law (through a definite minority) but continues to be so, with serious penalties for those who do not comply and a full-time department of the hierarchy to locate such transgressors. It is widely known that in Latin American and other "democracies" which also have the graduated income tax but lack effective location and punishment departments, individuals evade paying the tax on a grand scale.

Even more conspicuous examples of the law being imposed through force are described from the "peoples' democracies" and "socialist republics." The Soviet Union modernized itself rapidly, to a large extent by explicitly relying on raw coercion to force compliance with changes instituted by the dominant minority, the Communist Party. Certainly in the early days of the revolution, the majority of citizens were not privy or willing to accede to the quick changes required by the revolutionary movement. This was particularly true of the peasants who, like peasants everywhere, are much concerned with their private landholdings. It is claimed now that in the Stalin era the police executed hundreds of thousands of noncooperating peasants. The nature of landholding was effectively changed.

The process of change through force continues in all modern nations, although with much less brutality now. Laws are passed and police punishment is used to force compliance. If there were no question of morality involved, this kind of change might be quite desirable. Particularly as the Soviet example illustrates, it can produce widespread change in a relatively short period of time—the span of one generation. However, it does require the willingness of authorities to use force without hesitation.

The other kind of planned change is that which is accepted voluntarily by the recipients but planned by outside change agents. Before the twentieth century this kind of change involved either small-scale efforts or dealt with very specialized kinds of innovations. Colonial governments instituted small programs of voluntary planned change in the countries under their administration, although most of the change they effected was through direct or indirect coercion. Agricultural extension programs, which are by definition voluntary, began in the United States in the latter part of the nineteenth century. Organized Christian missionary efforts (change in supernatural beliefs) were greatly expanded from the sixteenth to the nineteenth century and, by comparison with previous missionization efforts, were based to a considerable extent on voluntary acceptance.

In the twentieth century, and particularly the last three decades, there has been a great increase in voluntary planned change. Agricultural extension, as well as community development programs, were increased enormously in the United States, and to a lesser extent in Europe, just prior to World War II. The colonial governments in Africa and Asia began to rely increasingly on

Cultural Change 81

voluntary, self-help programs in the territories under their control. And since the emergence of independent nations all over Africa and Asia, following World War II, voluntary development programs have reached even larger proportions. Also, voluntary or citizen-based community development programs have received much attention in the poorer areas of the industrial nations, particularly the United States. In fact, there is a tendency in urban, ethnic-based community development programs to attempt change without any input from the outside except money. If programs actually worked in this way, there would no longer be any diffusion of ideas. But since local people in community development councils consult "experts" there is a transfer of ideas although it is probably less than in a situation where a conscious change agent is working.

A final comment is appropriate in regard to planned coercive councils consult "experts" there is a transfer of ideas, although it seems that more voluntary change is going on now than in the past, this does not mean that coercive change is not being continued. In fact, government hierarchies find it next to impossible to abandon coercive change; and even when they give lip service to voluntary participation, they still tend to rely on coercive pressure. The degree of coercion applied will vary almost directly with the amount of power available and the moral position of the leadership group. However, this description of the change process will deal primarily with voluntary planned change.

4

The Change Process

The change process is regarded in this book as the transfer of a new idea or technique from one cultural group or subgroup to another, as one of the types of diffusion. Furthermore, it is pictured as a situation in which some representative individual or group is deliberately planning to introduce the new idea and will interact with the prospective recipients until such time as the innovation is voluntarily accepted and integrated into their cultural pattern.

By its very nature, an innovation cannot be something with which the prospective recipients are completely familiar. Even with the most idealistic change technique, classic community development, the local people are expected to identify their problems with the help of the community development specialist. They are not also expected to identify the exact solutions. Presumably if they could, there would be no need for any assistance other than financial. But if planned diffusion is expected to take place, some source of outside ideas also is necessary.

In actual fact, outside ideas, usually technical but sometimes administrative or sociocultural, are almost invariably presented even in community development. Also, such ideas are usually decided upon by members of the governing hierarchy, either overseas or domestic, and then developed into programs and presented to the final hoped-for recipients. At this point the primary problem is how to convince the ordinary man to accept the new ideas.

The obstacles to solutions of economic deprivation, poor health, lack of jobs, or poor education may well be partly financial. How-

The Change Process

ever this aspect of development gets plenty of attention from both donor and recipient groups. But all the difficulties which arise in the transfer of new ideas will not be cured by money. Problems derive from the nature of cultural systems and contact of the peoples concerned, the change agents and the recipients. In other words, such interaction characteristics as motivation, local leadership, and adaptation of an innovation to local patterns are as important as factors of finance.

What will provide success or failure in the rapid introduction of new techniques or ideas? This is the basic question for the change agent. Unfortunately, there is not yet a set of rules that will give pat answers; but a considerable body of helpful information has been gathered by social scientists and development specialists. Most such available case histories come from efforts to introduce innovations to communities of the agrarian societies of the world. And although there would be some differences, it seems likely that the main lessons learned from these could also be applied to project planning and operation in the poor areas of the industrial countries.

The cultural factors which influence the acceptance of a new idea can be considered either as obstacles or as a normal consideration in the change process. The approach selected depends primarily on the background and training of the change agent. For tactical reasons, and because other cultural ways are also valid, the second approach is suggested as the more fruitful one. It is similar to the attitude of the airplane pilot toward the weather. Certain aspects of weather cause him a great deal of trouble—such things as thunderstorms, fogs, headwinds, and turbulence. However, there are opposite conditions for each of the troublesome ones—such as clear air, tailwinds, and calm air. The weather can be either helpful or harmful to the pilot. It is really a way of looking at a range of conditions rather than a natural division. The pilot adapts to the weather. He flies around thunderstorms, goes to an alternate field when there is a fog, and alters his route and altitude to where the headwinds and turbulence are least. He can even find a tailwind this way. Recognizing that the weather exists, it is of no value to the pilot to condemn it and constantly fight against it, so he adapts to it.

In the same way, cultural systems exist. And although some customs can cause difficulties for the change agent, there are others that he can work with positively. In any event, they cannot be wished away, and the change agent who spends all his time fighting against local practices will probably get little else accomplished. The existing customs and beliefs will set limitations as to possible changes. If a given cultural group believes that animal life is sacred, as do some peoples of South and Southeast Asia, a project for setting up an elaborate system of slaughterhouses and meat processing plants is not likely to succeed. On the other hand, religious beliefs and institutions of the same people may provide the means of gaining approval for some other project. The brotherhood of monks may be the most highly respected group in the villages; if they back an idea, it would be well on its way to acceptance. A young agricultural specialist used this local condition deliberately in Cambodia. He would get permission from the Buddhist monks, as well as from secular leaders, to plant the new varieties of vegetables he was trying to introduce. Then he would give some of the first corn or cantaloupe or cucumbers to the monks. Because they appreciated the quality of these products, and had been considered seriously by the change agent, they would encourage their followers to plant the new crops.

What are the major components of the process of planned change? Although there is no map or complete list of categories, it can be understood by subdividing the various activities which a change agent will need to undertake:

1. Establishment of communication with the recipient people.
2. Selecting an innovation, particularly in reference to local motivation.
3. Adapting the innovation to the existing cultural pattern.
4. Utilizing project strategies.

Communication Channels

Most simply stated, the establishment of communication is to enable the interchange of information between the outside planner and the prospective adopters of some new idea or practice. In most instances the primary responsibility for setting up such

The Change Process

channels will rest with the change agent since he is hoping to influence the local people to adopt the innovation. It should come as no surprise that the methods of communicating would be essential for the transfer of ideas. The potentially most valuable innovation will be useless if no way is found to inform the prospective adopters about it, and moreover to convince them to try it. In fact, all other forms of interaction in the change process depend on the development of efficient communication channels.

And although communication channels are important in any social situation, it seems likely that they are particularly so in crosscultural circumstances. The difficulties of information transfer become larger when the people who are interacting have different cultural bases and values. For example, the rural extension agent can rely on the direct profit motivation almost exclusively when he is trying to introduce a new variety of cattle to Western farmers. He can expect to be able to convince them that a few high-grade cattle are preferable to many low-grade animals if the profit is demonstrated to be higher. He shares their attitude toward livestock. But he would have considerably more difficulty persuading herders in East and South Africa to reduce the size of their herds—for one thing because the numbers of animals give them social prestige. Also, the animals are directly involved in social and supernatural practices (Mahoney, 1961; Cassel, 1955).

What function does communication serve in the overall change process? First, it is obviously the main means of establishing working contact with a group. However well-meaning a person might be, if he does not have access to the symbols (language, primarily) of the group he is working with, he cannot touch them deeply. Second, communication is the means of learning more about their customs. A primary requirement for getting other people to accept an innovation is to adapt it to their cultural pattern. This is only possible if their cultural pattern is understood to some extent. Finally, communication is the means of both providing the potential recipients with information about the innovation and obtaining their response feedback, the first of which is absolutely required and the second is almost as necessary.

But how does one set about communicating with people of other cultures—and particularly in order to bring them beneficial new practices or ideas? The change process can be promoted by the use of the following communication channels:

1. The local language.
2. Formal addresses.
3. Mass media (audiovisual techniques).
4. Demonstration of the innovation.
5. Interpersonal exchange (face-to-face).
6. Intragroup (the gossip network).
7. Creation of a positive image.
8. Being predictable.

The Local Language

What to do about the local language is a problem whenever there is crosscultural contact, which means whenever outsiders are working in a community. If the change agent does not speak the local language well enough to meaningfully obtain and transmit information, he must rely on an interpreter, at least for information transmission. It is not here claimed that meaningful change can be brought about only if the outsider can handle the language; but if he does not, it is obviously more difficult to establish meaningful rapport, to obtain information in depth about the culture, or to influence the local people to adopt the given innovation.

Speaking the local language or dialect for social purposes only indicates that the outsider takes the local peoples' customs and way of life seriously, which does impress them favorably. This was partially revealed by the contrasting response toward two change agents in South Laos. Both were employees for the Agency for International Development, one an agronomist and the other a community development specialist. The agronomist had developed a disease-resistant variety of coffee, which was sorely needed and might well have been accepted on a wide scale if he had been more conscious of the problems of cultural diffusion. He was almost completely technically oriented, however, and paid little attention to developing transfer skills. He learned nothing of the local language except two or three greetings. Consequently, he

The Change Process

had practically no communication with local farmers or anyone else who did not speak English. His project was abandoned some two years after he started it.

On the other hand, the community development specialist made a genuine effort to learn the language as well as local customs. And although he never was able to learn the language with complete fluency, he did become competent to talk to villagers, Buddhist monks, and others in their language on development activities. He developed a technique of maximizing his use of the language for establishing rapport, while improving his speaking ability, and without depending on an interpreter. On trips to villages he would take along a driver/language instructor who spoke no English. Frequently, when he spoke to villagers, they would claim not to be able to understand (quite possibly true) and would ask the Lao driver what the American was saying. The driver, who would have been listening to the Lao spoken by his chief, would then repeat the message in more acceptable dialect. He would also interpret some of the expressions of the villagers in Lao, simplifying the terms for his chief. There would be a three-way conversation going on in Lao, with the driver serving as a dialect interpreter. The effect on the villagers was positive. Many of them, particularly the Buddhist monks, later visited the community development adviser, seeking his help on projects (Niehoff: field observation).

The problem of establishing rapport is probably the sole value of learning a local dialect, as in ethnic change projects in the cities of the United States and other industrial countries. In a city such as Los Angeles, the great majority of people can communicate in English. However, the lower class Afro-Americans and, to a lesser extent, the Mexican-Americans have dialectical patterns of speech. The outsider who wishes to work with them will gain an advantage by being able to use their speech patterns to a certain extent (unless they are very ashamed of them, in which case they would probably be insulted to hear the outsider attempting to reproduce their dialect; however, this kind of reaction does not seem too likely in the near future because of the new emphasis on cultural pluralism and subcultural integrity).

It is possible, of course, to learn about the local culture and even to help induce change, through interpreters. Speaking the local language is not absolutely required as are the direct communication techniques. The change agent must set up channels of formal (group meetings), interpersonal (face-to-face), or mass media (leaflets, radio) communication, but he can operate through an interpreter. Knowing the local language is no guarantee that project success will occur. There are many other needs which if ignored can leave a project just as thoroughly rejected as if no communication channels had been established. This has very frequently been true with Peace Corps volunteers, particularly those operating in Latin America. The overwhelming majority have learned adequate Spanish; but if they were not able or willing to adapt to the local culture or motivate the local people, their projects frequently failed to obtain the necessary cooperation. At the same time, relatively good rapport might have been established through use of the local language.

This kind of reaction also frequently occurs when the change agent is an educated civil servant of the same country, usually a high school or college educated specialist working with villagers. Such persons tend to emphasize government and technical requirements: although they are not as ignorant of local culture as Peace Corps volunteers, they may be even more intolerant. This kind of event was reported in an effort to convince village farmers to adopt phosphate fertilizer in Nigeria. The Nigerian extension agent spoke the local language, was a college trained specialist, and was highly enthusiastic about improving farming practices. However, he did no more in communication than to gather farmers in groups and lecture to them. Never giving them a chance to respond, he did not learn that they had many reservations based on past experience with fertilizer. Moreover, they were generally suspicious of government-sponsored projects, a not infrequent attitude with village people. Very few purchased fertilizer (Cohen, 1961). The suspicions and lack of cooperation might have been compensated for if adequate direct communication channels had been established, particularly feedback response. Knowing the local language is hardly enough if the change agent never uses it to listen.

Some innovations are intrinsically difficult to transfer for which

The Change Process

only intensive, long-term, or indirect measures will ensure adoption. Merely speaking the local language will be far from enough. Preventive medical measures seem to be of this type. A classic case has been cited from Peru in which a nurse attempted to persuade a group of mothers to boil their drinking water. Very few did, despite the fact that the change agent/nurse spoke their language and was quite popular. Among other objections, the mothers were not sufficiently convinced of the benefits, to be willing to undertake the necessary extra work in their primitive kitchens (Wellin, 1955).

A change agent who speaks the local dialect or language will be more likely accepted in the local community and thus will more easily be able to learn its patterns. Moreover, he will be able to transfer information about his innovation directly. But in order for actual adoption to take place several other change requirements will also need to be met.

Formal Communication

Probably the oldest form of communication associated with large groups is the technique of gathering an assemblage and lecturing them. It continues to be used in all societies, from the industrial to the agrarian. Examples in industrial countries are lectures in college classes, sermons in churches, political speeches, and addresses to PTAs; in agrarian countries many of the same kinds of formal addresses are given but there are also development agencies of one kind or another, the members of which give speeches to village councils or other assemblages of villagers or urban neighborhoods, trying to get them to cooperate in some kind of government endeavor. This is an obvious way to contact a large number of people; all that is needed is the ability to gather a group and get someone to deliver the message.

In general, it seems that formal communication can effectively introduce the knowledge of an innovation to prospective cooperators but will rarely provide the means to convince them to adopt it. The main difficulty is that formal communication does not usually occur in a setting where feedback is easy. The speaker can ask for questions but there is always only a limited amount of time; and furthermore, because of the lack of intimacy, the responder's ideas are heard by many in the audience. Unfortunately, the poor people of the world's villages generally do not speak out openly when government officials or other important outsiders are around. The local people may then cooperate only as much as they must in order to avoid punishment or to obtain future favors from the change agents. In Indian villages studied by the anthropologist, Dube, communication was almost exclusively from government leaders to villagers, and usually in formal addresses or audio-visual aids. There were speeches, addresses to meetings, and visits by VIPs. Dube found that there was very little means of finding out what the villagers thought of any innovations. Most of the new ideas were tried, although some to a very limited degree, but many were discontinued after villagers found there were few immediate benefits resulting. In general, the local people were afraid to take risks—and they visualized quite a few in connection with several innovations (1958: 22). If feedback channels had been open, some of the fears might have been learned in advance and there would have been the possibility of modifying some aspects of the project. But more than formal and mass media communications would have been needed.

Innovations which can be brought to the point of having their advantages demonstrated, however poor the initial communication, may still be adopted. An irrigation project in a Nigerian village illustrates such as occurrence. The scheme was explained to the village council in a formal meeting, and they agreed to cooperate even though they little understood what was to happen. They merely agreed because the government wanted them to. The dam and first irrigation channel were built by the ministry of agriculture and the advantages were soon apparent. In particular, the bathing facilities were greatly improved. Also, baptisms were easier to perform in this Christian community. In general, the villagers were positively convinced of the value of the new structure and built additional channels so they could begin to grow their crops under irrigation (Palmer, 1961: 44–45).

Thus, it is probable that unless there is a strong demonstration factor or people are very positively inclined toward the change agent, formal communication will not be sufficient to convince

The Change Process

them to adopt an innovation. However, it can serve as a useful means of introducing an idea, to be supplemented by other forms of communication.

Mass Media

Although having much in common with formal communication, mass media and its specialized subbranch, audio-visual communication, is associated with modern times and literate, urban culture. Most of the kinds of communication usually grouped under this term are products of urban industrial technology. In general, mass media communication is considered to be the transmission of information by means of mass-contact aids which have been specifically developed to influence group opinion. Some of the most familiar kinds are pictures, posters, charts, printed leaflets, loudspeaker systems, radio, televison, and films.

How does mass media compare with formal communication? Basically, it has the same advantage, which is widely recognized by all advertisers: that a large number of people can be contacted with minimum cost and effort. However, it has the same basic disadvantage also, which is that feedback is rare and when it does occur it tends to be fairly superficial. The most feedback that mass media disseminators normally get are the behavioral results they are trying to influence. Thus, in an urban culture they find out what percentage of people actually bought a given product or voted for a given candidate. Frequently, relatively superficial explanations for buying or voting are obtained and tabulated. But feedback during the process of decision making is not often obtained.

An added difficulty with mass media is that the forms most widely used have been developed in urban Western culture, and many of the symbols and even the media are unfamiliar to village people of Asia, Africa, and some rural areas of Latin America. The simple matter of relatively high illiteracy creates one problem. Even false perceptions, stemming from lack of familiarity with media mechanics, can cause unexpected difficulties. There is a widespread tale circulating among foreign aid specialists, which, though perhaps exaggerated, probably still has a grain of truth in it. A change agent in public health was showing slides to a group of Pacific islanders, illustrating the harmful effects of contamination by flies. There were transparencies of flies on human excrement and on food, and enlargements of the insect itself to show how the bacteria were carried. The audience watched attentively. At the end of the talk, the "expert" asked if there were any questions. There was reluctance to speak out (perhaps for fear of showing their ignorance) but finally one old man stood up and said, "We very much liked seeing your pictures. We were really amazed by the size of your flies. However, in our country, they are quite small and when they come around, we just swat them." The old man, and presumably others in the audience, perceived the full-sized close-ups as representing the actual size of the flies! Most mass media messages are not so widely misperceived, but lesser misperceptions of the same kind probably do occur in the villages and among the traditionally educated in the nonindustrial nations.

Innovations that are intrinsically difficult to transfer will need more efficient communication than those which tend to sell themselves. Furthermore, it may be surmised that mass media is much like formal communication in that it can introduce knowledge of a new practice but can hardly convince local people to adopt it. And the main problem is that since feedback channels are not easy with mass media, objections to innovations are not learned in advance often enough. This is particularly true with health innovations.

Consequently, in illness prevention projects, local people frequently fail to change their habits unless punishment is applied. Venereal disease campaigns have often had this kind of problem. A case history is cited of such a campaign in Tanzania where hundreds of copies of a pamphlet on the diseases were distributed at formal group meetings. However, the local people were not influenced enough to change their minds as to the seriousness of the ailment—they thought it no worse than the common cold. Also, they were little interested in changing their sexual practices, which were contributing strongly to the spread of the disease (Mtawali, 1951). This kind of change probably requires intensive communication efforts of many kinds over a long period of time. Use of mass media can hardly serve more than to get it started.

The Change Process

Mass media, like formal communication, serves the change process primarily in disseminating initial information about an innovation. However, adoption usually takes place only if other communication techniques are also used or if the innovation provides such clear advantages that it sells itself.

Demonstration

The villagers of the world, as well as the urban poor, are pragmatic people. Indeed, they have had to become so to survive. Nevertheless, the solid core of pragmatism is skepticism. The very practical person has to see how results are obtained before he can believe their value. This is the basis for demonstration, or the technique of showing in a pragmatic fashion the advantages of a new idea or practice. It is the most direct communication possible.

Demonstration techniques were highly developed in agricultural extension work in the United States, where the target group was the farm population and the innovations were improved agricultural practices. To a large extent American farming was transformed through this means, and innovations such as hybrid corn were eventually adopted by almost all farmers. It was not easy though, for the American farmer was a skeptic also. Conversations are remembered among Indiana farmers in the 1930s when this variety of corn was being introduced. They had seen the first scattered fields and were critical—the stalks were short, the roots were shallow, and the crop would blow down in a high wind (Niehoff: personal observation).

A former extension agent, who had gone into community development work overseas afterward, once explained how demonstration worked in Texas to help with this sort of problem. He said:

> There was one particular area of fairly well-to-do farmers who just wouldn't listen to me. I talked and talked and no one would try the new seed. Finally, I decided that I would have to stick my neck out. I found one farmer who jokingly told me he would plant some of the new seed on his farm if I would promise to pay the full difference in profit over the old variety. Although it was not a good practice in general, I decided I would have to do it this time if I

were to make any headway. I did know that the field he promised was in a good spot, in the middle of a wide valley, just along a paved road, where you could see a long way. As promised, he planted half the field with the old variety and half with the hybrid. Luckily for me, there was not much rain that year and the hybrid was a drought-resistant variety. By mid-summer the patch of hybrid corn was the only bright green spot in the valley. You could see it a mile away. My problem was solved. Not only was the farmer convinced, he became my unpaid agent. He invited all his friends to come and look and would even pick them up in his car. After that, it was no time at all before everyone in the valley was growing hybrid corn.

This particular community development adviser was quite successful overseas, primarily because the same kind of communication is valid in the agrarian village. These people too must see that an innovation will really be advantageous. Just as in Texas, it has been shown overseas that a successful demonstration will create a snowball effect. In the Vicos Project of Peru, one of the first innovations provided was the means for cultivating blight-free potatoes. A credit system was set up through which the local Indians could get the seed, insecticide, and other needed material, to be paid off with a share of the crop. Only a few farmers were willing to try the system the first year, but their yield was doubled. Within two years almost all of the three hundred families living there had switched to the new variety, and within six years the community had become the largest potato producer in the region, selling the surplus on the Lima market (Holmberg, 1960: 85-87). Such showing the consequences of a change is what agricultural extension people have termed a "result demonstration." It is not to be confused with merely showing something without any evidence of consequences, which has been termed a "method demonstration." For instance, if the extension agent in Texas had merely shown the farmers how to plant corn seeds twelve instead of eighteen inches apart, and without having them see the harvest, he would have produced an illustration or method demonstration only.

The key to this kind of demonstration is that the result becomes apparent to the prospective adopter. And since the value of this kind of communication depends on providing "proofs" to skeptical

The Change Process

individuals, it requires that conditions be convincing. In the village world demonstrations can legitimately take place only in the farmer's environment. There is a tendency for technicians to want their demonstrations in a controlled environment, and in agriculture this means the "ag station." Where experiment and demonstration are generally accepted techniques in a population, this type of location might be satisfactory. However, it is worth noting that the American extension agent conducted his demonstration in a farmer's field. Where the agricultural station or the techniques that are used in it are hardly known, it is not a very desirable place for demonstrations. The village farmer might believe that different soils, or water, or insect control are the cause for greater yield; but if a double crop is produced on a neighbor's field where the neighbor saw the whole process, the evidence is much more convincing.

The majority of case histories giving accounts of demonstrations have been in agricultural projects. This is no accident. The technique became the mainstay of agricultural agents in the now-industrial countries and many of them, like the man from Texas, have carried it overseas. Also, agriculture is particularly well suited to demonstration because "proofs" generally occur within one growing season and they are quite visible. Other kinds of innovations, such as those concerning many health measures, are much more difficult to demonstrate. The outer manifestations of syphilis, for instance, go away after a few months and a long period occurs during which the entire nervous system is becoming infected but when there are no visible symptoms. The person who would submit to treatment in such instances would not be doing it on the basis of a demonstration effect.

While positive results can bring about ready cooperation from a group, negative results can do much harm, the more so when there are reservations about the other techniques or the change agents. To fail in a result demonstration with an American farmer today is not so terrible since for the most part his occupational group is knowledgeable about and has accepted agricultural experimentation. But in the case of Asian or Peruvian villagers, the whole prestige of the new technology is at stake when a demonstration is made. If the new potatoes at Vicos had not survived the growing season, or had been smaller, the credibility of the Cornell University change agents would have dropped considerably and further cooperation would have been jeopardized.

There is a classic account of a strong negative effect in a pond digging program in India, though it was not designed as a demonstration. A government development worker was advising local people to deepen their all-purpose village ponds. He was not too knowledgeable about the local physical environment and advised several to go too deep, below the clay sealer level. Unfortunately, the villagers in these instances followed his advice, and when the ponds were dug to the sand/gravel underlying them, all the water drained out (Mayer, 1958: 100).

Any kind of technical project can run into unforeseen difficulties. This happens with the best construction firms in industrial countries. However, they make adjustments, and they are not primarily involved in producing demonstration effects. The change agent working in another culture is primarily in the business of changing people's minds, and the technical accomplishments are only a means to this end.

In sum, the result demonstration is one of the most important forms of communication in convincing people to adopt a new practice if the result or consequences can be shown clearly and in a reasonable memory span. Of all kinds of communication, this one most provides "proofs." Furthermore, if conducted properly, it can affect a relatively large number of people. However, in the same sense that positive demonstrations are very effective for getting cooperation, negative results can cause great credibility losses.

Interpersonal Communication

Up to this point forms of communication have been discussed which are widely and deliberately used in industrial society for influencing opinion. Although the value of reaching large numbers of people at minimum cost is recognized, there also are limitations inherent in these relatively impersonal ways of contacting people. The fact is that the most basic and common manner of communication is when two people come face to face and attempt to in-

The Change Process

fluence one another to do something, or not to do something, or just to create a favorable impression. Nothing is needed for this kind of communication but two people and a vehicle of expression, usually a common language.

So far as the change process is concerned, there appear to be two forms of interpersonal communication of significance: that between the change agent and the potential adopters, and communication among the adopters themselves. The first kind is the most commonly recognized. Interpersonal communication of this type is normally the home, field, or sidewalk visit of the change agent, in which he informally discusses the proposed innovation with one or a few people. The advantages of this approach over the formal and mass media methods is that the change agent can communicate as intensively as he wants, he can modify his approach as he judges the reaction of his audience, and he can expect to get a response (feedback). The one consistent disadvantage is that it obviously takes a lot more time and effort to contact the same number of people by this method than it would through audio-visual or formal communication.

It appears from the evidence available that decisions are made as a result of this kind of communication rather than the formal means. This is probably true because it includes the trust of personal relationship which mass media can never have. Moreover, in most of the world there is not much mass media and people are accustomed to this channel for most of their information.

The significance of interpersonal exchange is illustrated by two efforts in Somalia and one in Jordan to improve grazing conditions for herding peoples. In the Jordanian project the efforts were abandoned, while in one of the projects in Somalia the people were not cooperating and the results were just the opposite from what had been expected—they were overgrazing the land. The people in Somalia who were supposed to benefit from the project were not only not cooperating, they were cutting fences and dikes at night (Andrews, 1960: 19–20; Mahoney, 1961: 34–39).

The other project in Somalia got a very different reaction from the local people. After two years of efforts, village societies had been organized which were drawing up their own rules for preserving grazing land, including closing off certain areas for regeneration. Moreover, they had hauled stones, planted trees, and built roads to assist the conservation effort. The project had become so popular that neighboring communities had started forming societies for the same purposes (Ablett, 1961: 138–141).

It should be mentioned that in all three projects there had been positive demonstrations of the advantages of the conservation measures. So, how can such different reactions be explained?

Although there were other influences, one fact stands out clearly. In the two projects which failed to reach the desired goals, communication with the local people was the poorest possible. There is no indication that any interpersonal exchange existed between the technicians and the herding peoples. In fact, the conservation measures were carried out without the local peoples' participation, although they were allowed to graze their animals on the improved grass so long as they kept to the conservation restrictions. Obviously, there was no feedback. The reasons why the local people were cutting dikes and fences were learned only through "trouble-shooting" investigations by anthropologists. The communication from the technicians to the local people in Somalia had been so poor that the local people had a mistaken idea of what was the project goal. They thought it was a well-digging project, designed to provide them with water in the dry season, rather than a range management project.

In clear contrast, the communication techniques were quite effective in the Somalia effort which did achieve its goals. Formal classes had been held for officials and the herding people generally, and a short film was made on the project. However, probably of most significance were the numerous discussions held with chiefs, headmen, religious leaders, and the potential cooperators, in general. Intensive tours of the area were made for this purpose.

Intragroup Communication

In practically all instances a specialist who wishes to convince people in a local community to adopt some new idea will have to initiate communication. This can be either personal or impersonal, or some combination of the two. Whichever he chooses, however, communication will continue in the form of interpersonal contact

The Change Process

within the group. Its common name is gossip. What it means to the change process is that whenever any significant event occurs in a community, people start talking about it. Moreover, it appears that this talk is a powerful force in decision making which has often been overlooked.

Everyone knows that gossip exists, but most people just condemn or ignore it. The times it gets conscious attention is when by chance a change agent hears a garbled rumor of his efforts.

Gossip is private communication and an outsider is not freely included in such conversations. But if he works hard to gain acceptance and identifies key people, he can do much to tap the intragroup communication network. Gossip can be thought of as either positive talk or negative rumors, both of which are important kinds of information to the change agent. He can rest well assured that local response is favorable to an innovation if the gossip is positive.

A good example of an administrator who was clearly aware of the gossip in regard to his project is reported in a public health campaign on the island of Guam. The primary effort was intestinal parasite control in a village of 1,000 inhabitants. The change agent discovered that rat infestation was an important problem to the villagers, particularly because the rodents were responsible for a considerable economic loss. He decided to work on the rat problem as a means to reduce intestinal parasitism. After getting the approval of the villagers, he arranged for a team of specialists to help. They visited each home personally, and also held a series of informal discussions at the local school. The village people who became specifically interested then talked up the project to their friends and the school children carried some of the ideas home to their parents. The author of the report claimed the "bamboo telegraph" was so efficient that information was spread throughout the village shortly after it was given at any meeting. When the project was finished it is reported that over 90% of the homes inspected were improved, some 1,500 rats had been killed, and there was a drop in intestinal diseases (Cowper, 1958: 26–29).

It is suggested that change agents deliberately attempt to get information spread through such intragroup conversation. One such means is suggested in the above instance: of letting the children know so they will take the information home to their parents. Another means is to get the information to the gossip leaders, the barbers, midwives, itinerant merchants, and those who go to many meetings of different clubs and organizations. This is a possible way of compensating for the relative expense and difficulty of using interpersonal communication channels. There is a great multiplier effect in getting information into gossip networks, and in a sense the communicator obtains a large body of unpaid helpers.

Gossip can be negative also, in the form of false rumors. These are also important to know about. It is useless merely to condemn the spread of such rumors, since they do serve a real function in the local social group. In general, it appears that malicious rumors occur when something is happening in a community which the residents view as threatening and about which there is little information. Added to this kind of communication gap will be the lack of feedback channels. The local people just do not know how to contact the responsible individuals or groups for truthful information. Do they blithely ignore the situation? Not very often! A cultural system, including its communication mechanisms, is designed to make the world a logical place. One explanation for the function of religion and mythology is that they provide explanations for life after death, man's purpose in living, and the other aspects of existence which empirical observation cannot answer. In the same manner, rumor tries to serve the function of explaining the unknown events in everyday life. However false, it gives people explanations.

Although functional the rumor may be for the smooth operation of a local group, it can be quite harmful to the goals of a change project. There seem to be two actions that can be taken to compensate for rumors: to improve the quality of communication so the local people learn what actually is happening; and/or to modify the project itself. If there is something about the project which is particularly frightening but which is not absolutely essential, the wisest course of action would be to eliminate it.

Some rumors that have been reported seem farfetched but they indicate how far people will go to explain what to them are bizarre and threatening events. In most of the existing reports, the

The Change Process

effects of the rumors were counterbalanced, chiefly by improving communication. This means that there was enough feedback for the change agents to hear about the rumors in the first place. It is probable that rumors which have actually contributed to the abandonment of change projects have not often been reported. In those cases there was not enough communication for the change agents to learn anything about the gossip.

In a hookworm treatment campaign in Ceylon, information was first collected on the incidence of the disease, which made the villagers uneasy. They were afraid the information was being collected for tax or military draft purposes. Then the free treatment offered was in the form of capsules, with which they were not familiar. The rumor was generated and spread that the capsules contained little bombs which would explode after being swallowed. However, the project organizers then established better communication and persuaded local leaders to sanction their efforts, so that people did begin to take the pills (Phillips, 1955: 267–302).

A type of rumor which can easily occur in any urban environment where construction is taking place is described in connection with a community development project in Cali, Colombia. The project organizers, from a Latin American development agency, conducted a survey in a poor urban neighborhood where the inhabitants were squatters without title to the land. And although the outsiders suggested that a bridge, road, and drainage canals be built for the benefit of the residents, a rumor developed and was spread that it was merely a prelude to convert the neighborhood to a residential zone for the wealthy. Fortunately, these fears were allayed through persistent efforts by working through the leaders to convince the local people that the project was really for their benefit. The physical improvements were finally carried out on a self-help basis through local committees (Siloe, 1958: 1–29).

It may be noted that both rumors appeared just after surveys. Anthropological field workers have learned that for people who have suspicions to start with, a survey without some well accepted explanation is a particularly risky way to begin a project. Unpleasant events have often occurred just following a government or other large organizational survey and local people are justifiably suspicious of them. Something more positive must be done to gain acceptance before the survey is undertaken; and even then, the local people should be well informed as to its nature.

Interpersonal communication in change projects can be of two kinds: that between the change agent and the local people; and that within the local group itself. People tend to believe in personal messages much more quickly than impersonal ones. The disadvantage of interpersonal communication is that it requires much more effort and people to get a message across. One solution to this dilemma is to utilize the gossip network by informing the gossip leaders first so they will pass the message on to their communication followers. However done, interpersonal communication must be fitted into the change process. If it is not directed by the change agent, it will exist undirected and may be transformed into malicious rumors.

Communicator Image

Apart from the direct channels of communication which the development specialist chooses to work through and which will affect his acceptance by the local people, he also will be judged according to the kind of image he projects; that is, he or she will be judged according to *personal characteristics, sex, age, technical expertise,* and *organization affiliation.* Moreover, the local people will judge the outsider according to their perceptions of his status and role rather than what it actually is. In other words, he will be judged according to whether the local people "think" he is technically proficient rather than whether he has high credentials from elsewhere in this technical field.

Why won't people in another culture accept the outside change agent simply as an individual rather than judging him according to a stereotype? The fact is that they do not know him, and they have to make some kind of decision fairly quickly as to whether they will cooperate or not. Moreover, they frequently do not know his specialty, so can hardly use that criterion. So, they use the signposts with which they are familiar, thereby establishing what communication specialists call his "source credibility."

The *personal characteristics* of an individual make up what is

The Change Process

popularly known as his personality. They are the results of the individual's life history and make him outgoing or reserved, oriented toward social relationships or concerned only with "technical rationality." The individual's personal characteristics are principally what enables him to establish empathy with the local people. He is a "proper" kind of person if he fits the local cultural ideal. The man who is working in a Latin American country which emphasizes *machismo* and who shows extreme politeness and sensitivity in his treatment of all women would not be thought of highly by other men, while a "gentleman" in the antebellum South or England of the nineteenth century would have been considered uncouth if he did not treat women of his class with such deference.

Every culture has ideal patterns for personality characteristics and all individuals fulfill these to more or less degree. Naturally, the outsider will much more frequently be operating in situations where his personality is at variance with the cultural ideal. So, he will have to take deliberate conscious efforts to approximate the norms of the host culture or subculture.

The value of deliberate patience by a change agent is described in a change project in village India where factionalism was causing much discord. The block development officer did not rush the villagers (as government bureaucrats are frequently prone to do), but allowed them to slowly bring out the serious factional problem caused by a bitter headman who had recently lost his office. Besides joining local song fests and composing songs about the villagers' problems, the change agent also made daily visits to the deposed headman until he was willing to cooperate. An irrigation device and subsidiary projects were then completed (Link and Mehta, 1964: 13–23).

Most societies of the world have definite norms of what is proper for men and what is proper for women. And although there is in the urban, industrial world a blurring of such distinctions, these continue to be important elsewhere. Since it is obvious that sex cannot be changed—at least not very often—the most desirable alternative is to put people into working roles where their sex is "proper"; that is, men with men and women with women in societies which make strong distinctions. Otherwise, individuals can attempt to de-emphasize sexual characteristics although there are obvious limitations. It is apparent that in societies where women are kept rigidly apart from nonrelated males, no outside male, no matter how much he attempts to de-emphasize his sexual characteristics, will be allowed in the women's quarters or even permitted to speak to unattended women. Such was the case with one of the authors in a field study in India. Although he was able to establish good working relationships with Hindu men and allowed in their part of the house, only a couple of times was he allowed to be in the women's section, and then in the presence of one of the family males (Niehoff: field observation).

A new, sexless role and image seems to have emerged for Western women in non-Western cultures, particularly in those which have strong patterns of segregation, the Middle East and South Asia. Presumably because non-Westerners have seen the freedom which Western women have achieved, and because the ones who are seen are usually from a favored class, they have been given a role and an image very different from that of the local women, and approximating that of men. Thus, East Indians would allow and even invite Western women to ceremonial and social affairs as they would Western men, although their own women would not participate. Insofar as this is true, the sex image distinction would be less significant for women than for men.

Unlike the situation in Western industrial countries, the maturity and experience attributed to age is given much deference in agrarian societies. The older person is considered to be wiser by virtue of his greater years. This consideration will frequently be made irrespective of the technical or educational accomplishments of the outsider. Obviously, the change agent cannot change his age, but he can attempt to appear older and more sober if these are valued qualities.

Since Western industrial culture favors youth and specialized training for bestowing status, the role of the traditional elder is not given high consideration. This is particularly true with young volunteers from the industrial nations, such as the Peace Corps; but frequently traditionalism and age are held in low esteem by technical specialists of the agrarian nations also. And however worthwhile it might be to work with the youth in a village com-

The Change Process

munity on the assumption that they are more prone to change, it should always be kept in mind that the elders usually have the power to undercut a project merely by withholding resources. The same stricture applies to the image of the change agent. By emphasizing his youthfulness, he may lose the older decision makers. In the Philippines a project to introduce an improved rice cultivation system failed largely because the agricultural advisers could not create positive images for themselves. They were educated and socially distant; but most important, they were younger men whose technical training the local elders would not accept as outweighing their own practical experience (Covar, 1960).

One of the clearest descriptions of the influence of age, as well as sex, is provided by a young European women who was working in urban community development in South Africa. She said, "My youth, sex and single status considerably weakened my authority in the eyes of the older members. They had not yet come to value the acquisition of skills or expertise as giving authority. Each of these—youth, female, single status—meant lack of experience" (Junod, 1964: 28–35).

The disabilities of such image problems are not insuperable, however. This is partially indicated by the fact that the above mentioned community development worker was able to set up a functioning family welfare center and institute a number of projects for improving home life. She overcame her difficulties mainly by adapting her program to local conditions and relying on her African assistants to make most of the contacts with local people. One can also surmise that her personal characteristics were in her favor.

Most people who work to help develop other communities have been trained in some academic or *technical specialty:* health, education, agriculture, engineering. The primary exceptions to this generalization are the community development workers, whose expertise is usually expected to be in the analysis of social relationships; and the young volunteer groups, such as the Peace Corps or VISTA. But even the individuals in these organizations will receive some training in specialized fields, such as health or education, and they will be expected to call on full-fledged specialists if they need complex information. In any event, the normal change agent comes into a local community as a specialist in some aspect of development. Overseas he will often be referred to as an "expert"; but wherever located, he is expected to have particular expertise about the specialized field of his title.

Frequently, the technical competence of the outsider will be rated higher than it actually is. In such instances, he can bring about a negative demonstration and lose much of his credibility. Earlier described were community development workers in India who advised villagers to excavate below the sealer level of their local ponds, thus causing all water to run out. In general, the outsider usually starts with a fairly high image of technical competence; it behooves him not to destroy it by creating negative demonstrations.

Finally, although most change agents may think of themselves as the individuals they are, the fact is that very few enter another community except under the auspices of some organization committed to assistance or change. The usual change agent is a salaried person working as a government civil servant, for a foreign technical change agency, a church, or even a foreign or domestic business. Even the expenses of the "volunteer" groups are paid for by some organization, usually a government. Unless the outside organization is new, an image or stereotype will have emerged in the local communities where its members have worked. This image will be assigned to newcomers unless or until the individual does something to alter it. The individual will certainly not be able to change his affiliation but he will have the possibility of emphasizing or de-emphasizing it. Obviously, if a person or agency is currently genuinely concerned with development but has had other goals in the past, the individuals will usually be thought of in terms of the former stereotype. For instance, Christian groups, both overseas and in Euro-American industrial countries, until recently have been concerned almost exclusively with religious salvation, but they are now turning toward more worldly assistance. The religious leaders of many American churches have turned toward racial problems, while overseas religious missionaries have turned toward helping in socioeconomic problems. An example of such a positive image is described from Peru. The project was to introduce a credit cooperative which was sponsored by a Catholic missionary priest. His North American religious order was already highly regarded by the local Indians and they cooperated. The credit union was so successful that it expanded to other communities throughout Peru, and by 1966 was a national movement ("Everybody's Uncle," 1959: 20–24; *Time,* April 22, 1966, 75–76).

Before such a positive image was created, the Maryknoll Order and other development-oriented religious groups probably went through a transitional period during which they carried the image of prior religious orders which did not have such an interest. It is suggested that a change agent working under such circumstances not emphasize his organizational affiliation until he has achieved significant action of the new kind.

Concerning image, in general, it is suggested that five primary roles influence socioeconomic change projects, namely individual personality characteristics, sex, age, technical competence, and organizational affiliation. These are significant both for establishing rapport with the local people and for getting their cooperation on projects. Apart from originally assigning people with the most desirable image characteristics, it is suggested that once in the field the image characteristics be either emphasized or de-emphasized according to whether they are positively or negatively perceived.

Predictability

It is no easy task for an outsider to persuade people to change their pattern of doing things. However, they may be partially persuaded to try a new practice because there is a reward for doing so or because they want to please the change agent. He usually comes to their community as a person of high prestige or influence. But if a project is to require some time before it can be considered successful, the outsider will need to be predictable; in fact, a series of predictable persons will give this image to a whole agency which can then exert a real positive force.

Among peasant villagers, the poorer classes in cities, and the remnants of tribal peoples, there is a prevalent attitude of doubt and suspicion toward outsiders. Such misgivings can only be dispelled through continuous positive building by an individual, and a series of individuals, of a realistically positive agency image. Loose promises, ill-planned projects which must be abandoned, or unexplained behavior in general will only harden the incipient mistrust in such poor communities, creating a negative image which will be difficult to counteract.

The North American Indians in general seem to have generated from their experiences quite negative images of Indian service personnel, as well as a diffuse distrust of other Euro-Americans. Their attitude toward the Indian Service is undoubtedly a product of one unpredictable agent after another, which in the Indian mind finally becomes a general image of the agency. It does not matter that some or most of the programs were developed to help the Indians or that the individual agents usually were merely carrying out the directives of their supervisors. Thus, a program was undertaken on the Navajo reservation to halt erosion and to improve the quality of the Indians' livestock. The soil management technicians of the Indian service decided to reduce the number of animals to the carrying capacity of the range, which was reported to be quite overcrowded. The government bought and destroyed some 400,000 sheep, goats, and horses; land conservation projects were undertaken by the C.C.C.; sheep dipping procedures were started; and special grazing rules were established. Technically, it was a well-planned project; and since erosion was effectively halted, it could be considered a success.

However, so far as influencing the Navajos, both in a short-term and long-term sense, the project was a failure, mainly because the Indians never really understood what the technicians were trying to do. The ideas of range depletion and erosion due to excessive grazing were new to them; therefore, the complicated procedures for destroying animals and allotting pasturage were inexplicable. It might be noted that this reaction is almost identical to that of the nomadic herders in Somalia and Jordan, mentioned earlier. Someone once said that in the international development field, there is no memory. There seems to be some basis for this generalization, and it is certainly supported by the evidence that American technicians made identical project mistakes in different parts of the world over a 30-year period.

The Change Process

The Navajos who were involved in this project found the American administration and its agents completely unpredictable. One Navajo man is quoted as saying, "Before, in the six jurisdictions, you could go to your Agent. Now you go to Window Rock and you go to every department and never find out anything. I myself went to Window Rock many times to find out different things, and the longer I stayed the less I know—[they were] just passing the buck. I ask the superintendent—he sends me to office so-and-so. I go there and they send me somewhere else" (Spicer, 1952: 185–193).

Although this project achieved some of its technical goals, it undoubtedly had a very negative effect on the Indian community, a kind that has created an attitude of apathy among reservation Indians throughout the country. The unpredictability of change agents on special projects has undoubtedly been one of the main "causes" of such resignation.

The change agent must realize that his initial actions will be judged critically. If he is unpredictable or creates this impression with the local people, they will tend to withhold full cooperation on his project or future projects which appear similar.

5
Motivation for Change

Even before a change agent begins working in a local community he will have given some thought to the general kind of innovation he will attempt to introduce. Most such persons are committed simply by their technical training. The agronomist will work on agricultural problems, the public health specialist will work on problems of sanitation or communicable diseases. Probably the only individuals who are not committed to such specific areas are community development advisers and unspecialized members of volunteer groups. They are theoretically concerned with working on problems which are recognized as significant by the respective communities. One of the consequences of this latter kind of orientation is a concern with motivation; that is, what makes individuals have specific needs or wants.

Except for the community development type projects, it is probable that the kinds of innovations which agencies sponsor are selected, at least in general, before any change agent sets foot in a community. There is really no great disadvantage to such a procedure, with one provision: that the change agency really know something about the attitudes and behavioral patterns of the group and, specifically, their possible motivations for change. Otherwise, the actual field workers may be required to spend much energy in trying to convince people to change in ways for which they have no positive motivation.

But if motivation is taken seriously, innovations to be intro-

Motivation for Change

duced will not be chosen exclusively on the basis of technical considerations. This will happen most naturally in the community development type of project, which ideally attempts to find out what people want before innovations are selected.

In any event, the question needs to be considered very early in the induced change process, since all later reactions will reflect the amount of motivation that exists among the local people. At the very least, motivational considerations need to be made as soon as communication channels are established. Obviously, feedback channels will be most important for learning the wants of local people.

Needs

From a survey taken in one of the village areas of the world or in a poverty zone of an industrial country, it will practically always be possible to draw up a long list of conditions which need to be improved. If the survey is in public health, many deficiencies will be immediately apparent. For instance, in a village of Asia there may be no adequate garbage disposal and piles of trash may be lying in paths and lanes just outside the houses. There may be no system of drainage for waste water, it being habitually thrown directly out the door to form muddy holes where insects breed. The entire village area may go under water in the rainy season, due to lack of general drainage. The local wells may not be properly maintained, particularly on their perimeters, where ducks and water buffalo often puddle around in the mud. Many people will appear to have malaria and mosquitoes will be thick. The village people may go to the bushes just outside the villages to defecate. They may drink water from any available source, including polluted wells, nearby rivers, and even stagnant water holes.

A list such as the preceding could be made much longer. A similar one could be made by someone concerned with animal husbandry. The animals may be poorly fed. The villagers might not raise adequate forage crops for the cattle or give any special food to the fowl or pigs, expecting these animals to pick up whatever scraps they can find lying in the garbage piles. The chickens might be disease-ridden, and an epidemic may wipe out two-thirds of the flocks every year just before the beginning of the rains. Both cattle and pigs might also be subject to many diseases. Animals of all types are probably of low quality because there is little selective breeding. Conditions such as these can be noted in practically any of the village areas of the world.

The poverty zones of the industrial countries will have similar lists of conditions: overcrowding, poor garbage disposal, rats, inadequate heating in winter. And instead of animal problems which are economically important to the villager, the urban poor will have the economic problems of getting jobs, resulting from poor training and ethnic discrimination.

The first reaction of the development specialist who has a survey that was made in the community, or who makes one himself, will be to begin with what he considers the worst problems. In the village example, it is likely that the health specialist will decide the most severe problem is contaminated drinking water. The animal husbandry expert may decide that the villagers should start to upgrade the animals by bringing in new breeds and eliminating the existing low-grade ones. If the specialist has the proper government authority, and also offers some kind of special inducement for cooperating, he may get started on his projects and seemingly make some headway. However, the likelihood is that he will find the local people merely going through the motions of cooperation but doing nothing when he or his agents are not present. What has gone wrong?

When the outside specialist began his work, it was obvious to him that the local people needed help. And in a general way, they thought they needed improvement. However, their conception of what was needed was not the same as his. He had defined their needs, based on his own knowledge; and although other educated specialists would probably agree that these were genuine, the local people who had a different knowledge base could not see these needs as genuine or urgent.

The hypothetical health specialist who had decided that the most serious problem was polluted drinking water would start a program of purifying the wells and persuading the people to keep the perimeters clean. Furthermore, he would start a campaign to

Motivation for Change

stop the local people from taking water out of the local water holes, as well as to get them to boil what they did drink. However, according to the beliefs in that culture, water could not be polluted (at least not to the extent of causing illness), so these people would not really feel any need to go to the extra trouble. In the case of the animal husbandry situation, the local people would have been quite happy to see the handsome new breeds brought in by the specialist, but they were really not interested in reducing the number of animals in their herds. Cattle were sacred and also had important social functions for the group.

It seems to be an almost insoluble dilemma. The specialist knows what the people need, but they do not feel the same needs. There is a solution, however. When the villagers verbally agree with all the suggestions of the change agent but do not follow up with actual cooperation, he should remember that he has an image of being a powerful person who, among other things, can provide rewards of unknown amount; but the villagers are not by any means convinced yet of the validity of his technical suggestions. If he expects to get their cooperation he must win their confidence. *One way he can do this is to begin work on needs which they recognize.* He can look over his list and, on the basis of feedback which he obtains from the villagers, he can set up priorities. The health specialist may find that of the items listed, the particular one which bothers the villagers most is the lack of village drainage. They really dread the season when their houses go under water; they are aware of a specific need. The change agent can suggest and institute a plan of simple drainage. Then, after the rainy season, which the villagers will have spent dry for the first time in living memory, the villagers may be willing to try something less obvious but which the health specialist considers more important.

In the case of the animal husbandry situation, the specialist could try to inoculate the animals just before the epidemic season. The village people certainly do not want to lose their animals through disease. Thus, when the inoculated cattle or chickens survive the epidemic, while animals from neighboring villages die, the change agent will have produced a demonstration effect. He will be in a much better position to begin other projects that will not produce such dramatic results but which will benefit the villagers just as much in the long run.

A good illustration of such an occurrence is described in a village improvement project in north India. An epidemic of *hemorrhagic septicemia* broke out in 1949 in the region of Etawah. Before it reached there, however, the village development planners then working in the area instituted an innoculation campaign and 4,727 animals were inoculated. Not one of these died, although there were losses among those cattle which were not inoculated. The following year about 20,000 animals were brought in by villagers for inoculation and other projects for improving animal husbandry were then begun (Mayer, 1958: 256–259).

Over and over again, Western-inspired projects have been unsuccessful in the village world because of a failure to deal with needs of which the local people were aware. Public health specialists and young volunteer generalists, such as those in the Peace Corps, have reported instances by the dozens in which local people were taught to build new outhouses but would not continue to use them. In general, they would go through all this trouble to please the insistent change agents or to show their progressiveness. But with the open bush around, or where village custom decrees that a covering fringe of vegetation be left for common use, why should they use a very unpleasant hole in the ground which can soon become a breeding place for flies? In Burma people first felt the need for public sanitation when villages grew into cities and land speculation caused such common property to be divided, with the fringes of trees cut down.

Village people and others in poverty circumstances are frequently not aware of what is available through science-based technology. The disabilities and discomforts of poverty, low crop yield, sickness, high mortality, and weakness are accepted as inevitable burdens of life. Moreover, their belief system frequently gives them a philosophy which, at least in part, reconciles or consoles them.

But all people must recognize some problems in life because problems do occur and survival requires that the most serious ones be solved, at least partially. The motivationally sensitive change

Motivation for Change

agent will work on these initially. Then he will return to the original list because, from either a health or animal husbandry standpoint, the local people still have a number of important needs of which they are not aware. They are still drinking polluted water and overgrazing their land with low-grade cattle. But to get positive response in these areas, the change agent will need to convince them or generate needs. This can be done most efficiently in a gradual way, educating them and leading them from one project to the next.

Following the first success, the change agent might tackle the overall problem of drainage since the villagers will have learned that their houses can be kept dry in the rainy season. He might begin by trying to get drainage pits dug outside the houses and on the perimeters of the wells, relating this to their confort and desire for cleanliness. The animal husbandryman might try to work out a system for feeding chickens and pigs since these animals do not aggravate the grazing problem and the villagers will be able to recognize the benefit of maintaining them properly, an attitude that can be used later in improving the cattle and reducing their numbers.

How does the change agent find out what needs are recognized by local people? He obviously must have communication channels established so he can obtain relevant information from the local people. He absolutely must be able to listen to them. Then he can possibly identify one of the further needs and take appropriate action.

If he finds out that some problem exists in the local community which they have attempted to solve themselves, the change agent is dealing with a *demonstrated felt need,* a circumstance of one of the strongest motivational forces. An instance has been reported of farmers living near a river in India which had been flooding their land each year. The farmers had been unsuccessfully constructing dikes to prevent erosion. The change agents quickly offered their technical assistance, and strong dikes capable of withstanding the river's force were constructed by the farmers themselves (Mayer, 1959: 295–263).

More common, however, is what can be termed a *solicited felt need.* Local people hear of a change agency operating in their area and approach the proper officials to ask for help in the solution of their problem. One difficulty in depending on such an approach by the local people is that they may also be motivated by hoped-for rewards or subsidies which they think are granted by the change agency. Even so, if he is judicious, the change agent may utilize such motivation to advantage. Consider, for example, a development project in Uganda where local people approached the district officer to request that drilling rigs be sent to their villages to make wells. He informed them that such rigs were not available but that he would assist them in constructing self-help dams. However, they would have to do all the work. Enthusiasm ebbed at first but picked up again, and eventually the whole idea caught the imagination of the villagers. For one dam, 3,000 people were reported to have turned out for the first day's digging. Within several months three dams were finished and another was due to be finished shortly, although one was faltering through lack of participation (Coutts, 1953: 296–298).

Probably what is most common are projects decided upon through consultation between the change agent and the local people, based on what can be called *ascertained felt needs*. However, thoughtful consultation can elicit real motivation even here.

An example is provided in the rat control project on the island of Guam, mentioned earlier. The change agent was primarily concerned with lowering intestinal parasitism. On the basis of surveys and *consultations,* he learned that the local people were greatly concerned with loss of grain due to rat depredations. He then initiated a rat control project, knowing this would also improve health conditions. The local people cooperated fully and the amount of intestinal diseases was lowered (Cowper 1958: 26–29).

If a project is started where no positive motivation yet exists, it will be necessary to *generate needs*. When such is the case, more effort will be necessary, although it is certainly true that needs are created on a massive scale by advertising agencies in urban environments. In village environments needs can be generated by introducing innovations which are clearly demonstrated to be beneficial. It is reported that local farmers were satisfied with existing crop varieties in one district of India. However, when the

Motivation for Change

change agency persuaded some to try the new seeds, the observed advantages were sufficient to convince the farmers to continue growing the new varieties (Mayer, 1959: 239–248).

Direct Benefits

It has been frequently assumed by Westerners that the village people of Asia, Africa, and Latin America are as much or more interested in other-worldly concerns as in the practical needs of this life. One widespread Western belief is that rural people in these areas, as well as Indians in North America and some other ethnic minorities in the industrial countries, are fatalists, and uninterested in improving themselves in the standard economic fashion of the majority of Westerners. There is in fact a thesis in social psychology to the effect that the key to development is the existence of an "achievement motivation" in the traditional norms of the group (McClelland, 1961).

It is undoubtedly true that villagers in agrarian nations as well as most ethnic minorities in industrial countries accomplish less in economic production than individuals in the cultural mainstream of these cultures. But it is open to doubt that this relative lack of accomplishment is due to some innate disinterest in practical affairs. Other explanations are plausible. First, it must be admitted that the villagers of the world have lived for a long time in circumstances under which it was very difficult for the individual to improve himself financially; the difficulties in trying something new have been so great that it was hardly worth taking a chance. A peasant working under a landlord who got the major share of the harvest would have little incentive to increase his output, a situation widely prevalent in Latin America and Asia until recent years. Such an individual would have been helped little by adopting new agricultural practices.

There have also been oppressive taxes and restrictive government controls. But perhaps even more important have been the consequences of insecurity, in the continued unrest and instability of many countries. When such conditions exist long enough, an individual can put little faith in the future and particularly in regard to immovable property. For instance, there is a sharp contrast in the development of land in Laos and Thailand. The Thai, who have lived under one of the most stable goverments of Southeast Asia during the past several hundred years, have developed elaborate drainage and irrigation systems in the main valley of their country, the Menam. Land has been constantly improved there. In contrast, the Lao, who have been subject to depradations and invasions by one outside group after another, and have hardly known any stability during the same hundreds of years, have developed their main valley, the Mekong, hardly at all. In fact, during the 1950s, American technicians attempted to get one irrigation system after another started, none with any significant success. One large, expensive canal-irrigation system was abandoned in Saravane Province in 1961. Another was developed near the town of Luang Prabang, which could theoretically have doubled the rice crop as well as permitting vegetable production in the dry season. However, once this irrigation system was in use, the technicians discovered that the peasant farmers were growing the same amount of produce by merely cultivating only one-half the land they had tilled formerly. In such a situation it would appear that there was no motivation for economic improvement.

However, it is more likely that the chronic instability of the Lao nation had created a sense of defeatism among rural people—particularly so far as land improvement was concerned. By contrast, the Lao did take an interest in the one kind of innovation which is completely portable—education. Villagers were quite willing to cooperate with foreign advisers to help build and operate new schools. Illiterate men had seen enough of the advantages of being a civil servant and being able to read and write in general to want their sons to be educated. It is suggested that improving the land in their perceptions did not provide any lasting practical benefits. What is more, their judgment was probably more realistic than that of the agricultural technicians. Since the 1950s, the country of Laos has again degenerated into a state of great instability. Over half the land is now held by insurgents, and even the part which is in nominal government control is in a constant state of jeopardy. Roads are unsafe and the transport of surplus grain to market is a chancy procedure. The exaction of levies depends on

Motivation for Change

who controls the area at any one time. The Lao who cooperated on land improvement schemes suggested by American technicians would be reaping few benefits from it today. In the meantime, Thailand remains relatively stable.

In short, it is probable that the unwillingness of village peasnats to cooperate with outside technicians may not be any indication they are not interested in direct practical benefits, but simply that in their perceptions the suggested innovations do not sound promising. Moreover, local people may be correct in this judgment as often as the outsider, who tends to evaluate the practices as they would operate in his own social system.

A similar situation exists with the Amerindian, although perhaps with even more intensity. Not only was the cultural pattern of most Indian groups largely destroyed, the individuals were put into very difficult economic circumstances and subjected to vacillating bureaucratic control under the Bureau of Indian Affairs. After decades of such treatment, and with a manifest powerlessness to affect their own futures significantly, many Indian tribes have indeed become apathetic. In their perceptions there was little available that would provide practical benefits.

Despite this attitude, such groups will still respond to practical suggestions, although admittedly the situation for change would be better if such negative occurrences had never happened. There appear to be four kinds of *direct practical benefits* which people in local communities react to positively: *economic, health, educational,* and *convenience.*

The most common concern of poor people, villagers, rural disadvantaged, or urban ethnics, is whether a new idea or practice will effectively improve their economic condition. As individuals, they are not spurred to action by what will happen to the Gross National Product but what they think will happen to their family and kindred. Thus, an irrigation system that will improve the production of an entire district, but which in the perception of the indivdual farmer will not produce more rice in his own field, ordinarily will be received coldly.

The profit motive will usually bring about improvements in the growing of cash crops. Where people live primarily by subsistence farming, they often do not have the facilities to grow cash crops profitably; or they usually lack proper transportation facilities or adequate markets to dispose of them. However, once a region becomes tied to the national or world economy, with local markets to sell products, and if there is sufficient land, the villager is likely to adopt profitable agricultural changes as rapidly as he learns about them.

A clear-cut illustration of this process is reported from the Cayapas River area of Ecuador. The local rural population lived in villages along the river banks and practiced a subsistence economy based on growing corn, manioc (tapioca), and plantains (cooking bananas). In 1948 two fruit companies started a new marketing procedure for buying bananas, sending regular purchasing boats up the river about twice a week. The farmers had to load their bananas on rafts and canoes to meet the river boats at specified places, but they were assured a reliable, relatively high cash price. Bananas began to replace subsistence crops all along the river as far as the boats could go (Erasmus, 1961: 151–152).

The strongest economic motivation will be the one which promises to provide an advantage in the near future. In one region of Nigeria, new breeds of poultry were introduced which quickly demonstrated their advantages. The new varieties, along with new feeding and housing methods, were accepted enthusiastically when it became apparent that the birds weighed 40 percent more than the old variety and sold for almost twice as much on the local market ("Akowonjo Village . . . ," 1951).

Not only are practical considerations paramount in economic innovations, new health practices that are perceived as very advantageous are also adopted quickly. It has been recognized for some time that efficient new curative practices have been adopted widely throughout the world. Penicillin is known and used in even the remote villages of Asia and Africa, usually injected by self-trained medical specialists.

The same motivation does not occur with many disease prevention practices. It has been mentioned that village people do not adopt the use of latrines easily. Why such different reactions? The simplest explanation is that the benefits of latrine use are not

Motivation for Change 121

clearly apparent, certainly if the system does not include a modern plumbing and sewage system. The cause and effect relationships between ill health and defecation in the bush are much more difficult to show than those between penicillin injections and disappearance of yaws lesions in 24 hours.

However, the poor are very pragmatic. They will even go against their own folk beliefs once they are convinced a new practice is beneficial. In a maternity hospital for the poor in Ecuador, the medical authorities consistently ridiculed or forbade any folk medical practices for admitted mothers. However, the real benefits of the hospital care were so clear that the local mothers accepted even this treatment (Erasmus, 1961: 29–31).

In practically all countries, the poor—urban and rural—have accepted formal education for their children as a worthwhile goal. The usual underlying motivation is that the children so educated will get better jobs in government or business. There are even more practical considerations, particularly in the villages, such as the advantage deriving from reading, writing, and arithmetic for dealing more effectively with government officials and merchants. Adult literacy is usually desired, even though older people are frequently shy at being seen in the role of student. In a popular literacy campaign in Indonesia the primary motivation stemmed from a desire of individuals to check their own tax records and to read political tracts. Also, women were interested in reading in order to avoid being cheated by their husbands in financial affairs (Textor, 1954). A literacy campaign in the local language in Nigeria was popular, but the principal desire was to learn English, which was the language of urban shopping (Uzoma, 1948).

Most educational projects are concerned with children, but these also usually enlist positive motivation. Parents see the acquisition of education as the surest way to break the bonds of poverty. Thus, villagers are frequently willing to work on building self-help schools or all-weather roads so their children can get to school. Such projects were consistently the most popular choice of Lao villagers in community development projects in the late 1950s and early 1960s (Niehoff: personal observation).

Very few, if any, change programs are sponsored by governments or other change agencies with the primary goal of making existing activities easier to accomplish or more convenient. In spite of this, the motivation of *convenience* is reported to have been the primary driving force for many a change of habit or adoption of innovation. This has frequently been the case with the sanitary well. Local people not having Western health concepts have been little concerned with the health advantage of such wells, but they have appreciated the advantage of walking a short distance instead of hundreds of yards or several miles to get water in the dry season. This difference of perception is clearly described in a village project in Thailand (Andrews, 1960: 98–104). The same motivation has occurred frequently in regard to irrigation systems, where the initial primary use of the canal may have been to get household water (Palmer, 1962).

What should a change agent do in this regard—tailor all his projects to the motivation of convenience? Although for achieving the good life, there is no logical argument against such a procedure, it is not likely that any change agencies of the world will head in this direction. Still, it is only sensible to recognize this motivation and to utilize it when possible. Presumably, there are also other advantages with which the change agent is primarily concerned. Thus, people who work to build or use a new well because it is more convenient are still getting cleaner water. In fact, the project which combines convenience and economic benefit is not uncommon and it is only good strategy to emphasize the motivation which elicits cooperation most quickly. For instance, an electrical cooperative was established in a rural village in Costa Rica with complete cooperation from the local people. They primarily wanted electric lights (Summary Report, 1957), which provided both direct benefits in permitting people to study, figure accounts, and perform household chores, and indirect benefits in allowing people to socialize more at night. Many activities were made more convenient.

Thus, it is suggested that the principal motivating force for adopting innovations among the poor is perceived direct benefit. Immediate economic considerations provide the strongest drive, although health and educational considerations of direct practical advantage also bring positive responses. Finally, a type of direct benefit which frequently motivates people to adopt an innovation is simply greater convenience in accomplishing necessary or desired tasks.

Secondary Motivations

Although it is being suggested here that the poor of the world tend to be pragmatic and respond most quickly to economic gain obtained directly from adopting a new practice, they are also motivated by other forces. In general, it seems that people will act on the basis of these secondary motivations, but that they are not as strong. However, for some kinds of innovations, especially those whose advantages cannot be easily demonstrated, secondary motivational drives can be crucial. The ones of most significance seem to be *competition, reward* or *punishment,* and *novelty.*

Individuals and groups are motivated to adopt new behavior because they are in competition with others for the desired things of life. In most social groups there are some achievement goals for which individuals must vie with one another, usually some leadership role. This is not to say there are no cooperative tendencies; but except in an absolutely leaderless group (a not frequently occurring situation), there will be some differences in privilege. These are a source of competition. Also, communities will compete with one another for the most desirable things of life. If the government provides services to neighborhoods or villages, each will be in competition with the others for such. Any additional service or advantageous change in a community will put it in a better position in relation to the ones which did not get the change. The community with an all-weather road will be able to get its products to market the year around, while the small community with an industry will be able to provide jobs for all its inhabitants. The same is true of individual competition. The individual fisherman who adopts the use of an outboard motor will catch more fish than his paddle-wielding brothers. And in the poor district of a city, the individual who has a technical training will outstrip his peers who dropped out of high school.

Competition frequently takes the form of status climbing or prestige emulation. Most people attempt to gain recognition from their fellows. In fact, earlier it was stated that this is perhaps a biological drive which exists among other social mammals also. In practically all cultures and in all levels of society, there are approved methods for the individual to gain rank and recognition from his fellows, and few people ignore these. For instance, in cultures which are technologically simple, such as those of hunting and gathering people, where sizable surpluses are not produced, men are rewarded for generosity. This procedure helps to provide a form of food insurance for the group. The hunter gives meat from his kill and will receive some in return from the other hunters. A "big" man is a good hunter and meat giver, and it is he who gets the most desirable woman.

The significance of status differences increases greatly as cultures start to produce sizable surpluses and variety of goods. When this happens, there also is an increase in occupational specialization, which provides a means of indicating differences. Furthermore, class differences emerge. Most people attempt to work toward the status position of those in the higher prestige scale.

One anthropologist, Erasmus, claims that status emulation is the principal motivation for bringing about change and he produces a considerable amount of evidence to reinforce the idea. He describes a situation in Colombia, in which the Coffee Federation, acting as a change agency, provided three million dollars to carry out a hygiene program. This included housing improvements, latrines, a rural water distribution system, and some labor-saving devices for processing coffee. Also, many of the workers obtained new houses through the fund. When the area was surveyed a year later, it was found that houses near the roads and towns were well maintained; but the condition of houses in remote districts was the same as that of the inhabitants' previous houses. Chickens, dogs, and pigs again had the run of the buildings, most of the flush toilets were filthy, many were broken, and crude lean-tos had been attached to the sides of houses to serve as kitchens (Erasmus, 1961: 79–80). It appears that all the farmers were willing to move into new houses and accept new facilities but that only those whose houses were near roads and towns were willing to keep them in good condition. The most acceptable explanation for the

Motivation for Change

difference is whether the houses could be seen by others; that is, whether they served a display function. This behavior hardly differs from that of the middle class American whose first act with visitors often is to show them around the new house. It is his most tangible evidence of prosperity. If no one looked at his house, it is doubtful that he would spend so much time and energy in improving it. The cultivation of lawns in American suburbia can be viewed as a veritable cult built around the motivation of prestige emulation.

A very important factor influencing change through prestige motivation in most of the world is the influence of the city. Almost all new ideas which come to the agrarian countries are funneled through the cities where the national leaders reside. Rural people almost everywhere have become aware of this, and they do much to emulate city dwellers. The influence of the city in Greece is described as follows: A farmer who can afford it sends his son to town for an advanced education so he will become a tax collector, postal employee, teacher, or employee in a bank—all urban controlled jobs; the young man will not return to the village to live but will visit several times a year, bringing along new ideas; his village relatives will adopt some new ideas from him, both out of respect for his urbanity and to appear sophisticated; villagers who have no city relatives will try to copy those who do. Thus the whole village will be affected by city ideas. In one village in Boetia, which was intensively studied by an anthropologist, some of the new ideas recently adopted in this fashion were city dresses, shoes, toilets, and even the practice of going to the hospital when ill (Freidl, 1959: 31–35).

Another strong influence on the process of prestige emulation has been the emergence everywhere of a new middle class sustained by the development of bureaucracies and the growth of industrial urbanism. Status seeking in this social segment has long been recognized in the United States and the industrial countries of western Europe. Moreover, this social level now includes the majority of the population of these countries and is often cited as the primary base of their economies.

Until recent decades there were no middle classes in the agrarian nations of Asia, Africa, and Latin America. Instead there existed social systems containing only two important classes: a small circle of the very rich, and a large mass of the very poor. Today, due to the growth of large cities, the development of civil services, more widespread educational opportunities, and the expansion of mercantile and professional opportunities, an intermediate class has emerged and is increasing both in numbers and importance. The new middle class consists primarily of urban people, usually composed of persons with the equivalent of at least a junior high school education. These people often have no hereditary status in the older social system and their education usually is Western-oriented. They are thus relatively amenable to change, hoping to improve their own positions thereby. What they do is observed and frequently imitated by people of poorer classes, mainly in the cities themselves but ultimately in the villages also. Such imitation can be harmful as well as advantagous. It has recently been noted by nutritionists that mothers in the "peri-urban" areas of the agrarian nations are giving up breast feeding their babies because of medical recommendations, advertisements, and because that is what middle class women do. Unfortunately, most such mothers are poor and not well educated, thus providing too little substitute foods for their babies, particularly protein. Undernourishment of babies in these areas is reported to be occurring widely now (Protein Advisory Group, 1970).

A good example of the effect of emulating middle class ideas, (in this instance, useful ones) is reported from a study of water boiling practices in a Peruvian town. A public health nurse worked with two hundred families during a two-year period, to improve their health practices. In particular, she tried to get the housewives to boil their drinking water. Fifteen of the two hundred families were already boiling their water when she entered the scene. Five of these had been influenced to do so by city relatives. The housewives of two other families had worked on a plantation for an upper class woman who had taught them the habit, and which they continued after their period of employment with her. The other eight boiled water because of a local cultural belief that sickly people should not take "cold" foods or drinks (as unboiled water was classified). This belief, incidentally, had nothing

Motivation for Change

to do with the modern concepts of contamination since it implied that healthy people could safely drink unboiled water, irrespective of its degree of pollution.

The nurse concentrated on another twenty-one families and in two years convinced eleven more housewives to boil their water. Seven of these eleven were converted, mainly because they valued the close relationship with the nurse, who in Peru is a member of a middle class. The other four accepted the new idea after hearing lectures from the public health doctor, who was also of the middle class. None of the people changed because they believed the theory of contamination that the public health people were teaching. In all cases, except with those who held the old folk belief, the people who became water boilers did so because they were influenced by city people or had accepted ideas that had come from middle class health specialists (Wellin, 1955: 73–92).

Communities and other social groups also become involved in competition for status or for resources. Those who have described projects have tended to emphasize the harmful nature of such competition, presumably because one of the major development philosophies, community development, uses cooperation as its action mainstay. Competition within villages or other small communities, usually described as factionalism, is decried by most developers. And it is true that such competition can produce a negative influence on a community development project. Thus, in a case history from India it was claimed that six feuding factions existed in a given village and prevented any community wide effort. However, it must be noted that the community development worker early identified himself with one of the factions, which alienated the other five (Link and Mehta, 1964: 33–39).

But there are reports of the positive use of factionalism also, which would seem to be the most strategic way to deal with it. One such report is in reference to community development in Palau, Pacific Trust Territory. The population was described as split into several factions with varying loyalties and prejudices. The change agents attempted to channel these divisions into clubs and teams for constructive competition. Prizes and trophies were offered as inducements for the accomplishment of development goals and the reporter felt the effort was successful (Koror Community, 1953). It must be stressed that with this kind of approach, the change agent simply cannot identify himself with a specific faction.

Competition exists among individuals and groups and can provide a significant secondary motivation for change. Individuals frequently will adopt new ideas for status emulation or to try to obtain leadership roles in their group. Status emulation is particularly associated with urbanism, rural people attempting to imitate city people. Also, the expansion of the middle class in agrarian nations promotes status emulation, individuals from poor classes emulating those of middle class habits. Finally, groups also compete with one another, providing a force which can be utilized by the change agent if he does not become identified with a specific group.

Individuals will readily cooperate on a change effort if they perceive some positive value in the innovation itself. However, they may also take part because they expect to receive a *reward* of some kind from the change agency or a *punishment* if they do not participate. Certainly in the past, punishment has been widely used as an inducement for people to cooperate. This is the kind of change identified earlier as taking place through coercion, and which has continued in the form of police power to enforce legislation. Socioeconomic change since the end of the colonial period has been more oriented toward change based on voluntary participation, but the idea of providing rewards or punishments has been given up completely by only a few change agencies. Which of the two is more frequently relied upon is difficult to know for certain; although because of the existing philosophy of what the ideal form of change ought to be, reward as an inducement is openly mentioned much more frequently than is punishment.

Where reported in successful projects, reward usually seems to have had a secondary influence, though providing the initial impetus for adoption. It can take two forms: either small gifts or prizes offered for cooperation, or substantial subsidies to cover significant proportions of the cost of self-help projects. An example of the first was the provision of a cigarette to each person who would swallow a pill in a health campaign in Uganda (Jordan, 1957). An example of the second type is a rural community de-

Motivation for Change

velopment program in south Laos in which approximately one-half of the cost of materials was supplied by the change agency (Niehoff: field observation). And although it is suggested that the second type of reward would provide a somewhat greater promise for continuation since there is greater value in the materials, both kinds appear to provide a weak motivation for the actual transference of new ideas or techniques. If no other motivation for continuance exists, people will tend to abandon the new behaviors when the rewards cease.

Punishment appears to have involved much the same response, except in those instances where it has been continued over long enough periods for the innovations or fear of penalties to be internalized. Thus, in a venereal disease campaign in Northern Rhodesia, the local chiefs applied coercion to get people for treatment. However, they were acting under pressure of the European medical authorities and had little interest in continuing threats of punishment against their followers once the campaign was over. The tribal people consequently stopped treatment and dropped all the precautions that had been promoted during the campaign (Evans, 1950).

The sheer novelty of an innovation can attract or repel. Normally this effect is mixed with other types of motivation, especially rewards or punishments. An example of such a novelty attraction combined with a reward motivation is provided in a poultry improvement project in Laos. The villagers seem to have participated both because they were impressed by the unusually large size of the Leghorns and Rhode Island Reds, and because they received the birds free (Niehoff: field observation).

Any very new practice introduced into a village community can produce suspicion. This behavior is a part of the complex of conservatism which helps to insure cultural continuity. If people simply adopted any new thing that was offered them, the cultural cores of their systems would rapidly disintegrate, resulting in systemic chaos. Nevertheless, some basically new practices may provide real benefits; but they do require more patient and knowledgeable communication efforts on the part of the change agents. For example, part of a nutritional improvement program in Guatemala was to take blood samples. The Indian villagers reacted quite negatively since they believed that blood once lost could not be regenerated (Adams, 1955). This belief is quite logical in the absence of Western physiological knowledge. Patient explanation by the change agents and a reward motivation of getting free food for the children sufficiently allayed the villagers' fears.

In sum, it is suggested that reward or punishment and novelty are of secondary significance so far as final diffusion of an innovation is concerned. Reward in the form of gifts or subsidies certainly can be used to obtain initial cooperation; but unless there is a continuing advantage to be derived from the new behavior, cooperation will tend to be discontinued when the rewards are stopped. The effect of novelty seems to be significant mainly in the early stages of a project.

6
Adaptation Techniques

Efforts to induce change are by nature in basic conflict with existing ideas and customs. Moreover, the forces of conservatism are strong in many places because however poor the local life standard may be from the change agent's point of view, it is a successful adaptation to the local environment and enables the people to get by. The new requires risks, and the poor have little margin to take chances. Add to this the ethnocentric bias built into all cultures, and the result is that the new generally has no attraction simply because it is new. The local people may want to have a better life but they fear changing an arrangement which they already know and trust.

Certain innovations provide dramatic demonstrations and these tend to sell themselves. Some examples that have already been mentioned are penicillin, outboard motors, flashlights, firearms. The change agent has merely to show these items to the local people.

Unfortunately, there are large numbers of innovations which would undoubtedly provide real advantages in the long run, if adopted, but which do not produce any dramatic immediate results. Health and preventive medicinal innovations are particularly susceptible to this kind of difficulty. It seems advisable in most such circumstances to build new ideas and practices on the old ones. By completely discounting the traditional, by defining it as irrational and superstitious, the change agent merely creates distrust between himself and the people he is trying to influence, making them less willing to try anything new. All peoples are pragmatic enough that they will most probably adopt an advantageous change if given the opportunity to observe it. However, if the new practice is presented to them along with a demand to immediately abandon the old practice for that life problem, the local people may well refuse to observe enough to find out its advantages.

To adapt the new to the old may be bitter medicine for many Westerners and people from other cultures who have received Western-oriented educations, since Western culture has a strong bias of exclusivity in it—probably stronger than that which exists with normal ethnocentrism. It has been suggested earlier that the predominant Western religion, Christianity, contains a strong notion that its ideas are the only correct ones and that other supernatural ideas are either superstitions or ideas of "false gods." Further, it was mentioned that other religions, particularly those of Asia, are quite eclectic and are willing to take in a variety of supernatural notions. This same kind of belief has been carried into social organization and politics. For instance, the most powerful industrial states, the United States and the Soviet Union, try to convince others that there is only one true ideal condition—their own: capitalism and socialism respectively. And finally, Euro-American science and technology has gone the same way. The idea has been spread that health, agriculture, education, etc., can be "right" only if it becomes like the Euro-American versions. In other words, Euro-American cultural patterns do not really have tendencies for permitting combinations. In the religious sphere one is a Christian; in politics one is a communist or democrat; and in technological matters one is scientific. It is not proper in this way of thinking to be a Christian/Buddhist or a communist/capitalist or scientific/traditional.

Thus, it is hardly unnatural that technical specialists of Euro-American orientation have rarely attempted to adapt scientific ideas to those of other cultures. However, apart from the fact that much of Western science and technology is based on arbitrary but frequently unstated assumptions, adapting an innovation to existing practices can be considered merely as good strategy; the inno-

Adaptation Techniques 133

vation requires some new behavior but does not require that the old behavior be given up at the same time or as a precondition.

This necessity has been recognized by a few specialists of Western orientation in the immediate past, including even a few of the medical profession. It has been graphically stated by G. Morris Carstairs, M.D., who came to know East Indian culture well:

> In the immediate future, it devolves upon those who are introducing western techniques in public health and medicine how best they can adapt the roles of the doctor, the pharmacist, and the public hygienist to fit into cultural expectations. In the process, they may have to consent to assume the mantle of the priest or magician. This does not mean, of course, that they will themselves subscribe to nonrational beliefs, but simply that they will accept the inevitable fact that their own techniques of healing will be accepted "irrationally," as indeed they are for the most part in the West. [1955: 133]

It may well be, as a number of social scientists have suggested, that economic development will not come to the agrarian nations until they accept a fair number of Western practices. However such replacement can be gradual and need not be complete. And those cultural practices which are not critical for socioeconomic change may as well be left alone.

Thus, it is suggested that traditional culture be treated as something which exists and that it needs to be taken seriously on purely pragmatic grounds; by ignoring it, the change agent merely reduces the chances for successful innovation. Moreover, the local cultural system needs to be taken into consideration throughout a project—early, in order to select the innovation; and later, during the interaction period, to adapt it to local customs.

Selecting an Innovation

Efforts to produce socioeconomic change in local communities of the developing nations, and among the poor in the industrial countries, usually begin in the planning offices of development or technical specialists. In such circumstances it is hardly surprising that the main configuration of programs is determined before interaction begins on a local level. This pattern of selecting changes will affect all later stages; and in fact it would take the most brilliant field worker to succeed with an innovation chosen in the central headquarters which is basically unrewarding to the local people. It may even be impossible to succeed. Therefore, this initial selection needs to be carefully considered.

It is probable that most technical specialists will regard the change process, when they consciously regard it at all, as a simple matter of replacement. In this manner of reasoning, uneconomic or "irrational" practices should be replaced by "rational" (Western) economic ones. Unfortunately, what appears to be rational to the outsider may not appear so to the potential adopter, particularly if there is a significant cultural difference.

Every cultural system is a functional whole even if it is operating on a relatively low level of productivity. Customs are interwoven so that an economic or technical practice is related to religious beliefs, social structure, and general values of the functioning system. A change may disrupt a related practice and if the disruption is enough, it might be rejected. Thus, villagers of certain castes in India are reluctant to raise chickens commercially because the bird is ritually unclean (Fraser, 1963: 98–100), while Zulu tribesmen have been reluctant to use powdered milk because it did not come from their own cows, a vital exchange item in the kinship system (Cassel, 1955: 26–29). So it is evident that ritual considerations can influence economic behavior in India, and kinship concerns can influence economic behavior among the Zulu.

The point being made is not that the local practices are better or worse than Western ways but that the simple technique of replacement merely complicates the change process and increases the possibilities of rejection. So the first thing that must be done in the planning office is to answer the question of how an innovation will fit into the local cultural pattern.

There are several ways in which innovations can be classified, such as their complexity, degree of benefit, timeliness, etc. One criterion of great significance seems to be that of compatibility with or degree of similarity to existing technologies or behaviors. Therefore, a threefold classification of types is proposed: *adaptive, additive,* and *replacement* innovations.

Adaptation Techniques

An adaptive innovation is a modification of a set of existing beliefs or practices; an additive innovation has had no comparable beliefs or practices in the local cultural system; and a replacement innovation will theoretically replace a set of existing beliefs or practices. The key to the difference between the three types is the amount of new behavior required and the amount of old behavior which must be discarded when the new practice is adopted. It can be assumed that the greater the changes required, the greater will be the problems of incompatibility with other parts of the system and consequent conflict. Examples of the different types are the following:

Adaptive: Improved varieties of existing seeds, plants, and animals.
Traditional healers trained as modern medical corpsmen.
Improvement of existing roads, houses, or canals.
Additive: Vegetable gardening where none existed before.
Animal husbandry among horticultural people.
Treatment of syphilis with penicillin where no treatment previously existed.
Replacement: Vegetable gardening to replace tree crops.
Brooder chicken raising to replace the open flock system.
Medical corpsmen to replace traditional healers.

Innovations in the adaptive group will pose the fewest problems of acceptance, while the replacement innovations are potentially the most problematical. The adaptive innovations will conflict least with existing customs and will require only a minimum of new behavior.

However, one other significant influence can temper this hypothesis, namely, the degree of advantage obtained from the new practice. If something is obviously advantageous, it will probably be adopted irrespective of its compatibility. Such was the case with the steel axes adopted by stone-using Australians. So also is this true with modern "wonder drugs." Penicillin has been adopted throughout the world, despite conflicts with local practices and objections of medicine men, to cure such diseases as yaws (Erasmus, 1961: 26–27; Niehoff: field observation).

Thus, it is suggested that the adaptive characteristics of a new idea or practice, unless its advantages are very apparent and great, should be considered by program planners. The adaptive innovations, which require the least behavioral change, should be adopted most quickly; while those requiring the most change, replacement innovations, will be least quickly adopted; and additive innovations, which require new behavior only will be intermediate in acceptability.

Local Leaders

Although the initial selection of an innovation is quite critical, there is still the necessity to introduce it to the adoptive group. Here again the change agent is faced with a choice of ignoring the local cultural system or working through it. It is suggested that the former is most effective for the same reason that the innovation selected for its adaptive characteristics is most acceptable. The change agent can work through local leaders instead of ignoring them, or he can modify the innovation to fit local social values rather than opposing them. There may be other reasons for not adapting to a local cultural system but an innovation's acceptability is not one of them.

The leadership pattern is undoubtedly the most significant element of any local culture to work through in presenting new ideas. Leaders influence opinion and they have vested interests in their positions. If powerful influences come into communities without the sanction of the leaders, their position is threatened. An outside change agent does not really have the option of ignoring a local leader, because if ignored, the leader has the choice of either accepting a position of powerlessness or opposing the outsider. Since few leaders willingly relinquish power, the usual reaction in such circumstances is to oppose the outsider.

Normally, in the initial stages of project development, the outside change agent works through official government workers. Such officials can be expected to have more or less accepted the specialist even before they begin working together, or at least to

Adaptation Techniques

have a common interest to bring about change. Nevertheless, no matter how amicable the relations are between the two, the change agent will still need to face his chief hurdle: to take his message to the population, the peasant villager or the urban poor, where there will be other government officials but also other significant leaders. His chief responsibility at this stage will be to identify the persons who actually influence local opinion, and to get them committed to his project goals. The influential persons described most often in case histories of change are the following *administrative, educational, religious, civic, noninstitutional.*

In the villages of nonindustrial countries there are basically two kinds of *administrative leaders:* traditional headmen, and appointed bureaucrats. This distinction reflects the continuance of an old system while a new one is forming. The ex-colonial governments of the world are constantly trying to increase their authority, and one of the principal methods is to assign administrative officials ever more widely. Such appointed officials are persons whose positions depend either on modern education or relationship with the political group in power. They are also allocated the power distributed by the central authorities, the most important of which is the police force. However, in many of these villages the traditional leaders, who are inheritors of the kind of authority that existed before the modern civil service system was begun, have also remained. Such traditional headmen frequently have much credibility with the villagers but relatively little power from the government. Consequently, both types are important for change. The degree of their importance will depend on local circumstances.

An instance of successfully working through such leaders is reported in a case history of one of the erosion control projects in Somalia, mentioned earlier. The change agents held advance discussions with local chiefs, village headmen, and the people in general before they held formal classes on the erosion problems. Then, with the sanction of the leaders, local development committees were organized which drew up the rules for controlling land utilization (Ablett, 1961: 138–141).

The lack of cooperation by leaders can be almost as harmful to a project's success as their open opposition. Such lack of cooperation frequently results from the leaders not visualizing any advantage for themselves. They will then simply go through the formalities with the change agents but do little or nothing to sway their followers. It may be a desirable ideal to picture leaders as persons exclusively dedicated to help those who follow; but the facts of social organization indicate that normally some personal benefit is expected from a leadership role. This reaction probably most often occurs with bureaucratic or political leaders. Thus, a community development project in rural Colombia, sponsored by the government with the assistance of Peace Corps volunteers, was expected to operate through local leaders. The religious and civic leaders cooperated, but the mayor and governor actively opposed the project. Evidently these individuals did not believe they could gain any political advantage from association with the effort. Fortunately, in this instance, the local priest was aggressive and concerned and was able to counteract the administrators' negative influence (Stein, 1964: 179–197).

The local *educator,* teacher or headmaster, may be a very significant person for implementing new ideas. This stems from several basic reasons: he is educated and usually interested in modernization; he is not opposed to change, at least as long as it does not challenge his position; and he works, and frequently lives, in the world of the rural villager or the urban poor, thus having advantages over the county, district, or city official who remains a distant, outside figure. The local educator is most capable of closing the gap between the higher officials and the poor to whom they hope to introduce change. Also, the teacher usually has a relatively good image among the poor because he brings a highly desired commodity—education. And furthermore, the educator is in a very favorable position to put information into the informal communication network. He can present it to his pupils with the expectation that a considerable amount will be carried home to their parents. For this reason, teachers were brought into the early stages of a public health program in Guam, to give students special assignments in sanitation and to lecture them. The children in turn influenced their parents to adopt some new health practices, and a significant reduction in intestinal diseases occurred (Cowper, 1958: 26–29).

Adaptation Techniques

Local teachers frequently initiate change projects themselves and are normally able to get a fair degree of cooperation from their neighborhoods or villages. They can be fairly effective as combination leader/change agents. Thus, a teacher took an active role in developing an agricultural cooperative in a rural area of Jamaica. The market for the previous cash crop, tobacco, had been destroyed by a price decline on the international market. The teacher heard that there was a good market for tomatoes in Canada. He requested a specialist from the agricultural department for technical advice. His position as a trusted leader in the community enabled him to overcome the initial skepticism to plant the seeds and ultimately to develop a financially sound cooperative with 15,000 growers on some 80,000 acres of land (Millard, 1950: 42–45).

The difficulty with teachers as promoters of change is that they can accept outside ideas too freely, and frequently without having the necessary technical background to fulfill the demonstration requirements. An index of the judgment of the headmaster described above is that he obtained the necessary technical expertise from a qualified technician. The effort of a well-meaning teacher in Costa Rica was just the opposite because he attempted to act as the technician without the requisite background. Trying to get local farmers to cultivate vegetables, he planted a demonstration garden which failed to prove the value of the new varieties because the soil was not proper. The village cultivators' opinion was confirmed that the teacher was not an agricultural "expert" and they did not adopt the new practice (Alers-Montalvo, 1957: 3–4).

Although bypassed in many modern governments, the *religious leader* and his organization remain as powerful forces in most of the world. This is particularly true of the established world religions—Buddhism, Hinduism, Christianity, and Islam. The leaders of these groups possess at least four attributes which make them important. First, they are members of large organizations which cover not only whole nations but also whole world areas, which gives them the potentiality of being communication centers. Second, they are well accepted in most of Asia, Africa, and Latin America because they bring another commodity which is appreciated by the majority of men—supernatural aid. Third, almost all local education in the past was in the hands of religious groups. And fourth, recreational ceremonial gatherings, such as the fiesta in Latin America, have often been the only focus of common interest for all community members.

Although religious organizations have been quite important in the world of the villager, this does not mean that they are still the most dominant force. In fact, much of their power has been sapped, both by the secularization of governments and by the growth of extra-village, middle class influence (Gillin, 1960: 53–54). Still, religious leaders in the village world often have enough influence to affect public opinion. The planners of the Etawah Pilot Project in north India took advantage of this situation in a strategic way. Although they took no overt steps to work directly with priests in the village projects, they did name the development newspaper *Mandir Se* (From the Temple). Its masthead showed a villager greeting the rising sun in traditional posture, standing beside a Hindu temple (Mayer, 1958: 188–193). The coverage of the paper was mostly news items and practical advice to villagers, but the layout probably had a secondary effect of bringing Brahmin priests to the cause of change.

Since theologies by their nature tend to be conservative, the most one could normally expect from religious leaders is sanction or approval of secular change efforts. But this role can be very important because village people tend to look to religious leaders for advice on all kinds of problems. An instance is provided by a case history from India. In a vaccination campaign the change agents ignored the local religious leaders and frightened the villagers by their aggressive tactics. The Brahmin priest advised his followers not to cooperate but instead to sacrifice a goat for placating the smallpox goddess. Fortunately for the project, the priest's nephew became ill and the medical people offered to cure him if the priest would sanction the vaccinations. When this was done, the villagers cooperated (Link and Mehta, 1964: 62–67). It is probable that the Brahmin's resistance would not have existed or would have been less if the change agents had actively tried to obtain his sanction from the beginning. As it was, he visualized the vaccinations as merely an alternate technique for preventing illness, but one which would compete with his ritual method.

Adaptation Techniques

Religious leaders also can be activists in mundane affairs. In the last decade many have become deeply involved in the racial discrimination issue in the United States. Religious leaders are openly involved in political issues and even development problems in other countries also. Christian missionaries no longer concern themselves exclusively with the search for religious converts, but work on agricultural, health, and economic problems faced by local people. The potential for an activist role probably also exists in other religious groups. For instance, there was a well-drilling effort in south Laos which was a failure primarily because villagers did not maintain the new wells. However, two or three were put into temple grounds by accident. These were the only wells in the entire project that were properly maintained. Their surroundings were kept clean and dry, and broken parts were replaced (Niehoff: field observation).

Civic leaders are dedicated by nature to development of their communities, so it should be expected that they would work with an outside change agent. They are leaders in such organizations as farmers' clubs, cooperatives, PTAs, youth clubs, and welfare groups. However, they tend to be found in much greater numbers in urban communities than in rural areas because of less extensive kinship relations in the cities. The leaders of these groups can be expected to both sanction and assist in implementing change efforts. The one disadvantage is that these individuals tend to be young and in traditional communities, where age is still given deference, their views may not carry too much weight. However, they should be utilized as much as possible. In a World Health Organization (WHO) project in Egypt, existing local health committees cooperated with the government efforts and significant health gains were reported (Bogue and Habashy, 1952: 1–49).

The *noninstitutional leader* is the person who owes his position to personal achievement in wealth, religious merit, political manipulation, or some other culturally approved criteria for gaining prestige. Such a leader does not have an organized body of followers, but his prestige or respect may still be great enough that he will be listened to, sometimes even over the heads of the formal leaders. Thus, a water improvement project in Ghana was held up for two years because the formal leader, the village headman, opposed it. He even went so far as to consult the local fetish and then reported to villagers that anyone who would work on the project would die. An elder in the village disagreed; he obtained the assistance of the local teacher, and initially persuaded one-fifth of the villagers to help in cementing the base of the spring. When the misfortune predicted by the headman did not materialize, the other villagers were persuaded to cooperate (Yao, 1962: 69–71).

Thus, it is suggested that working through local leaders is of central importance for the successful diffusion of new ideas. Administrative leaders are most important because they are most directly concerned with development, but religious leaders and educators are also significant, mainly because they bring desirable services—education and supernatural aid. The educator is particularly important because he is normally committed to change of some kind. It is, of course, possible to substitute new leaders for old ones and this is normally done in revolutionary change. But if change is not to be forced on people, it will be necessary to deal with old leaders because normally they will not relinquish their base of influence.

Social Structure

Earlier, social organization as a central ingredient of culture has been discussed, including the three primary bases for such group patterns: kinship, territoriality, and special interest. Also, it was indicated that most leaders are the heads of social institutions. Apart from the leadership characteristics, however, there are patterns of conduct for each social institution, and these make up what we call the social structure. In other words, one can have the same type of leader, authoritarian, in a religious or a political organization but the function with an appropriate pattern of conduct of the first will be to propitiate the supernatural while in the second it will be to manipulate power.

Change will basically conflict with the existing patterns of conduct. If the conflict is too great, local people will probably resist the new. If the innovations are modified to fit the group patterns, there will be less resistance. But the group is important for another reason. The only way there can be assurance that a new

Adaptation Techniques

idea or practice has diffused is when it has been incorporated into the overall behavior patterns. As long as only a few individuals adopt the idea, it can disappear when they do, or when they lose interest.

People have strong and deep feelings about social organization and the values that support them, and they impose the standards of their culture on other cultures almost automatically. For instance, most cultures of the world do not claim that all people should have equal opportunities, but this idea has been carried forth by many Western change agents and attempts have been made to impose it on other people, even when the innovation is supposed to be about health or agriculture. Anthropologists and social psychologists do not think that ethnocentrism can be changed in most people by a little study of other ways of life, but they hope that men attempting to cross cultural boundaries will at least learn to recognize when they are applying ethnocentric standards.

The kinds of social behavior which seem to affect innovation projects most are those based on *kinship, caste* (or class), *ethnic group membership, politics,* and *central authority.*

The basic *kinship* unit in the world is the nuclear family of husband, wife, and children. Furthermore a special characteristic of this group in the less urbanized cultures, particularly in Asia and Latin America, is a fairly strong distinction between men's and women's behavior. The man is supposed to be the provider and protector of the woman, but the woman in turn is expected to be obedient and remain primarily in a family or female context. This pattern of conduct existed with some minor differences in European and American cultures prior to the intense urbanization of these countries. And although women's liberation movements and other kinds of equalizing forces are again becoming aggressive in urban societies, women have already obtained more rights in urban societies than in any agrarian ones. Most of the world continues to be much nearer the other pattern, where men and women have different positions and the woman usually is obedient to the man. Unless the Western or Western-oriented change agent makes a choice in this kind of situation, he may encounter unexpected resistances. He can either attempt to adapt the innovation to the local cultural pattern; or he can attempt to require a social change along with adoption of the innovation. It is a question of values. But to unwittingly impose social changes on another kind of innovation—health, agriculture, education—is behavior unworthy of a change agent.

Obviously, if the innovation is of prime consideration, then adaptation is recommended. The role of the male as protector of women was adapted to positively, in a latrine project in Maharashtra, India. As usual, the villagers had shown little interest when the latrines were first suggested. But one day the change agent noticed that the place where women relieved themselves had become quite public. A new road had been built through the area and the lights of passing trucks were shining on the squatting women. The change agent then concentrated on appealing to the role of men as protectors of females, suggesting that they build latrines to provide privacy for their women. This produced a positive reaction which the early sanitary appeal had not (Link and Mehta, 1964: 84–89).

Unlike the situation in urban cultures, the kin group remains as a force of stability and support in most of Asia and Africa. In these societies people become quite unhappy with the impersonal treatment administered by Western institutions. In time of crises, such as sickness, they want to be with their kin rather than separated in a hospital—a sterile, lonely place. The kin group can be included in some manner even if it disturbs Western ideas of sanitation to some extent. Dr. Schweitzer reported that even though he used the least amount of discipline possible in his Congo hospital, the local people still made every possible effort to avoid going there, mainly because they would be separated from their kinfolk. Lepers would visit the clinic only to get medication for home use, and many patients would hide symptoms of ailments that would cause them to be isolated and put under supervision (1931: 110–117).

This emphasis on personal relations and kinship has produced one other significant conflict with a Western innovation, namely, community development, which is expected to depend on impersonal community cooperation. However, kinship concerns frequently exist at the expense of community loyalty. The inhabitants may be loyal to their own village when it is in competition with

Adaptation Techniques 145

others, but before village loyalty they have family loyalty. This kind of situation has been reported often from Latin America. In one instance, an anthropologist attempted to introduce a communal health clinic to a Mexican village and although there were other problems, one primary difficulty was reported as resulting from the strong self-sufficiency of the family, which worked against the idea of an all-village cooperative endeavor (Lewis, 1955: 403–433). An effort to introduce irrigation facilities into a highland Peruvian village area suffered from the same handicap. The tightly knit family relationships, added to the dispersed settlement pattern, made community cooperation quite difficult. The goal of providing irrigation facilities was not achieved (Castillo, 1963). There is nothing sacred about a village or any other kind of settlement, so the change agent need not limit himself by deciding in advance what the ideal cooperative unit ought to be. If it is the family or kin unit rather than the settlement group (village), he can focus his efforts on the former as the cooperation group.

Much the same observation can be made of the next larger social unit, the *caste* (or *class*). However, Western or Westernized change agents are even more deeply ethnocentric regarding this kind of social distinction than they are in regard to the kin unit. It can only be emphasized that the change agent should do all he can to try to learn to recognize when he is imposing his own values. Of course, as cultural relativists, anthropologists hope that change agents do not try to impose all their own values; but as realists, they must accept the fact that many will find it impossible to avoid some ethnocentric actions.

Although equal opportunities are emphasized in industrial societies and class distinctions are not viewed favorably, in most of the world there are clear distinctions based on hereditary position, relative wealth, and education. Such caste or class groups have certain patterns of conduct which distinguish them from other groups within the same hierarchies; moreover, the members of the upper levels practically always have vested interests in their positions. And the basic reality is that resistance is produced when such interests are violated through the introduction of innovations which require equal treatment for all.

Individuals in other cultures desire to preserve their traditional ways as strongly as Westerners desire to impose their values. Moreover, even village people have considerable manipulative powers to sidestep the pressures of outsiders. When the American military forces took over the administration of Palau in the Pacific, they instituted a system of free elections, which of course has a very high value in American culture. The Palauans, had been accustomed to a two-class system of elite and commoners. However, they had long lived under a series of foreign governments— Spanish, German, and Japanese—and had become accomplished manipulators. They did not openly object to the elections; but after the results were tallied, the Americans were surprised to learn that the same persons who had held the offices by hereditary right were still in power. Some were removed by the American administrators because they violated American values too much, but their replacements were later found to be merely "front men," still controlled by the elite in the background. Some changes in power structure did take place; but in general, the traditional two-class hereditary system persisted (Useem, 1952: 79–80).

It may well be that the future of man's culture will require equal opportunity for all, but there is no clear evidence that the industrial world will not return to patterns of hereditary positions. In any event, they still persist elsewhere and the change agent will have to resist them strongly or accommodate to them. The American Friends (Quakers) have a particularly strong egalitarian philosophy, that all men are "equal under God." So when they introduced wells into the Indian village area of Barpoli, they also made a requirement that the installations should be accessible to all, irrespective of caste. The high castes objected due to fear of ritual pollution from low caste well users and consequent weakening of the social system. The Friends attempted to change this attitude; but when they realized that to insist might cause the project to be abondoned in entirety, they dropped this egalitarian requirement and had separate wells constructed for the low castes (Fraser, 1963: 96–98).

Ethnic groups, as subdivisions of societies, are like classes or castes except that they tend to be larger, in most instances there is allegedly a common ancestry, and usually there is a distinct language or dialect. They also have a certain body of customs and

Adaptation Techniques

beliefs of their own which distinguishes them from other ethnics or the dominant majority. In the agrarian nations, ethnic groups may be tribal enclaves, migrant groups, or regional subdivisions, which have not been absorbed into the locally dominant cultures. There are ethnic survivals in industrial countries, such as the Basques of Spain or the Bretons of France; or they may be large and politically significant segments of modern nations such as the French Canadians, Walloons of Belgium, or Texans of the United States. The term as used here would also include what have come to be renamed "racial groups" in industrial cultures, and particularly the United States. As mentioned earlier, such groups do sometimes have a racial component, although for purposes of achieving a desirable social status one part of the ancestry will be emphasized over another. American "Blacks," for instance, now emphasize their African ancestry even though their group is probably at least equally derived from Caucasoid and Negroid ancestors. But most Afro-Americans do have some cultural characteristics in common, including a dialect of English.

Ethnic groups which are conscious of their common culture and ancestry normally have some vested interest in their uniqueness. If they did not, they would not claim ethnicity and would try to merge into the greater society. Moreover, many are in a lower or minority position in the whole society, frequently being exploited economically by the majority. But an ethnic group, even though it constitutes a minority in the total society, is usually large enough to exert considerable force, and more often than not, this is political. The change agent who ignores ethnic wants does so at the risk of project failure. The range management project in Somalia, cited before, in which local people not only failed to cooperate but took direct action to negate the change efforts, owed some of its difficulties to tribalism, a form of ethnicity. The technician began with no consideration of tribal boundaries or desires. Water catchment basins were built in restricted areas and many adjacent tribes were neglected. They brought pressure on their political representatives, who put pressure on the prime minister, who stopped the project. Continued action by the tribal politicians was threatening the entire project (Mahony, 1961: 34–39).

Ethnic considerations today frequently become involved in local *political* organizations. Also, class and caste interests get political expression. Furthermore, since political groups are designed to manipulate power, they can have much influence on a change project. The local political party is stirred to action either because the change proposed is against its interests or the change agents have ignored it. However, political organizations, like individual leaders, can hardly let significant things happen in their communities without their involvement; to do so means to abdicate power, which is unlikely for a political group. Therefore, where they visualize that their position would be weakened or where they do not perceive any advantage by backing a project, political groups tend to resist. Thus, the effort to establish a cooperative medical clinic in a Mexican village was abandoned by the change agent when the local political party, which had not been included in the plans, put up strong resistance and spread damning rumors about it (Lewis, 1955: 403–433).

Finally, a group attitude of crucial importance is the regard of the local people toward the *central authority* of their government. Of course, there are change projects sponsored by other agencies; but the overwhelming majority come under government auspices even though there may be outside assistance. Whether people are positively or negatively inclined toward efforts of their government will depend primarily on the past treatment they have received. In the past, central governments in the agrarian nations have pricipally been instruments for land regulation, tax collection, support of the wealthy, and military conscription. In most of his dealings with a government official, the villager has lost something. Consequently, his attitude toward the government has usually been negative. In the industrial countries the ethnic minorities have been treated to a lesser extent in this fashion and some have also developed negative views toward the government, or at least toward certain of its branches. In the United States this situation seems to be particularly true in regard to the Amerindian and the Bureau of Indian Affairs.

Where such negativism exists, there is a "credibility gap" and local people will not readily believe representatives of the central government. This can be damaging to project cooperation, even in a project designed for the benefit of the local people. It is

Adaptation Techniques

suggested that the attitude will be changed only through cautious and successful innovations or services sponsored by government authorities. The change agent should be aware of the general attitude and be doubly careful where it is negative. A diet improvement project in Dominica, West Indies, suffered from the local people's constant suspicion of the government's motivations. They refused to participate in "Achievement Day" shows because they were afraid the government would tax them more for the better animals they had raised through the project. However, they participated in other ways once they realized their diet was being improved (Christian, 1953: 20–22).

In sum, it is evident that local social structure can provide serious resistance to change projects unless efforts are made to adapt to it. Where significant caste-class, ethnic, or political groups exist, the change agent can simplify the change process if he takes into account the vested interests of these groups. Any attempt to impose egalitarian or impersonal relationship patterns on societies with caste-class inequalities or strong kinship relations will probably impede the transfer process.

Economic Pattern

Although an economic pattern is merely another kind of social organization, it is special enough to be treated separately. This is particularly so because the primary interest all over the world is to produce socioeconomic change, with the accent on "economic." The main interest of both change agents and adopters of new ideas is improvement of their way of life, and this is usually meant to be in economic terms.

An economic system is a pattern for allocating natural and processed resources, and is a set of cultural rules of behavior as for any other social institution. Moreover, however deficient a tribal or peasant people's economic system may appear to the man from the industrial West, it does permit its followers to survive. The deficiency that is frequently noted by outsiders is more often in technology, which the economic pattern must reflect to some extent. Differing economies with similar technologies (capitalist, socialist) can achieve comparable levels of development. It should be emphasized, finally, that the economic pattern is probably more vital than any other part of the culture of the poor. It is only the rich or the desperate who can afford to experiment without much careful consideration. Consequently, no outsider should expect people in poor communities to accept innovations which will disrupt their traditional economic pattern unless there are compelling reasons for doing so. Some of the more important aspects of economic systems that become caught up in change efforts are *work methods, schedules, groupings, proprietary rights, and distribution and consumption patterns.*

Everywhere there are traditionally learned manual techniques that will enable local people to produce the goods necessary to sustain life in the accepted manner. One of the most important of such *work methods* are the traditionally learned motor habits. Alteration of such habits will cause some resistance simply because people will need to go through another learning process to change. So usually, new habits of work will be undertaken in proportion to the degree of perceived advantage of the innovation.

As might be expected also, work habits are harder to change with older people than with the younger. The old have learned the traditional techniques too well and do not have as much continued learning capacity. As an example, in the 1930s the Mexican government established trade schools in rural areas to spread the knowledge of labor-saving techniques, including the potter's wheel. Some years later the government learned that the wheel had not been adopted in Michoacan villages, where circular motions had not been used in pottery manufacture previously. The adult potters either would not take the time or could not master the new technique. In villages where rotary motions had been used, the wheel usually had been adopted (Foster, 1962: 88).

When advantages are considerable, people are more likely to adopt new practices but future advantages will rarely be as important as immediate consequences. The poor cannot always wait long periods of time to get compensation for their labor. An irrigation project in highland Peru failed to stimulate cooperation, largely because the proposed benefits were not apparent, while considerable immediate changes in agricultural methods were required by the adoptees. If the local people had had more confi-

Adaptation Techniques

dence in either the change agents or the proposed innovation they might have been willing to wait longer for the benefits; they did not cooperate enough to find out (Castillo, 1963).

A vital necessity in all systems is that work be *scheduled* in some fashion. The industrial cultures are controlled very largely by clock and calendar schedules. The nonindustrial cultures of the world obviously could not arrange schedules in this manner because, among other lacks, the great majority of people do not have clocks or watches. This does not mean that they have no schedules; but in such cultures work tends to be scheduled according to seasonal variations, the requirements of the agricultural cycle, the natural light conditions (they largely lack electricity), or temperature. Many of these choices turn out to be quite "rational," given local conditions. For instance, working in the early morning and late afternoon, with a rest period in mid-day (the siesta) uses the times most conducive to hard work in tropical climates.

It is suggested that innovations be introduced to fit with local scheduling requirements on all possible occasions. This minimizes potential resistance. Albert Mayer, one of the earliest community development specialists in India, was well aware of this need and worked it into many projects. He helped start a brickmaking cooperative to function in the agricultural off-season, he sponsored a project to build roads in village areas during the period of seasonal unemployment, and he introduced vegetable gardening between the rice harvest and planting time for the winter harvest (1959: 272–277, 239–248, 166–169).

Although most innovations do not quickly produce dramatic results, those that do usually can be introduced without much adaptation, including to local schedules. For example, an agricultural improvement project among Arab farmers in Israel was quite successful after the first year. On the basis of this harvest, which was much greater than usual, they began planting before the rains, a time innovation for them, and at the end of four years all were planting at this season (Turan, 1956: 79–85).

Work is also controlled by who will do it. Although much work in agrarian societies is done by family members or kinfolk, there are also some traditional *work groupings* not based on kinship. A considerable amount of development work, particularly community development and cooperatives, is expected to be done by communitywide groups. Where kinship and personalized relationships are strongly adhered to, local people are reluctant to risk their resources or even their labor with such groups. An effort to introduce a communal health clinic in a Mexican village was abandoned by the anthropologist/change agent, to a large extent because families were self-sufficient and did not want to work in a villagewide cooperative.

Creating work groupings on a model familiar to the change agent and ignoring the possibility of locally existing ones is not a recommended procedure since there will be little natural basis for cooperation. Two cooperatives were organized in a development scheme in India in which caste membership was ignored. The cooperative which was formed by the American change agents with mixed caste membership failed to find willing cooperation and was termed unsuccessful, while the one which was based on the membership of a single caste (Chamar) became one of the most successful ventures of the project (Fraser, 1963: 98–100).

Although there is a wide range of *proprietary rights* in the cultures of the world, the most important kind which concerns international development is the ownership of land. Moreover, proprietary rights in land are quite important because (except in the socialist countries) they are linked with caste or class privilege. Although in many places landlordism produces a negative influence on innovative behavior, it can nonetheless be adapted to without necessarily favoring the privileged. Another choice is to deliberately oppose the landlords, but the change agent will need considerable power at his disposal to do this effectively. An interesting example of adaptation to local conditions is described in a community development program in the Philippines. The construction of a self-help road, desired by the lower class villagers, was impeded by the landlords, who were unwilling to give land for the right-of-way. A compromise was reached by tracing the road along the edges of property so landlords on both sides would donate small strips. Although the road was not straight, the compromise allowed the construction of some kind of road (Orata, 1954: 12–14).

Adaptation Techniques

Insecurity of tenure and very small landholdings can create serious problems in making farmers unwilling to take any chances—they are not worth the risk. In fact, if the holdings are very small, the farmers hardly have the choice of taking part out of production, even temporarily. Thus, in one East Indian village project a proposal to plant trees for fuel made little progress because the farmers were in need of immediate returns on all the land they possessed (Dube, 1958: 59–67, 102–131).

However, even in circumstances like this, adaptations are possible if the change agents keep the farmers' needs in mind. Thus, a project to plant vegetables in a tobacco growing area of Puerto Rico ran into difficulties early because the farmers were reluctant to take any of their small plots of land out of commercial production. A compromise was reached when they agreed to grow vegetables on the edges and in the empty spaces of the tobacco fields (Roberts, 1963). To have initially insisted on utilizing whole fields might have jeopardized the project's outcome; presumably if the vegetables proved more profitable, the farmers would expand their cultivation from the edges.

All cultures must contain *distribution patterns* to spread the fruits of production throughout the population. The two most important in most cultures are the market system and transportation facilities. Although there is the very widespread distribution pattern based on kinship, the assemblage of traders which makes up the traditional market is of most significance for modern socioeconomic change. Also, there is the prime necessity for getting the goods to the market, the means of transport. If the producer has no means of selling part of his production, and cannot consume all of it himself, he will have little incentive to adopt changes that will produce an increase.

Thus, road building projects are frequently inspired by trading needs, and tend to get willing participation from local people. This was the primary incentive to build a six-mile road from a Filipino village to a nearby market center. The particular village was dependent on cash from home-produced mosquito nets which were sold in the city. They built a new road by contributing one-fourth of the cost and all the labor (Einseidel, 1960: 60–62).

Although villagers are strongly motivated by economic advantages, they still tend to cling to traditional, personalized ways of doing business even when these produce less immediate advantages. But from their point of view there are "rational" reasons for such behavior. In many parts of the nonindustrial world the patterns of trading are dominated by moneylenders or traders who buy low and sell high but who also provide services for their clients that are not available through impersonal, Western economic institutions. In particular, they lend money to poor credit risks and for purposes that a Western financier would not consider economic. Such moneylenders have strong vested interests in their positions and will fight against innovations which threaten them. The main innovation is the Western style cooperative, which is usually sponsored by the government or other outside agency. If these are integrated into the local social fabric, provide considerable benefits to the members, and have strong backing by the government or other strong institutions, they can be quite successful ("Everybody's Uncle," 1959; Khan, 1962). However, if the government or sponsoring agency does not give them strong support, the moneylenders will be able to keep the villagers away. This is reported from two producers' cooperatives in Vietnam where the moneylenders were powerful Chinese. The villagers chose to deal with the latter who had undoubtedly manipulated against the new institutions (Montgomery, 1959: 78–91, 144–162).

Ultimately, there must be as a part of the economic system some standardized ways of using the goods that have been produced and distributed, and these are the *consumption patterns.* The ones that have been reported most often in change projects concern food. Although economic considerations seem to be primary, there also are the consequences of long habituation so that people resist new choices simply because they taste, feel or look different. For instance, where production is relatively low, as with village people in the agrarian nations, most of the diet will tend to be the local grain or root staple, rice, wheat, kaffir corn, maize, yams, or cassava. The poor will tend to eat very little meat, primarily because it is relatively costly, and few vegetables either because these take a relatively large amount of attention in cultivation or do not fill a person as much as the grain or root staples.

Adaptation Techniques 155

Thus, when innovations are introduced in conflict with such traditional diets, and/or production, and which offer no other appreciable advantages, they are not quickly accepted. Vegetable gardening for health improvement has often found little response among subsistence or low-production producers. This was clearly the case in an effort to persuade Costa Rican coffee farmers to devote part of their small farm areas to vegetable growing. They would not divert even a small corner of their fields from the coffee production, which was their mainstay, and they claimed they were satisfied with the existing diet which included few vegetables (Alers-Montalvo, 1957: 3–5).

On the other hand, when the innovation consists of increasing or improving the existing foodstuff, there will tend to be a much more positive response. An effort to introduce improved vegetable varieties to Indian villagers was considerably more successful because plant products are the most accepted kind of food for orthodox Hindus, one of the few people who incline toward vegetarianism on ideological grounds (Fraser, 1963: 98–100). Also the Vicos Project of Peru was quite successful with its basic food introduction, potatoes. This is the staple of these Andean highland peoples and the innovation was merely a new variety with new cultivation techniques (O'Dea, 1958: 48–51).

People will change in proportion to the degree of perceived personal gains. In a large-scale irrigation/drainage project in East Pakistan, villagers changed from rice to wheat consumption as payment for their work. There was a considerable amount of grumbling initially at the suggestion to take one-half payment in wheat, but when the amount of wheat was increased so that they got twice as much as they had of rice, they changed their diet. They still preferred rice, and some even claimed they would die if they had to subsist on wheat, but the economic advantage was enough to produce change (Khan, 1962: 4–9).

In sum, local economic systems are normally tailored to the existing technologies of a people and cannot be changed without careful consideration. Moreover, because the poor are less able to take risks, the acceptable innovation will need to have a relatively high benefit. Of the economic behavior described, work patterns and proprietary rights appeared to be least changeable, the first because motor habits and accustomed ways are involved, and the second because the change threatens existing social positions.

Belief Patterns

Besides particular practices of social or technological nature, all cultural systems embody patterns of belief. In fact, a particular belief exists for each custom. For instance, some cultures have a practice called polygamy, or having several spouses simultaneously, while others have the practice of keeping only one wife at a time, known generally as monogamy. These respective cultures have a belief that many spouses are most proper, or that one is, according to which of the alternatives they practice. However, there are also a few kinds of beliefs which seem to be more significant than the practices which stem from them. In the main, these are concepts which explain man's role in the universe; they give individuals a rationale for their acts and a feeling of confidence in their way of life.

The kinds of beliefs which appear to be most significant in socioeconomic change projects are those which explain the *supernatural,* those which concern *health* and disease, and those that relate to the *possibility of change.* However, none appear to produce high resistance if there are clearly perceived advantages for changing. However, where the gains are marginal, the resistance from such beliefs can be significant.

Supernatural beliefs, with their consequent actions, can be subdivided into three classes: theological, derived from the great world religions; spiritual, derived from ideas about the spirit world; and magical, beliefs used to manipulate events through ritual. Supernatural beliefs are utilized most where cause and effect relationships are least clear. Consequently, it is found that they exert the strongest influence on medical or health programs. The advantages of these kinds of innovations are quite difficult to demonstrate. And when there is an existing belief that explains the condition, there is really little incentive for change. Added to this is the difficulty that health workers normally tend to rely on "rational" explanations to persuade local people to change habits, and it can be seen that the problem is considerable. There is a

Adaptation Techniques 157

well documented effort to improve health conditions among the Zulu of South Africa, one part of which was a tuberculosis campaign. After nine years a minimum amount of cooperation and positive results were obtained. A local belief and "proper" action to cure the ailment already existed, to wit that the illness was caused by an "ill-wisher" who poisoned one's food through ritual means. The traditional treatment was a responsibility of the medicine man. The change agents knew about this belief and attempted to counteract it by using "rational" persuasion, showing posters and models of the anatomy of cattle and goats to illustrate that the stomach was not connected to the lungs (Cassel, 1955: 29–34). It should be noted that they were not producing a result demonstration with their models, and moreover that the local people would be taking a big risk by abandoning the medicine man before they were convinced of the efficacy of the new treatment. There was no indication that the change agents conceived of the possibility of adapting the new treatment to the traditional beliefs or even of working out some cooperative arrangement with the medicine men.

In general, the most effective strategy for introducing innovations seems to be to adapt to (or at least not to directly oppose) such beliefs. If a new idea or practice is more effective, it should eventually replace the old idea by its demonstrated merits. Thus, in a health campaign in village India, the change agents encountered a belief that dysentery was caused by the anger of a local deity. And although they used some "rational" explanation for convincing the village people to take the new medicine, they also presented it as a gift of a local goddess. Furthermore, they participated in a village prayer meeting to get the goddess' sanction before the distribution. The medicine was accepted and regular health education started soon after (Link and Mehta, 1964: 33–39).

Supernatural beliefs are frequently relied upon to explain *health* and to cure sickness. But peoples in all cultures also have other ideas to explain the nature of the human body and physical ailments. Moreover, since health is of great concern, such beliefs are quite common. Most are based on seemingly plausible cause and effect relationships. People in South and Southeast Asia believe that clear or running water is pure and fit to drink. The fact is that when water is brought in from water holes, shallow wells, or the river it is frequently put into earthen vessels where the mud can settle to the bottom. Drinking water is then dipped from the top. This is a rational procedure if no microbe theory of disease exists.

In Latin America there was a local belief that water could be "hot" or "cold," a condition not dependent on its actual temperature, and that a well person who drank boiled water was looked down upon. And since there were no other clear advantages for taking the trouble to boil water, few people did so.

New health ideas can be merged into old ones, but perhaps even more important is the need to provide significant benefits, at least until the local people have accepted the validity of the new kind of medicine. It has been mentioned that in a maternity hospital in Ecuador, the medical people deliberately violated or ridiculed all folk beliefs, but that the advantages of hospital treatment to mothers were so apparent that they came anyway (Erasmus 1961: 29–31).

People in poor communities, either in agrarian nations or in the poor districts of industrial countries, tend to have less faith in the *possibility of change* through self-effort than do the more favored educated or middle classes. There is fatalism in all cultures, based either on supernatural beliefs or experiences in the world of the here and now. Fatalistic concepts normally help to explain why unpleasant things happen, rather than the reverse. They relate why someone died or why the crop failed rather than why someone remained healthy or there was a good crop. When such beliefs are based on the supernatural, they tend to explain the events as "God's will" or "the wheel of Karma" or "kismet." Otherwise the explanation will simply be that it was "fate." People like to have causes for everything—even if they are sometimes only a word. Cultural systems do not often condition people to say that things have happened for unknown reasons.

It appears that fatalistic concepts are used most often for after-the-fact explanations; that is, most people in the world will try as hard as they can to control their own lives but when unpleasant things still happen, they will claim that it couldn't be helped since

Adaptation Techniques

it was caused by fate. However, fatalism does have some negative influence on change and should be understood by the change agent.

One kind of fatalism is based on real conditions and can aptly be referred to as situational apathy. People have tried hard to change things for the better without success and have finally given up. Thus, the Indians at Vicos had practically abandoned any efforts toward improvement when the Cornell group of change agents came. They had been living in a crushing socio-economic system in which only a precarious existence could be expected (O'Dea, 1958: 48–51). Another direct example was the reclamation project in North India where villagers had tried to restore their land only to see their efforts washed away each rainy season. They were disillusioned and apathetic when the change agent arrived (Mayer, 1959: 259–262). In these instances, and in most others of which there is record, changes were brought about anyway. However, these were probably managed by the better change agents, since they knew enough about the local people to recognize the existence of such an attitude. Although people of most cultures can suffer failure and still try again, where they have suffered many disappointments their risk inclination usually is lower.

One of the most significant attitudes which is perhaps even more serious is a kind which can be aptly termed "project negativism." It exists where people have had unpleasant experiences from cooperating on prior change projects, and in particular have lost some money or goods in the process. A good example is described in an effort to introduce tractor cooperatives in East Pakistan. The villagers were initially distrustful because they were asked to deposit some of their money, and they had seen similar cooperatives before when other villagers had lost money. The change agency could not persuade the whole community to cooperate initially but was able to get a few important men to begin from whom lines of family trust were utilized to get more depositors. Since there was a recognizable gain from membership, a large number finally came in (Khan, 1962).

In sum, although local beliefs must exert an influence (often negative) on change projects, this does not seem to be exceptionally strong. It is suggested that this is due to the adaptability of the cultural mechanism and the requirement for the viable culture to have provisions for change. Of the three kinds identified, health beliefs and attitude toward change seem most important since supernatural beliefs seem to be used mostly as a means of providing after-the-fact explanations. Other peoples' medical beliefs are based on seemingly plausible cause and effect relationships which probably should be allowed to coexist with any new beliefs. The negative attitude toward change requires only that the change agent be extra concerned that projects be successful, in which case a positive attitude should be developed for future development.

7

Secondary Strategies

The topics of the previous three chapters, communication, motivation, and adaptation, constitute the main influences in the guided change process. Anyone concerning himself with the transfer of ideas simply has to deal with communication; motivation for change will be critical whether or not he considers it; and adaptation to the existing customs and beliefs will be the simplest way to reduce resistance. There are, however, some other influences which appear to be secondary in significance. They are significant enough for independent, although briefer, discussion.

Participation

It is indeed surprising how many failures have occurred in the development field because change agents have not taken the trouble to involve the local people thoroughly in the projects. In this manual, development is considered to be a type of diffusion, of the guided transfer of ideas. Thus, it can be considered as an informal kind of group education. If all development people thought of it in this way, there would be very few problems, since not many educators could conceive of transferring information to students without their participation.

Unfortunately, there are two other facets of development, one or both of which have often been given more attention than this educational strategy. One is the fact that projects are frequently handled by technicians who tend to emphasize the technical aspect of their jobs over the human factor. Too often this has resulted in installations of great efficiency which have never been fully accepted or understood by the expected users.

The average technician, particularly overseas, is highly specialized; from his point of view the local needs are clear. Moreover, he wishes to get something done, for his own career's sake as well as for providing assistance. He tries minimally to explain both the needs and solution to the local people. Sometimes they do not understand as quickly or as well as he wishes; but he is still convinced he knows what they need, so he pushes ahead with the project. Rarely will they openly contradict the technical adviser, for to them he is high on the ladder of important people and they are used to authoritarian directives coming from above. He may request little effort from them, in which case there will be few problems. They may give the bare minimum but discontinue all further effort when he departs.

The other difficulty with development (and this includes domestic programs as much as those overseas) is that the same agency which dispenses the technical knowledge usually also dispenses money or goods. Minority or poverty groups in industrial countries, particularly the United States, will not often bestow such esteem or deference on a technical or any other kind of "expert," but they will be aware, as their counterparts in the worlds' villages are aware, that financial assistance is controlled, directly or indirectly, by this person. And if this is desired (as it practically always is), overt noncooperativeness is poor policy on their part. But they may still provide only minimal effort.

To the person interested in idea diffusion, participation by local people in all stages of a change project means simply that they are being committed to its goals by their giving something, and that they are learning something about the nature of the innovation before the change agent withdraws. Diffusion means integration of a new idea or practice into another culture after a project is completed. Several kinds of such participation can take place, such as the contribution by local people of *labor* or *material* or the development of *organizations* or even nothing more than *passive compliance*.

The contribution of *labor* and/or *material possessions* in the

Secondary Strategies

form of money, land, or locally produced goods is the most common kind of participation asked for and required. The poor of the world can give their *labor* easiest, since it costs them nothing but some time and energy. Even so, such participation should create a strong commitment to continue. Fortunately, there are available two good examples of opposite reactions, resulting primarily from this influence.

As was mentioned in the section on religious leadership, a well project in South Laos failed to produce any lasting results except for the two wells being managed by Buddhist monks. As a matter of fact, there had been a previous well drilling project in the area, sponsored by the same American agency. Three years previously the Lao public works department, with advice and financing from this agency, dug and dynamited seven wells through layers of solid rock, capped them with concrete, and fit them with good pumps. There is no evidence that any participation by local people was required. The wells were used heavily, since a need for convenient water sources was clearly recognized by local people. However, since no one was assigned responsibility, and they had been put in by the public works department, the wells were evidently regarded as "government" installations. Within two years all had broken down and there was no effort by local people to repair them. That year the American regional agricultural adviser repaired them, but still failed to designate any responsibility. In another two years all were out of order again.

In the meantime, the other well installation project was undertaken through American financing and technical know-how in the same province. This time the work was done under a contract with an American driller, using a deep bore rig. His technique was to consult with Lao officials to find out which villages had the greatest need for wells. He would then move in with his rig and crew to drill and cap the new well in a few days. About fifteen were drilled, five of which were at government installations or at the homes of Lao officials. (Any efficient grass roots official learns quickly how to divert some funds or services from dispensing agencies which keep loose records and control.) With the other ten, the villagers were quite pleased and used them heavily as long as they were operative.

Within a year, however, at least half of the village wells were out of order. Usually the breakdown was of a minor nature and could have been repaired locally, either through the public works department or through local machine shops. But the government assumed no responsibility for such repair, nor did the village leaders, with the exception of the two taken over by the monks. The villagers undoubtedly considered these as "government" wells also, just as had the townsmen in the earlier project. After all, they had not been consulted except where to locate each installation, nor was any other kind of participation required of them. And as mentioned before, where the monks took responsibility, the wells were continued in good repair. Also, those drilled on private land continued to be operated efficiently. In those cases the Lao officials assumed responsibility, regarding the wells as their own property.

Could anything have been done for the continuance of these wells? It is suggested that some kind of participation and involvement other than merely pumping water would have helped. Although villagers could not actually drill the wells, they could have managed their maintenance as well as keeping the grounds around them clean. As it was, overflow water was ignored and muddy holes were created around all the village wells. Some kind of training and responsibility could have been initiated for well maintenance early in the project. Also, concrete work might have been required of villagers. They were quite capable of this kind of task, for in a community development program in the same area they put down many school and market foundations in concrete. In short, the users should have been required to commit themselves by actively participating in the well construction and management.

Fortunately, to offset such cases, there are on record instances where the change agents did successfully enlist the active participation of the local people. Although change programs on Amerindian reservations have not often been noted for utilizing the participation of the Indians, there is one such conservation program on record. It took place between 1947 and 1949 on the Papago reservation of Arizona. Several thousand acres of land were reclaimed for pasture. As is not unusual, the change agent had already conceived a plan of action; but before initiating activity, he

Secondary Strategies

presented the idea to the district people. He even located two informal leaders—a bus driver who lived in the district, and an extension employee—and explained his plan to them with the expectation that they would take it to the headman and local people. This seemed to have worked well since the group agreed to build the earth dikes suggested. At this point the change agent/conservationist brought in an engineer to survey the area. The Indians objected to the results. Fortunately, this change agent was sensitive to local sensibilities—he recognized his error in not consulting them in advance about the survey. So, in trying to reassure them that the project was really theirs, he had the survey redone. Only a minor change was made, but the Indians then accepted the whole survey. From that time on, the change agent emphasized his role as that of adviser, not planner. The Indians did the work promised; and when the rains came that fall, the dikes held as predicted. The program was intensified the next two years and proved to be quite successful (Dobyns, 1951: 209–223).

Material contributions probably indicate a greater degree of commitment, however, since individuals are risking some of their own wealth in so participating. In some community development activities, village people are expected to provide local materials as well as the necessary labor. Thus, in Laos, in 1959–1960, villages which chose to build a school on a self-help basis were provided with cement, nails and other hardware, and galvanized roofing sheets. They had to provide all the labor necessary, as well as sand and gravel to make the concrete, and wood for frames and siding. This combination worked out quite well since there was a strong motivational force for education (Niehoff: field observation).

Apart from donating the very tangible commodities of labor and material possessions, there are some kinds of change efforts which require *organizational participation*. As used here, the term means participation in organizing groups for the continuance of a proposed innovation. It takes some commitment and effort to either incorporate a new practice into an existing institution or to create one for its administration. Creation of an institution is no easy task even if the work involved is not so obvious as the manual tasks that are included here under the term, labor. One of the main advantages to organizational participation is that it helps to ensure group continuity. As mentioned earlier, relying on the adoption of an innovation by only a few individuals is risky because if they lose interest or die the new practice will also disappear. Once it is incorporated into an institution, however, it has a superindividual base. Also, organizational participation is required with group based projects, such as community development and cooperatives. The participation in such instances is the visiting, talking, and arranging necessary to create group mechanisms. For most projects, participation by donation of material goods and/or labor is also necessary, but organizing the local people and persuading them to take over the new responsibilities themselves is of the essence.

A relatively ambitious project in community development in nine Fijian villages during 1950 and 1951 is an example. It was a pilot effort to promote agricultural, health, and educational improvements. A cooperative was organized, agricultural projects started, and a medical clinic put into operation. Considerable amounts of labor and goods were contributed, the most important of which was a donation by villagers of 50 percent of the copra crop, to be used as a development fund. After agreement by the most important of the local leaders, a development committee was formed by electing a member of each participating village as well as appointing the headman and minister. This committee then became responsible for planning and implementing the projects selected. The change agents did little more than offer technical advice once the committee was functioning (Hayden, 1953: 2–12).

One disability to organizational innovation not inherent in the other types of participation is the fact that commitment takes from the local people nothing more than some of their time and manipulative energies. Consequently, people may organize or join development institutions merely because it appears to be an easy means of obtaining subsidies or donations. It is advisable to distinguish active participation from mere joining.

A final type of participation can be termed *passive compliance*. This is a willingness to be present when requested, or to allow some activity on one's person or property, but without changing one's active behavior. In general, it is a poor indication that a new idea is being transmitted since nothing is sacrificed but time, and often little of this. The adoption of new forms of behavior require stronger forms of participation. Thus, if wells are being installed or irrigation channels are being constructed, during which time the local people do nothing more than permit the work to be done, there will be little vested interest in continuance nor will new forms of behavior have been learned.

There are a few types of projects, however, which need little more. These are chiefly in the public health field where the passive compliance is the acceptance of such new measures as inoculations or vaccinations, or allowing houses to be sprayed with insecticides. Of course, the continuance of this kind of innovation depends on outsiders (sprayers) doing the work, although people presumably will learn over a period of time that this is an alternative, more efficacious method of solving this kind of problem.

In sum then, participation in change projects is vital because this is the principal way that local people learn the necessary new behavior. Furthermore, it shows their commitment and decreases the possibility of discontinuance after the project is terminated. Contribution of material goods or property indicates the greatest commitment because it is hardest come by, with the contribution of labor of second greatest significance. Organizational participation is important for group-focused projects and because organizational incorporation helps to assure continuity. Passive compliance is useful only when no active behavioral change is required by individuals for the perpetuation of the innovation.

Flexibility

The importance has been stressed of learning as much of the local cultural patterns as possible and then adapting to them. However, the fact is that no full-time field researcher can predict all reactions that can occur in a culture; and a change agent, who will have far less time or experience for such study, will know less. Although it seems likely that even a change agent working with people of his own culture would need to have some leeway to modify his projects, when he is working in a system considerably different from his own the need for modification will be correspondingly greater. But in order for modification to occur, efficient communication is essential, and specifically feedback channels. If the change agent does not know what objections the local people have, he will have no sensible basis for modification.

Unexpected occurrences should be accepted as a normal part of the change process and provisions taken accordingly. The Israeli approach to technical assistance actually uses as a primary technique the ability to improvise considerable changes during the introduction process (Laufer, 1967: 53–59). This is, of course, built-in flexibility.

It is not here suggested that a project will necessarily succeed only because there is flexibility on the part of the change agent. Other factors, such as an unwillingness to adapt sufficiently to local cultural traditions or inherent difficulties of the innovation, may still prevent acceptance. In a health education campaign in Pakistan, an outside change agent had a series of simple pamphlets made and put on the market at popular prices. Initially, the local people would not pay even the low prices required, primarily because this kind of mass media communication has little persuasive power. The health specialist then began giving the pamphlets away. Though they took them free, this did not solve the problem of creating a need for the information. They used pamphlets for a purpose meaningful to them—wrapping market purchases. Finally, the change agent gave the pamphlets to village schoolmasters for distribution to literates. But as has been indicated earlier, new health concepts are difficult to transfer and it is extremely unlikely that a series of pamphlets distributed to literates will do the job. It was reported that even then no significant change in attitudes occurred (Shamsudeen, 1956: 60–61).

But as with all change influences, flexibility can help to produce a positive response and is valuable even when there is only a class or educational barrier separating the change agents from the potential adoptors. Such an instance is described in an effort to persuade Indian farmers to plant an improved seed variety. In this case the change agent, a district officer, even went against bureaucratic regulations to bring about change. Seeds were supposed to be distributed through the government store but there

Secondary Strategies

was not enough interest by the farmers to come for them. Therefore, the district officer went against official instructions and had his assistants take the seeds to the individual farmers, thereby establishing interpersonal communication. The project was then carried to a successful conclusion (Singh, 1952: 55–67). The extension agent in Texas, whose actions were described before, had also gone against customary procedures to get the first farmer to plant hybrid corn.

In sum, it is suggested that project flexibility is desirable because no one can predict all responses of a local group to a new idea. Moreover, it is probable that greater flexibility is required when the cultural difference is great and the benefit of the innovation low.

Timing

Whenever affairs are working out well within a cultural system, or for individuals, there is not much incentive to make changes. However, when there are unusual occurrences, and particularly those which come to the point of being crises, there is a natural tendency to try new actions. After all, if the old ways are not adequate, new ones provide the only possibility for improvement. Thus, crisis timing has been used as a primary technique for innovation, even when crosscultural problems have not been involved (Aguilera, 1970).

The use of timing to introduce an innovation requires that the change agent know a fair amount about the local scene—he has to be able to recognize a significant occurrence; otherwise he might just as probably introduce an innovation at an inappropriate time as the reverse. When that happens it is apparent that he has been little concerned with communication in general. Thus, a Filipino village level change agent, very mechanically following the instructions of his superiors, ignored the fact that an animal epidemic was just beginning in local villages into which he was instructed to introduce an improved variety. He went ahead anyway; and when village pigs died, the local people blamed their death on the new animals as the disease carriers (Einsiedel, 1960: 34–38). The epidemic was mere coincidence but it was hard to convince the villagers after their hogs were dead. The change agent might have waited or tried to prevent death among the animals instead of blindly following instructions.

More significant than such negative instances, however, are the times when a change agent has attempted to help in a recently developed threatening situation. If motivational forces, and particularly felt needs, are considered seriously, the change agent automatically learns about crises. In such instances, the local people inform him what their most serious problems are. In a range management project in Somalia, response was quite positive and significant changes were brought about. The area chosen had been beset by two famines during the previous ten years and another was impending. Most of the cattle had already been lost and the herding people were reduced to cutting trees for charcoal as a means of livelihood. It is apparent that a crisis was in existence and anything which could demonstrate some progress would probably have received support (Ablett, 1961: 38–41).

To introduce an innovation when a local cultural system is facing serious difficulties provides a strong base of support because change is required for adjustment. The special occurrence, particularly the crisis, is therefore an ideal time for innovation introduction.

Continuity

Formerly, in the agrarian nations, and now beginning in the cities of the industrial countries, administrators and specialists have started projects only to abandon them after local people have committed themselves. In fact, where change agencies have been present for many years there is frequently a standard belief that discontinuity is normal. Such a stereotyped attitude is described for north India. The local people believed that demonstrations (primarily of method) and cooperative work group projects were the whims of government which would last for only a few days; therefore, it was best to comply, at least minimally. The local people realized also that the village level workers were government officials, however low in the hierarchy, who were paid and who had to show something to their superiors for the money.

Secondary Strategies

To help make a showing, the villagers would cooperate; by obliging these local officials one might obtain a favor later on (Dube, 1958: 126–128). However, the soakage pits dug for official visits would slowly deteriorate, the compost pits would not be used, and the habits of the people would be little changed.

When a change agent begins a project and then fails to follow through, with or without modifications, his project is not only a failure but he is also building a negative attitude in the people he is trying to influence. This was earlier described as "project negativism." Any successor will find an apathy and lack of confidence that will be hard to counteract. No person can foresee all the consequences of a projected change, but even in the worst of situations he can attempt to keep some element of the project going, maintaining a sense of continuity.

Continuity, or persistent effort, can compensate for many other missing innovation strategies. The Christian missionary movement has been largely based on this strategy, and it must be admitted that many people in Asia and Africa have been converted. The fact is that the message of Christianity has not been readily acceptable to people with very different religious beliefs but the missionaries have simply kept at it without let-up. They also had the continuity of one missionary following another, each carrying almost the same message. Some modern political movements are transmitted in the same fashion. And the prime example is commercial advertising, which also repeats its messages tirelessly, endlessly persistent. Many of the messages of advertising are not at all convincing to a rational mind; but with enough persistent effort, whole populations can still be persuaded to buy the products. The great majority of Americans select specific brands of toothpaste despite the fact that dentists claim they are practically all the same except for flavor and amounts of abrasive.

The positive effects of continuity have been well demonstrated in the Vicos Project in Peru. In 1952 Cornell University took over a hacienda in the highlands with the approval of the national government. It was done with the expectation that the Indians would take over their own administration when the project had run its course. Many achievements occurred in technological, economic, nutritional, health, and educational changes, due in no small part to the excellent continuity of effort. In 1957 the *Vicoseños* took control of their own community as a cooperative (Holmberg, 1960: 82–95).

Continuity, or persistent effort, is essential if a positive attitude toward change is to be maintained in a local population. Persistence can actually compensate for the lack of more sophisticated innovation techniques.

Maintenance

The only final proof that an innovation has been accepted is when the local people are using it as their own, are teaching it to one another or to their children, and the change agent can discontinue his efforts. In order for this to happen some patterns for maintenance usually need to be established. There seem to be at least three different kinds needed: *new skills, organizational responsibility* and *sources for new materials*. These requirements should be fulfilled by getting local people to participate in the implementation process so they will keep the innovation in process automatically when the change agent's stimulus is withdrawn.

The well projects in Laos were described as having been failures, abandoned by the local people as soon as something broke, primarily because none of the above requirements were met. Skills required to keep the perimeters clean and simple repairs were not taught to anyone, although some such requirement probably could have been met even with no outside training. The Buddhist monks and Lao officials kept their wells operating without any special training from the American operator. There were no provisions made for replacement parts, but even this lack probably was secondary as is indicated by the fact that the monks, and perhaps the officials, did manage some simple repairs on their own. The monks in one instance replaced a pump handle part, originally made from cast iron, with a carved wooden piece. The most important maintenance pattern lacking on this project undoubtedly was the absence of any designated responsibility, the social control necessary for the operation of any technical device used by a group.

The requirement to have organizational maintenance patterns in existence at the termination of a project is not easy if a change

Secondary Strategies

agent has taken the initiative throughout and without requiring appreciable participation by the local people. This is so even when the advantages from accepting the innovation are appreciable. Reluctance to take over has often been reported in the formation of cooperatives, presumably because the form that is introduced is usually fairly complex and based on Western models. The local people do not understand exactly how the operation takes place and they see no particular advantage in taking over the time-consuming responsibility of administration. An illuminating instance of a dramatic step taken by a change agency to shift such responsibility is described in an agricultural cooperative project of the American Friends in Israel. The Arab farmers had reaped considerable economic benefits from the new forms of agriculture, but after four years showed no interest in taking over the cooperative. This was despite the fact that young men had been trained in farm machinery skills, and participation in administration had been an integral part of the project. When the farmers showed no willingness to take over, the Friends decided to push them to concern by starting negotiations to sell the project machinery to the government. The villagers quickly organized themselves, and with the training they had received, they were able to operate and maintain the machinery and administration effectively on their own (Tur'an, 1956: 79–85).

In the agrarian nations two special kinds of materials in continued supply are frequently needed for innovation projects, namely, replacement parts for new mechanical equipment, and sources of reading material. The first is required for newly introduced devices, such as the wells in Laos. The second, reading material, is required primarily in connection with literacy projects. It is all very well to teach literacy to a population where previously the majority were illiterate, but it has been well recognized that if no source of reading material is accessible, the new literates will not maintain their skills. Several such projects have been described in former British colonies of Africa. In a combination literacy and community development campaign in Tanzania, the change agents helped to produce follow-up literature for new literates—pamphlets on pottery manufacture, tree and grass planting, and hide and food preparation. Most of these were technically too complex, but a locally established newspaper was more successful (Mason, 1952: 9–14). A literacy campaign in Buganda was quite similar in maintaining the supply of reading material, the follow-up literature totaling almost forty titles. Also a Buganda version of *Today,* an illustrated magazine, was produced and sold at a subsidized price. Particular attention was given to literature distribution by stocking shopkeepers with materials and organizing traveling booksellers (Carr, 1952: 144–148)

The final integration of a new idea into a cultural system is most significantly achieved where patterns of maintenance are established. Innovations can be maintained if new skills are transferred, sources of needed new material are provided, and responsibility for continuance is established.

Conclusions

In the last four chapters a number of suggestions have been made as to how new ideas can be most efficiently transferred across cultural lines. It is not pretended that these are the only possible ones but that they appear at this time to be most important. Furthermore, in order that they be brought together as parts of a whole process, they will be here presented as a series of guidelines. It is suggested, therefore, that diffusion of new ideas into communities of other cultures will occur most easily if:

1. Channels of communication are established by the change agent which provide an efficient two-way flow of information, and particularly including feedback channels.
2. Innovations are initially selected which will meet existing felt needs of the recipients, preferably of problems they have tried to solve on their own.
3. Innovations are selected which will provide practical benefits in this world as perceived by the recipients. Usually these are economic benefits.
4. Innovations are selected which will tend to be compatible with the cultural patterns of the recipients so they will not need to give up great amounts of old behavior or learn large amounts of new behavior.

Secondary Strategies

5. The introduction methods will involve adapting to and working through local cultural patterns, particularly existing leadership.
6. The recipients are involved in full participation, particularly in planning, working, and giving some material goods.
7. The change agent is flexible in his approach.
8. The change agent establishes patterns of maintenance for the continuation of the new idea.

8

The Underdeveloped Areas

Shared Characteristics

Although the culture of each country in the less productive areas of the world is unique in many respects, there are some characteristics which almost all of them share. And to a lesser degree, the ethnic minorities that have not been absorbed into the mainstream of the industrial nations reflect some of the same characteristics. This is mainly due to the fact that they have experienced a common history in the past four hundred years in their relationship to the industrializing Euro-American countries. Although it is known that the nations of Asia, Africa, and Latin America had problems before the appearance of the first Westerners, their current problems, particularly in productivity, are due chiefly to the impact of the West. Indeed the only reason they can be called "underdeveloped" or "developing" is in comparison with the "developed" nations of the industrial West. It is of value, therefore, to know what took place after 1500 when the first Westerners appeared in these countries.

The Colonial Past

The technical advances that the Westerner brings to the developing or agrarian nations sometimes have the unfortunate appearance of being measures designed for the advantage of economic

The Underdeveloped Areas

exploiters. And in the narrowest sense, a change agent is in another country for some interest of his own organization or country, not to mention for him personally. This is generally recognized. Villagers do not expect their own officials to act purely from the goodness of their hearts, so it would be surprising if they expected such of outsiders. In many places overseas, Peace Corps volunteers have had an image problem in this regard—the local people did not know why someone would work as a volunteer, and with "peace" as the exclusive goal. The situation was ameliorated to some extent by the fact that from the villager's point of view, the American was not really working for nothing, but still was working for quite a bit less than other opulent Americans.

The self-interest of the development specialist definitely includes the requirement that he try to improve the conditions of the community where he is assigned. And although there are undoubtedly other criteria applied, part of the success of the change agent depends on the achievement of the local communities where he is working. In this sense, the effort is cooperative rather than one-way, as has been the case too often in the past.

However, the particular danger to the change agent's program does not arise from the merits or demerits of techniques being applied, nor for any personal dislike toward him, but because the weight of the past is frequently against him. The history of contact between the industrial Western countries and the agrarian, mostly tropical, nations is long and has not always been pleasant. It has given rise to certain important widespread attitudes which it would be folly to ignore. The change agent must deal with them in some measure and for this he needs some insight.

Economic development is not new in the world, and particularly in its coercive form. The history of contacts between the Western and non-Western countries is strewn with the indications of past attempts at development, some having produced long-lasting effects while others have left nothing more than the relics of abandoned projects. Many of these have been well intentioned, although most were undertaken for the clear benefit of the colonizing powers; if the local cultures also received benefit, that was considered no more than an added bonus.

The record of colonialism shows a considerable measure of

success in producing change. Most of the great cities of Asia and Africa were built first as trading enclaves by European powers, later becoming the industrial and administrative centers of the new or newly independent countries. Places such as Saigon, New Delhi, Karachi, Lagos, and Nairobi either did not exist or were no more than provincial towns before the beginning of the colonial period. Elaborate transport systems, such as the railway networks and road systems in India and Pakistan, were built by colonizing powers. Asphalt roads, the only kind of paved surface known in many countries, were unknown before the Western impact. Seaports were constructed, industries begun, plantation systems set up, and educational and administrative systems were organized in most such countries. But the developments of this era are inseparable from the record of wars, conquests, seizures, uses and abuses of natural and human resources, headlong economic booms and busts in prices of raw materials or plantation products, colonization at breakneck speed, and "openings" which have filled the period of Western European expansion and which have taken the Westerner to every corner of the earth.

A glance at the history of European expansion since 1500, and particularly what they found in the rest of the world at the time of discovery, is worth the effort. The productive inequality between nations which exists today really came into being during this period and provides no insight into the state of the local civilizations that graced Asia, America, and Africa before Columbus. The Spanish conquistadors marvelled at the empires of the Aztec in Mexico and the Inca in Peru, comparing the cities of Tenochtitlan and Cuzco favorably with their own urban centers. The chief reason these Spanish adventurers labored so mightily to get to these capitals was for the gold and silver they had heard about—a report that was amply true, especially for Peru. At that time also the excellent products of China and India were in great demand in Europe, which was one of the reasons that European nations initially strove to set up trading centers in Asia.

Even sub-Saharan Africa, which Europeans once characterized as a dark and savage land, in the light of recent scholarship presents a picture of stable and complex native societies. The chaos of the nineteenth century, during which time Africa was being

The Underdeveloped Areas 179

partitioned by the colonial powers, dates not from time immemorial in a "continent without history" but rather from the combined onslaught of Arab and European expansion and the commercial slave trade both of these peoples trafficked in extensively. Considering Africa's past relations with the West, it is not difficult to understand why countries such as the Congo and Nigeria have been so turbulent in the 1960s. It has been estimated that by the end of the nineteenth century at least fifteen million Congolese had been exported as slaves, while the coast of Nigeria was the major trade depot for slaves in west Africa.

Much of today's poverty and disease in poor countries is indirectly a product of this European expansion, especially the serious overcrowding of some of the Asiatic, Caribbean, and Middle Eastern countries. In general, the birth and death rate of these countries is thought to have been stabilized until Europeans introduced relatively simple improvements of epidemic disease control, transportation, and communication—thus unintentionally affecting the death rate. Previously, famines were a frequent occurrence in the large Asian nations, which undoubtedly helped to hold populations at a level where their resources were adequate, but were steadily decreased through the colonial period. The new transportation systems alone could help to avoid the most lethal effects of famines since with a railway food could be shifted rapidly into a famine threatened area which previously would have had to depend almost exclusively on its own resources. And as nothing was done about the birth rate in this period, a rapidly increasing population resulted.

The common experience of the nations of Asia and Africa, as well as the ethnic groups controlled by European powers in the New World, has been that they were pushed and pulled, willingly and unwillingly, toward economic and political incorporation with the alien West. Sometimes as colonies, sometimes as free dominions, republics, or unconquered native kingdoms, they have moved toward entry into the community of nations led by Western countries. Even countries such as Thailand and Japan, which were able to remain independent through the period of Western expansion, have been able to survive on their own only because they adopted many Western ways. The movements in this direction were sometimes propelled by overt force (as with Commander Perry's opening of Japan to Western trade) or sometimes through more indirect pressure (as with the competition of England and France over economic control of Thailand, with that country working to remain independent from both). As to the direction they would go, however, few of these nations had much choice.

The pressure to which they have been subjected has brought the destruction of many local values but it has had its constructive sides as well. Although local civilizations had achieved much before 1500, there has also been much progress in production since then, particularly from industrialization and the usage of science-based technology. As mentioned before, transportation has been greatly improved, a "good" which all peoples recognize. Thus, where 400 years ago people traveled by foot, canoes, or oxcart, it is now possible to travel by train, bus, or airplane, all products of the industrial revolution. The benefits of the new medicine (even death control is a "good" if birth control is also applied) have been cited a number of times and are certainly a consequence of Western developments and expansion.

Whether a people have remained independent or have gone through a colonial period, whether they maintain still-living civilizations now undergoing modernization (as in Asia, the Middle East, or Africa), or whether they are developing their own amalgams of Western and other traditions (as in Latin America), they are alike with regard to pressure from the industrialized West. They have been pushed toward conformity to international law, production for world markets, universal literacy and education, disease control, mortality reduction, and nationally integrated government forms which, even if not always democratic or representational, are based on constitutions and centralized bureaucracies.

Not all this influence has been one-way, as is true in all acculturation situations. The West has received a great deal from these other nations since 1500—raw materials, new domestic plants, new ideas (technical, moral and artistic), and people. But the main direction of pressure and power, and the demands for change and conformity, have run the other way. The Asian,

The Underdeveloped Areas

African, and Latin American countries have had to accommodate themselves to these pressures. They have not had the choice of ignoring the West. The present-day technical change programs are treading this old path, already marked by the group attitudes of a long history of accommodation.

Nationalism

Each culture tends to be ethnocentric, to regard its own traditions and values as better than those of others. This is an attitude which gives people a drive to work toward the goals of their society. And a measure of ethnocentrism exists irrespective of the actual achievements of the system. Thus, the nations that are weak as producers will tend to emphasize other values. But at the same time they recognize their vulnerable position in the world and, with their memories of the colonial period still fresh, they have an emotion-backed drive to achieve a respectable place among nations. It is a position that has been denied them for four hundred years and which, now that political and military independence have been attained, seems possible at last. Despite probable need for a supernational power in the world, national aspirations and hopes are still universal and the agrarian nations are especially intense in their desire to achieve them. But most of this nationalistic drive is found among the educated class. Few of these countries are integrated sufficiently, or the population informed enough, for such aspirations to be widespread through all classes. Nationalistic feelings will undoubtedly spread as literacy increases, communications improve, and the elite class continues to try to influence the majority, but in many countries this is not yet the case.

A kind of three-phase cycle has occurred in many such nations. At first the local people have resisted changes other than attempting to obtain material goods and new techniques of obvious utility. Frequently, between this first resistant stage and the next, an acceptance stage, there has been a strong build-up of pressure from outside and a polarization of individuals on the inside. The leaders have been divided on whether to "open the door" or "slam it shut." The door has been opened everywhere, although in some instances only after struggles between the inside groups. The alien ways in the "open door" period have been accepted with least reservation by the younger people because they are not so committed to the values of their culture. The elders have frequently been taunted as old-fashioned, and there has been an urgency to accept the new as rapidly as possible. Then the third stage has occurred during which time it has been realized that the local people could not participate fully in the Western pattern, largely for economic reasons. The traditional culture has then reasserted itself to some extent (Foster, 1962: 40–41). The countries of South Asia and the Middle East have gone through most of these phases already and the newly independent African nations seem to be just moving into stage three.

When cultures reach this latter phase, they have learned enough of the technical superiority of Western ways to convince them of the advantages, but this is not necessarily so with nontechnical ways. The reassertion that will take place will practically always be in the nontechnological aspects of culture: in costumes, language, folklore, artistic styles, sports, and religion.

Local cultures will look back at their past, hoping to find indications of greatness. And in quite a few places these still exist even though they have been neglected by recent generations. One area where the greatness of the past remains is in the archeological ruins. It has been noted that during the period of colonialism or Western domination, excavation, reconstruction, and maintenance of ruins of past civilizations in Asia and the Americas was left to outsiders, either the colonial masters or other Western industrial states. Thus, in India and Egypt it was the British, in Indonesia the Dutch, and in Indochina the French. Also, of course, they took quite a few archeological treasures back to their museums. When independence came, the Indians, Egyptians, Mexicans, Peruvians, Cambodians, and Thai have turned their interests back to their own monuments. At this stage, such ruins stand as visible symbols of national greatness; both schoolchildren and foreign visitors can be escorted through them for the promotion of nationalism. Under colonial or dependent status such ruins only indicated more sharply how far such nations had fallen. Of course, in many countries such sites also have an economic function as tourist attractions.

The Underdeveloped Areas

Such motivations of nationalism and ethnocentrism can be understood as required to some extent by a viable culture. But the old traditions may be overstressed. Although it is not suggested that the nations of Asia and Africa westernize themselves, or for Latin America to "go *Yanqui*," there is evidence that some aspects of their cultures, particularly in social and religious behavior, will have to change if they are to develop urban, industrial economies. It is well known that the traditions of Western European nations, and later North American ones, were changed in the process of their economic expansion. The patriarchal family, religious control, and government by royalty were the norm in the preindustrial age. These are either gone or else only vestiges remain. Similarly, change of some traditional ways may be part of the price that must be paid for the agrarian countries which intend to obtain the wealth of industrial production.

For instance, dependence on kinship is a method of organizing human affairs which is still the norm in many of the agrarian nations; and few of these really visualize the possibility of substituting the Euro-American type of small family, even while this unit seems to be decreasing in importance in urban society. In such kinship societies the individual is controlled or powerfully influenced in his choice of mate, much of his money is absorbed, and the major decisions of life are largely made by the extended, property-holding family. Although there are undoubtedly other influences, this pattern must affect the initiative of the individual, as well as create favorable conditions for nepotism in government and familialism in business. It may be that such a unit is not helpful toward producing the spirit of saving and investment which assisted in making industrial expansion succeed in the West. The individual who does not derive the benefits directly has less incentive to risk his precious wealth. Moreover, where such kinship units are dominant, there is a tendency to spend considerable amounts for ceremonies and ceremonial giving, and for elaborate weddings and funerals. The kinds of simple ceremonies performed by a justice of the peace or in a chapel in urban cultures are hardly acceptable in kinship-based societies. It is not suggested here that such ceremonies be eliminated immediately, even if they could be, because of the risk of sudden deculturization. Nevertheless, to create conditions where capital can be accumulated and investment made more possible, either by individuals or the state, it may well be necessary to de-emphasize ceremonial expenditures and perhaps even to favor the small family unit.

Even religious beliefs may have to be modified or de-emphasized. This has already occurred with Christianity and Judaism and it is to be expected with other religions. The Western personality traits of thrift and hard work, whether secular or derived from religion, may contrast sharply with the traditional generosities of Islam, the other-worldly emphasis of Buddhism, the asceticism of Hinduism, and even the wealth-consuming religiosity of Latin American Catholicism. It has been argued, chiefly by economists, that such doctrines are not calculated to produce industrious workers, thrifty capitalists, or daring promoters (Hunt, 1955: 318). And though other social scientists do not agree in entirety with this idea, they usually see some validity in it.

To expect the people of the agrarian nations voluntarily to abandon all their institutions just to obtain the material advantages of the West is unreasonable, but it is well to recognize that some habits and ways of thinking may need to be altered. The parts of a culture which are of less significance to economic change—music, costume, language, literature—can remain untouched. However, the drive toward nationalism and national revival may end up in nothing if no room for change in basic behavior is made. The fervor of emergent nationalism in the agrarian nations will seem sometimes shaky, sensitive, and exaggerated. It is nonetheless a potent force that should be considered in all plans for change.

Plurality of Society

National aspirations and hopes are universal today. Remote villagers and awakening tribesmen are leaving their isolation to establish contacts with the world community, both through direct experience in travel and trade and also by incorporation into the national consciousness. Such consciousness of state citizenship varies in intensity throughout the world. Most of the countries of western Europe achieved unified central governments during the Renaissance and Reformation; for the rest it occurred be-

The Underdeveloped Areas 185

tween 1870 and 1918. The citizens of these lands, whatever their provincial language, dialect, or cultural heritage, consider themselves to be first of all Britons, Frenchmen, or Spaniards.

The history of centralization and consolidation in the United States is much more recent and there were two great movements of special ethnic types of a kind that did not occur in Europe: namely, the importation of African slaves and the immigration of Europeans in the nineteenth and twentieth centuries. In connection with the latter movement and the absorption of its people, the concept of "the melting pot" arose. Almost all of these people did develop a strong national consciousness as Americans. The descendants of Africans and, to a lesser extent, Mexican-Americans did not develop so strong a feeling of inclusion in the new nation; but except for a very few extremists, the majority of even such disadvantaged minorities hope to become fully incorporated into the national society. It is to be noted that the common names even for those still struggling for their rights are "Afro-American" and "Mexican-American." Many nations have been built by amalgamating and hyphenating prior separated "ethnic groups" in a broader inclusion.

Many of the agrarian nations are still in the throes of achieving such national consolidation. Large numbers of people do not yet know that they are citizens of a large nation state. Many nations of South and Southeast Asia make up what social scientists call *plural societies;* that is, they contain several cultural systems, each with an independent language, religion, or cultural heritage, within the confines of one nation. Sometimes these countries contain several ethnic groups, often with considerably different cultural heritages. India provides a good example, where in religion alone there are Hindus, Muslims, Parsis, Jains, Sikhs, Christians, and adherents to many tribal belief systems. There are over a dozen major languages, each spoken by more than a million people and some spoken by over a hundred million. There is also a basic and very old cultural difference between the people of the north and those of the south. And finally, the population is subdivided into numerous caste groups which maintain separate cultural heritages by not allowing intermarriage with other groups. Even a comparatively small country, such as Malaya, possesses several cultural subgroups—Muslim Malayans, Chinese, East Indians, and tribal people of at least two basic kinds.

Such groups may not yet have come to place their common nationality above their particular group allegiance. In India, for example, there have been difficulties ever since its independence in 1947 as to what the official government language would be. Agitation and rioting has occurred on numerous occasions, the most recent being the Sikh demands for Punjabi to be on an equal status with Hindi. The national government has found it expedient to create official provincial languages including, for example, Punjabi alongside the major national language. And the picture of the language plurality in India becomes even more complex when one realizes that the most common medium of communication between educated men from different parts of the country is neither the national nor one of the provincial languages, but English. Malaya too, has had its problems with an unassimilated plurality, the Chinese. The island of Singapore has been separated and made into a separate nation, principally because the population is chiefly Chinese, who feared being assimilated by the Malayan majority of the mainland.

There are nation states which exist because the colonial masters merged them into units for their own administrative advantage irrespective of the ethnic background of the population. Tribal units with strong group consciousness, sometimes quite large, continue in such places. Burma is a country of this kind, with Shans, Karens, Chins, Burmese, Chinese, and East Indians, each group having its own language and traditions. Another is Nigeria, where Yoruba, Beni, Ibo, Fulani, Hausa, and multitudinous smaller groups live adjacent to one another, each with its own cultural distinctiveness.

Remote tribal groups may not only have no desire to become a part of a nation, they may not even know there is such a unit. Such people of the hills and other marginal land areas may be quite isolated except for the few goods that pass in trade and the visits of occasional government police officials. If they know anything of the national government, it is as some kind of distant authority which is best avoided. The shift from colonial to independent status has meant little to them. The remote authority,

The Underdeveloped Areas

whether of foreigners or of the upper class officialdom of the valley ethnic group, has always exploited and attempted to dominate them.

Laos is a constitutional monarchy and the king is theoretically the defender of the faith, Buddhism. It should be noted that this is the faith of the Lao, not the tribal people. However, the king has far less symbolic importance than does the queen in Britain because few people outside the cities and large towns, which are all in the Lao area, know that he exists. An important activity of the United States Information Service in the late 1950s and early 1960s was to assist the Lao government to distribute posters of the king as widely as possible so that at least people would have seen an image of their nominal head of state. And however little the remote Lao knew of their king, it is certain that the non-Buddhist tribal people knew and cared less; and it was believed that these people were more numerous than the lowland Lao whose king headed the state.

The situation is much the same in the greater part of Africa, where people probably identify themselves more readily by their tribal than by their national name. And they do not yet usually use hyphens, in calling themselves Yoruba-Nigerians or Hausa-Nigerians. Until recently, Middle Eastern religious communities lived side by side under their own laws for centuries, even in the same towns and cities, although in different quarters. The Israeli-Arab conflict owes a considerable part of its origin to the plurality that existed until the formation of the Jewish state. The population in Latin America may be divided between a Spanish-speaking *creole* or *ladino* cultural majority and several Indian or Negro minority peoples who are only partly "hispanicized." Amalgamation of such culturally diverse minority populations (an old process in European nations) is in an early stage in most of the developing nations.

Thus, in all these areas the stir of nationalism is abroad and the multiplicity of separate traditions is under attack. In one way or another the emergent nation states are attempting to gather the diverse peoples of their still plural societies into more homogeneous units. The young, educated, and internationally oriented seem particularly dedicated to refashioning their nations and the world after the national model. Not even the remotest hill tribesman can any longer avoid encroachment on his former free isolation from the centralized, self-conscious government and its enthusiasts.

The new nationalizing central governments, attempting to create unity by binding all the elements of their society together, certainly experience real compulsions. They feel the need to utilize the whole of their populations toward achieving productive positions in the world comparable to that of the wealthy, industrial nations. Uncommitted pockets, not integrated into the whole society, weaken their potential. Then too, nonassimilated minorities are a constant source of political and military weakness, particularly in the modern context of world power struggles. The tribal areas of Laos and Vietnam, for example, have been thoroughly infiltrated by the Vietcong and Pathet Lao serving as the principal base of supply for the insurgent forces.

The central governments use customary means of propaganda to reach these groups. But even more common, they try to extend their authority over them by the appointment of ever more government administrators and the stationing of police and military forces among them—administrative measures patterned largely on Western institutions. Military force is used when deemed necessary, particularly when separatism is threatened. The Ibo-Nigerian insurrection was of this order, when by means of a military campaign and a food blockade resulting in starvation, hundreds of thousands and probably even millions of Ibo were killed. It is to be noted that only a very few other African states supported the cause of the Ibo, probably because they too fear the dangers of tribal separatism.

One of the primary functions of national school systems is to disseminate information about and get children committed to the goals of the state. To help fulfill this need, each new nation hopes to build a system of universal education. Besides actual civic training in such schools, literacy and the national language can be taught, media through which the central governments hope to communicate with all groups more efficiently, and thus to assimilate them.

Also, in most of these countries tribal and unassimilated groups are currently being tied to the central government through ex-

The Underdeveloped Areas

tension of the national economies. The villages which were once remote are now ever more attached to provincial and national seats of government through improved markets as well as new products, both those manufactured in each country's cities and those which have been imported. Many such products—the cigarette lighter, the transistor radio, factory-woven cloth, the safety match, kerosene, the bicycle—have come to be in great demand, useful rewards both of modernity and national consolidation.

Transportation systems are vital for such assimilation. New roads, bus lines, and railroads make it easier both to get goods to the cities and to travel for pleasure, visiting relatives and friends. Airplanes also contribute to tying a new nation together and have some advantages lacking in ground transport. No roads or railroads are necessary to establish a system, and over very mountainous terrain the cost of such construction can be prohibitive. In fact, it is doubtful that any new railroad lines will be built in the new nations, if anywhere else in the world. Many peoples in Asia, Africa, and Latin America, who have never seen railroads, have become fairly familiar with airplanes. A dramatic sequence exists in the documentary film, "Mondo Cane," which shows a New Guinea tribesman staring through a cyclone fence at a four-engine passenger plane just landing. Later, he and his fellow tribesmen are shown operating a simulated airstrip, with a control tower, to bring the "cargo" plane down to their runway. It is significant that the Melanesian tribesman has moved from the ship to the airplane in his conception of "cargo." Railroads simply do not exist for him and, except for short distances around port cities, neither do automobiles.

In the countries of Latin America, Africa, and Asia, the DC-3 with the national emblem on its side has become an important symbol of the central government. Each of these countries very much wants its own airline. It is no accident that when governments in agrarian nations are overthrown through revolutionary action, the two things taken over most quickly are the airplanes and radio transmitters.

While the process of consolidation of plural groups goes on apace in the agrarian nations, in the industrial West there now seems to be a tendency to move back toward more pluralism. In

Britain, for example, Scottish and Welsh voices again are asking for greater regional recognition. In America the idea of a "melting pot" is no longer so popular, and replacing it to a certain extent has been the idea of cultural pluralism and ethnic autonomy. This idea has been particularly attractive to Afro-Americans, but also to Mexican-Americans and Amerindians, all groups which have been least assimilated. In any event, they now call for "self-pride," meaning cultural autonomy, and attempt to support customs of their own group through education and publicity—such things as hair styles, costumes, language or dialect, and even eating patterns. It is worth noting that there are few suggestions of alternative patterns of technology. This difference in suggested change may be occurring because industrial technology, despite the deleterious effects of not controlling it (a socioeconomic rather than technological problem) is really very productive. So the ideal pluralism is proposed for the nontechnological parts of culture.

No one knows yet whether the world will gravitate toward more pluralism, as encouraged by several ethnic minorities in industrial states, or toward continued centralization, as promoted by the emergent states in Africa, Asia, and those of Latin America with large Indian populations. Currently, the major thrust of the developing nations is certainly toward greater centralization, whatever may be afoot in the developed ones.

The Urban Elite

The change agent in an agrarian country must be ready to cope with another social consequence of the pressures of Westernization. This is the cultural distinction between the educated classes which have been exposed to Western education, and the rural and other poor folk who have been educated primarily in their local traditions. It can be thought of as a world tradition and native or local tradition.

When the colonizing powers took over the countries of Asia, Africa, and Latin America, they created, sometimes deliberately and sometimes accidentally, a group of people who could serve as intermediaries between themselves and the traditional elements of society. At first these individuals were employed as civil ser-

The Underdeveloped Areas

vants of the colonizers; but with the growth of new cities and expansion of the new style of education and commerce, this group of people grew in numbers. They remained as the backbone of the civil service after independence but also branched out to become the merchants, politicians, army officers, and even technical specialists of these countries. This is the class of people with whom the change agent will conduct most of his dealings, at least initially. If he has an appointed counterpart, it will be from this class.

In many agrarian nations this class of people is tending to become like a middle class in industrial countries. They are thus distinct from the few very wealthy who tended to be the leaders until two or three decades ago. In India one of the old traditional signs of wealth and power was a stable of elephants. But elephants are expensive to feed and the members of the new middle class do not have that kind of money. Consequently today there are few elephants owned by private individuals.

The middle class in these countries is still small compared to that in Western nations or Japan, but it is growing in influence and numbers. It should be a few percentage points greater now but even by 1957 the middle class was estimated to be between 5 to 15 percent of the whole population of most underdeveloped countries (Smith, 1957: 361). This compares with approximately 65 to 80 percent in the industrial countries. And although much smaller comparatively, the middle class of the agrarian countries can be considered, together with the much smaller percentage of very rich, as an urban elite in contrast to the more traditional rural villagers.

What are characteristics of this group? In the first place, the great majority are urban residents, either in the few large cities or much more numerous provincial towns. Their relationship to the rural areas is usually restricted to landownership and administration. Since most often there is a stigma to manual labor, members of this group rarely do any physical work, on the farm or elsewhere. Those who do own land will have peasant cultivators doing the work, either on a sharecropping basis or as renters.

This elite is comparatively well educated. Despite low levels of literacy in their countries, most individuals in this group—and practically all the males—can read and write. Furthermore, they usually speak the European language of their colonizers: English in India, Pakistan, Burma, and former British Africa; French in former Indochina and the ex-colonial dependencies of Africa; Dutch in Indonesia; and Spanish and Portuguese in Latin America. Latin America is a little different from the other continental areas because it was colonized about four hundred years ago and, with the exception of the high density Indian civilizations, the local people were either eliminated or absorbed. In most of these countries all persons, rural or urban, speak the same language. In Asia and Africa the foreign language is spoken primarily in the cities, and by the elite class.

Because of their education and the general influence of the urban environment, the members of this elite are oriented to a large extent toward the West. This is particularly true of the men because they get most of the outside style of education and work in the Western type environment—city offices and shops. They wear shirts and trousers instead of such traditional garments as the *dhoti* of India, the *sarong* of Malaya, and the *burnous* of North Africa. It is interesting to note that although a few traditional cultural revivalistic leaders returned to indigenous garments (Gandhi, U Nu), the great majority, including those with strong policies of nationalism, continued to wear the Western garments they assumed in their formative years (Nasser, Jomo Kenyatta, Sukarno, Nkrumah). In many countries a pattern has been developed of wearing Western clothes in public but of donning more comfortable local costumes at home. In most places the women of the elite class have been more resistant to change, probably because they have had less education and less exposure to outside ideas.

In the height of postindependence nationalistic fervor there has been some reversal to this tendency in costumes, particularly in the new African nations; that is, the members of the elite (usually the politicians) now deliberately wear traditional garments to assert the integrity of their cultures. Frequently, however, they will assume a national costume which is acceptable to European standards even though in pre-European days this did not exist. Thus, the toga-like garment now worn by nationalistic

The Underdeveloped Areas

Nigerians is actually a Yoruba garment. The men of the southern tribes (especially those in the southeast) wore loincloths.

Elite food habits and patterns of consumption reflect this international influence. Most of the traditional diet may be maintained in the home, but these people are also familiar with and use some Western foods and drinks. Partially this is because they can afford it, but it also reflects the fact that they know about such items. For instance, milk is now consumed in the cities of Southeast Asia, an area where traditionally people drank no milk at all and where rural villagers still do not milk their cattle or buffalo. Breakfast cereals are used very widely in both dry and cooked forms. There is hardly a city in the world now where corn flakes cannot be obtained for breakfast. A wide variety of canned and other processed foods are obtainable in such places. It was mentioned earlier that this influence is even carried to babies, with unfortunate consequences, when mothers refuse to nurse their infants and instead feed them processed baby food in Western style. The pattern of alcoholic consumption in the city also is different. Village people all over the world make and consume alcoholic beverages, such as palm or *maguey* wine, rice or millet beer, local rum, or rice whiskey. The city elite now tend to consume standard beers and whiskies made in their countries from European formulas, or if they can afford them, imported beverages. Scotch whiskey and French brandy or champagne are now preferred drinks among the elite for any kind of important occasion in most of the agrarian nations. At weddings of officials in Laos, locally-made rice wine or whiskey was never served. Instead they had scotch, champagne, and European style beer.

Another significant characteristic of urban elitism in these countries is that it is strongly universal, while peasantry is localistic. For instance, the urban members of various religious groups in a country such as India—Hindu, Muslim, Parsi, Sikh, and Christian—will have a considerable number of cultural habits in common in contrast to the rural people of the same religious groups. Hindu, Muslim, or Sikh civil servants in New Delhi may well have as much in common with one another as they have with villagers of their respective religions. Their behavior even extends to having a common international pattern. The government official in India would have a great deal of behavior in common with his counterpart in Ghana or Colombia which the rural villager of those countries would have considerable difficulty in comprehending.

Although the elite class is a minority group in the total population, the political, military, and commercial leadership of each country is drawn from it. These are the planners and organizers, and (most important for the readers of this manual) the contact men with outsiders. Unfortunately, a problem exists in that compared to the industrial countries, this class is too small and many individuals are not well trained. Independence came suddenly to these lands and the people who had administrative responsibility under colonial rule had done little more than subordinate jobs. They were not the primary decision makers and were in fact discouraged from taking such responsibility. The situation has improved some in the last twenty years but a different problem has tended to partially replace it, namely, the "brain drain." Many young men have gone to Western universities for necessary training but have found after getting it that their career and salary opportunities were much better if they remained in the industrial countries. They have chosen not to return to their native lands, thus causing a drain of the best trained minds.

A final disability of the members of this class is that with Western style education and urbanization, they have tended to break contact and lose understanding with the majority of their countries, the village peasants. This situation is partially a carryover from colonial days and it may be improving somewhat since independence, but it is still to be reckoned with. The villager now is being given more consideration by the elite since it is recognized that if he does not become more productive, the nation as a whole will not; also, if he is not fully incorporated into the national consciousness, he will be susceptible to dissenting and insurgent movements.

The Rural Peasant

If a country has 50 percent or more of its working males engaged in farming and related pursuits, it is considered to have an

The Underdeveloped Areas

economy based on agriculture. Such agriculture has been termed *archaic,* to differentiate it from the mechanized form found in Western countries, which can be descriptively called *industrial agriculture.* Despite the tremendous productivity of industrial agriculture and the small proportion of the population involved, about three-fourths of the world's peoples (almost all of them in the tropical or subtropical zones) still have an economy based on the subsistence form of agriculture. In the countries where these peoples live, only little more than 10 percent of the population is in the cities, just the reverse of the situation in the United States, which has less than 10 percent of its population living on farms.

In many of these countries the peasant lives in a cluster of houses which will contain anything from a few hundred to a few thousand people. This village is a type of social unit that has existed even before the rise of the first cities, for 9,000 to 10,000 years. It is stationary and practically always dependent on agriculture for subsistence. It is by no means the same thing as an independent tribe, such as those of most North American Indian groups previous to the European and Anglo-American destruction of their social systems. The agricultural village was historically the base on which the wealth and power of the ancient cities were built, but during this process they came under control of the cities.

The peasant village is not an independent settlement but rather only a part of a greater social unit, the agrarian state. Although he has considerably greater self-sufficiency than the farmer in an industrial society, the village peasant has always been dependent on the city for specialized goods. The city was and is the focus of commerce and manufacture and provides the peasant with the things he cannot produce himself. In return the peasant sells his surplus agricultural production and some other locally produced specialized goods. There is then a two-way economic relationship, although the city merchants usually benefit considerably more then do the village producers. At the same time the city officials attempt to administer and control the villager. From this the peasant has characteristically developed an ambivalent attitude toward the city. He wants many of the good things only available through city merchants and other contacts; but at the same time he must avoid the exploitative tentacles of the cunning merchant and exacting administrator.

In contrast to the member of the urban elite class, the rural peasant is oriented more toward traditional values and customs. Because the average villager is illiterate and his level of education quite low, he knows comparatively little of outside ways. He cannot even take advantage of most of the new devices he learns about because of his poor economic circumstances. For instance, the airplane which is now important in these countries is used primarily by members of the elite class. The average villager speaks only his own language, follows his regionally limited traditional dietary patterns, and depends mostly on home remedies and local practicioners for medical assistance. His knowledge of the world is usually confined to a circle of villagers, in which his own is the center, and perhaps one or two nearby market towns or pilgrimage centers.

Such ideas as the villager may have concerning national or world affairs will come through communication channels controlled by the urban elite. However, even with the best of intentions, it is not easy for members of the elite class to establish meaningful contact. The dialect forms, symbols, and image of the officials frequently have little meaning to villagers.

The technology of the peasant is primitive and, on a per capita basis, he is not a productive farmer. He may get as much from the land as is possible with his technology, but this is still very low compared to what an industrial farmer can produce. His technique is "labor intensive" in contrast to that of the Western farmer whose technique is "machine intensive."

If the agricultural year has been good, the peasant produces enough to get by and some little surplus to sell to the town market for buying the special goods which are not produced in the village: the bicycle, galvanized bucket, factory-made cloth, kerosene, and a few religious objects. If the year is bad, he may have no surplus and may even lack the food required until the next harvest. Then his only recourse is to get money from relatives or the moneylender. However, his relatives may be as poor as he is, in which case only the moneylender will be left. Even the few peasants who are relatively well off tend to use their extra wealth in a nonproductive, traditional manner. They may try to get more land, but in the densely populated rural areas this is not easily available. So, the extra wealth is hoarded, usually in gold or silver jewelry. These villagers are either unfamiliar with banks or do not trust them because they are remote and impersonal. They rely on personal ties to relatives, patrons, or moneylenders.

The social group the peasant depends on above all others is the family and kindred. He is tied to this circle of people economically, socially, and ritually; and whatever insurance he has will be as a member of the kinship unit. They tend to rise and fall together. A villager in India, and even a townsman for that matter, will stay with kinfolk when he travels. Hotels are places for foreigners and very rich Indians. The idea of kinship is so strong that they will create fictive relationships where no blood lines exist. Thus, Indians who went overseas as immigrants to Trinidad and other British colonies established a relationship of "ship brother," meaning someone who came over on the same ship.

When he cannot depend on kinsmen, the peasant tends to depend on people he knows well in a personal way. He does not understand the value of impersonal relationships (employer-employee, banker-client, broker-customer) and initially distrusts the stranger. This attitude is a result of the peasant's long history of exploitation by people from the outside, almost always from the city. This is not to say that some villagers have not been exploited by other villagers but such exploitation has been more limited and more comprehensible to the peasant.

The peasant's socioeconomic situation has been restricted in many directions, which has resulted in a kind of suspicious independence by the kinship unit toward other kinship groups. It has been argued that the "economic pie" of peasantry is too fixed to be divided other than to make one man's gain another man's loss. And it is true that resources, particularly land, are often quite limited and that unless there is change in method, the production remains constant and barely adequate. Greater production by someone else is in these circumstances looked at suspiciously (Foster, 1962: 52–53). This seems to be the case primarily in areas where the population is dense and land is scarce. In areas where these are not the exact conditions—most of Southeast Asia,

Negro Africa, and the less densely settled parts of Latin America —competition is not so fierce.

The rural peasant tends to be oriented toward the traditional religion far more than does the member of the urban elite class. Secularization has developed along with Westernization in the cities. The villager supports his mosque, temple, or church as a vital part of his life. He also supports a large body of folk beliefs which are not necessarily part of the formal tenets of his religion, chiefly various kinds of spirit beliefs. He has not been exposed sufficiently to outside ideas to seriously question most of these beliefs.

The Economy

Most of the agrarian nations lack two principal kinds of development: their agricultural practices are inefficient, and they lack adequate industry. Shortly after independence, most of these nations felt that their lack of sufficient industry in respect to twentieth century expectations was their main problem and they concentrated on getting industries started. However, in the last decade practically all of them have come to the realization that agricultural production is even more basic and they have concentrated on this need. There now seems to be more or less of an even balance: to increase the productivity of the village farmer and the much fewer commercial farmers, and to stimulate some industries in the cities and towns.

There is more logic to this approach than to the former single-pronged drive toward industry. There are a lot of problems to be solved before real industry will be created, two of which are the dearth of local working capital and the disinclination of outsiders to make local investments. Usually the economy of these countries is not attractive enough for investors to be willing to take significant risks. Industrialization alone will not solve the problem of greater food production, a lesson learned by a number of countries in recent years, notably India, China, and even Russia.

One particular problem that continues to plague non-Western lands is the coexistence of the old and new economies. The older, subsistence economies are still to be found, much changed by out-

The Underdeveloped Areas

side influence but still operating fairly independently alongside the economic institutions of the world market. Thus, in whole areas in West Africa, village farmers can be found who spend most of their effort growing yams, cassava, and maize for their own subsistence and who gather some palm oil, a part to be sold at the market. Adjacent to these villages there are oil palm, rubber, and cacao estates of many hundreds and even thousands of acres each, where a single crop is grown by specialists, exclusively for the world market. The native Indian village communities have persisted beside the spreading plantations under foreign and absentee ownership in Mexico. When rubber cultivation was introduced to Indonesian and Malayan village farmers, they remained in their ancestral villages because they were able to keep pace with the production of the great Dutch and English rubber plantations. And although the peasant village was never entirely self-sufficient, even before the period of Western influence, it was nearly so; furthermore, almost all its economic ties in the pure agrarian state were limited to the cities and towns of the nation. The economy found in this relatively self-sufficient, traditional society may still rule a good part of the lives of people upcountry, in the "boondocks."

Tribal, village, kinship, or religious groupings, not direct economic considerations or administrative and political divisions, are still for many people in such areas the real lines of their affiliations, loyalties, and interests. However, the incorporation of their nations into the modern world has given rise to organs of central government and caused networks of economic influence to be developed by plantation owners and landlords. In this process there have appeared credit-granting merchants and moneylenders as well as agents of foreign mines and plantations. From the national capitals and trading centers, the economic interests of the educated elite now reach out into the villages. But while planning officials may be absorbed in developing productivity similar to that found in industrial nations, they run into the inescapable fact that the subsistence village economy is not adequate for this task.

These forms of government, business, and the professions, so easily recognized by Westerners, are new to villagers, being alien, urban consequences. In Southeast Asia and Africa, for example, the first local representatives of a monetary economy are usually shopkeepers and traders, often Chinese, East Indian, or Syrian immigrants who have different customs from the local populations they serve. The educated officials, merchants, plantation or mine operators, and other trained professionals, may be either native or foreign born, sometimes of the local race, religion, and language group, and sometimes not. Their exact origin does not make much difference; these men of the new occupations are the intrusive agents of a world economy and world civilization, pushing their way into the old cultures of agrarian or tribal villagers.

There was undoubtedly much that was good in village life before the impact of Western-derived institutions and an international money economy, but the situation should be assessed realistically. The surviving subsistence economies, village and tribal ties, ethnic and religious groupings have deep roots and command strong allegiance; but the old way of life of which they were the base is disappearing. Neither Westerners nor they can turn back the clock. It was an interesting experiment for Gandhi, a revered nationalist, to attempt to revive preindustrial occupations (spinning and weaving on hand wheels and looms) but it was hardly more than that. Whatever the negative aspects of uncontrolled industrialization, cloth made on power looms is much better and cheaper than that made by hand. When Gandhi died, the home spinning and weaving movement also went into decline.

Apart from the economic verities, which no one can wish away, a great majority of the elite in these countries will be satisfied with nothing less than a standard of wealth and economic conditions that approach those achieved in the industrial countries. And even the villagers have had enough contact with outsiders that they too want some of the advantages the world economy can bring, despite the fact that there are some disadvantages for such participation. And for these goals a minimum requirement will be change toward more industrialization and commercial farming, with a constant decrease of emphasis on subsistence production.

Rising Expectations

There is evidence that men in all stages of culture have been interested in acquiring whatever new things and techniques would

The Underdeveloped Areas 201

benefit them in a practical way, but the desire for such improvements was probably never at such a pitch or on such a worldwide scale, as it is today. Satisfaction with the old way of life, at least measured by material goods, is rarely found in the modern world. The fact that other people often do not accept improvements brought to them from the outside, even when the change agents are convinced that direct benefits would so result, may seem to belie the above statement. However, when such occurs, there are usually other explanations rather than that they did not want material improvements.

Many change agents explained the reluctance of Lao farmers to grow more rice or vegetables as due to Buddhist complacency. The same explanation was advanced to explain Cambodian lack of economic drive. However, such arguments ignored the fact that both countries were underpopulated and there was no strong competition for land, as in such densely populated countries as India or Pakistan. Also, markets and transportation were poor and the future was very unpredictable, a premonition which has been amply borne out. The Lao would not invest in their own territory for the same reasons that a foreign investor would not invest in a country marked by past political unrest and promising to have future uprisings.

Occasionally hopes were raised, only to be dashed by conditions of new instability. During the several decades of French occupation, a greater rule of peace was established than the Lao had seen for a long time. Among other things, transportation was improved somewhat and new agricultural projects were undertaken. In south Laos, the French built a 50 kilometer paved road into the center of the rich plateau of the Bolovens where some French, and other plantation farmers introduced new crops and agricultural methods. The Vietnamese, Lao, and tribal Kha farmers soon followed suit. Coffee, pineapple, corn, and temperate zone vegetables were grown as cash crops, using the new road for transport to a fairly good market town.

Unfortunately, the French period ended just when the agricultural economy had started to boom; and political chaos, as bad if not worse than before, ensued. The roads became unsafe, making the markets inaccessible, and it even became precarious to be in the fields for fear of being captured or otherwise mistreated by either the insurgents or units of the Royal Lao army. One after another, the newly developed farms were abandoned, reverting to the bamboo forests from which they had been cleared.

The Lao were caught up in the wave of rising expectations that has swept through most of the world's cultures, but to meet these expectations through increased agricultural production had become well nigh impossible. Industrial jobs did not exist, since for all practical purposes there was no industry in the country. The only remote possibility was higher education and a government job. Only by this means could they hope to get one of the bicycles, radios, imported cloth, sewing machines, or other devices they had learned about in recent decades.

Even tribal people will go to great lengths to participate in the new world economy. A dramatic example of such an occurrence has been documented by Dr. Margaret Mead on the island of Manus in the South Pacific. She made a study in 1928 of a tribal people who subsisted primarily on horticultural products and fish. They settled most of their disputes by magic curses, and their religion rested on a type of ancestor worship that required them to store the skulls of deceased kinfolk in their houses. These people had no writing system and are reported to have had no remembered history or knowledge of geography beyond the confines of their island group. Their political arrangements were only elaborate enough to unite 200 to 300 people (Mead, 1956: 32).

By the 1940s new desires were already emerging, primarily through missionaries and from travel to work on plantations. However, intensive contact with the Western world occurred when a large occupation of American military forces was established in the region. The people of Manus then saw for the first time the elaborate equipment of the West. They saw the American soldiers knock down hills, blast channels, smoothe out airstrips, and tear up miles of brush. They also experienced a new kind of social relationship, being treated with much more equality than they had received from outsiders before. Instead of being treated as "boys" as had been the case on the plantations, they were treated as "good Joes" by the G.I.s. There was probably some condescension on the part of the American soldiers but it was evidently much more acceptable than the previous formal subordination

The Underdeveloped Areas

which plantation owners exacted. It is to be noted that the Americans were not interested in developing an economic relationship with the local people, exploitative or otherwise, which goes far to explain their relatively accepting attitude.

When the Americans left, the people of Manus were changed. They had experienced such a growth of needs that they decided to remodel their culture. When Dr. Mead returned in 1953 they had moved their village to the mainland from the earlier site where houses had been located on piles along the seashore. They were even trying to landscape it. They were by this time committed to Western concepts of law with a police force, and they had set up a system of education. They had even rejected the former ancestor cult, tossing the skulls into the sea and replacing the old belief system with their new version of Christianity (Mead, 1956: 241).

This case is of special interest because of the unusual rapidity in the growth of new expectations and the efforts of local people to fulfill them. Most tribal and peasant people cannot be expected to go so far so rapidly, particularly if they are a segment of an important national culture, and often of a broader, international cultural context. In such cultures there will be more of a tendency to retain some traditions of the past, and certainly the religious beliefs. It would be most unlikely for Muslims, Hindus, or Buddhists to give up their traditional beliefs just for the sake of material goods, but they will otherwise exert themselves to obtain these benefits.

The growth of expectations is intimately related to the degree of communications. If the islanders of Manus had never seen the American soldiers it is unlikely they would have moved so fast. The most rapid growth of needs occurs in cities, chiefly because city people are the first to learn of new ways and usually have more capacity to acquire them. The village people will be influenced primarily by observing urban types.

Population Pressures

It has been indicated at several points that the expansion and influence of the West has both directly and indirectly affected the population of the agrarian nations. The Western nations have carried their high value of individual human life to these nations by establishing health facilities where people could get relatively inexpensive treatment, and by instituting public health measures such as spraying for disease carriers and establishing pure water supplies. Also, some technological innovations, particularly in transportation, have decreased the specter of famine. So the death rate has dropped much faster than the birth rate.

Previously the high birth rate barely kept pace with the high death rate and the cultures of these lands were adjusted to this balance, providing social support for producing babies. For instance, married women in India, and in most other village cultures, have traditionally had little status until they had produced a child, preferably a boy. This attitude is believed to have contributed to the customs of early marriage, the dowry, elaborate wedding ceremonials, and other kinds of behavior which support the institution. Among other things, ritualistic beliefs among Hindus required a man to have children, particularly a son to conduct his death rites and other posthumous ceremonies. Also, land inheritance and extended family management required male children. All this worked satisfactorily as long as birth and death rates were fairly well balanced. But modern conditions have upset that balance. Many new medical and technological improvements have resulted in fewer infant deaths. Meanwhile the birth rate has remained the same because village peoples' attitudes have not changed so fast.

An ever-increasing population is a world problem today, although it is most grave in the countries of low production. The nations of western Europe are densely populated, with some (such as Holland, Belgium, and England) having more people per unit of area than most nations of Asia and Africa. However, these Western countries are industrialized and wealthy by world standards. The density of population in Bengal, Java, the Nile River delta, and Iraq is much more serious however, because in these areas there is the least per capita wealth and productivity. This is one of the consequences of introducing organized commerce, public health measures, and famine control without any introduction of birth control.

The Underdeveloped Areas

In the past there seem to have been cycles of population growth based primarily on technological innovations. When significant technological changes have taken place, there has been a sharp upswing in the rate of population growth, followed by a leveling off to a more stable, slower rate of increase and even a real ballance between births and deaths. The populations of England, Germany, and the United States went through such cycles during their agricultural (mechanization of agriculture) and industrial revolutions. With the increased food and materials available, as well as improved health facilities, the populations rose rapidly, the birth rate remaining high while the death rate came down. However, at the end of each cycle the birth rate also came down and large families went out of fashion. Some demographers believe that urbanization is a strong contributory influence to this process while others think it is primarily reorganization of family structure. It must be admitted that children in urban, industrial cultures contribute practically nothing financially to the family group and very little in any other way except by carrying a name and perhaps exchanging some affection. The ritual and economic ties of the traditional peasant family are completely gone in the industrial urban context.

It is possible that the agrarian nations will go through such a cycle, although no one is at all sure it will come rapidly enough. The margin between available food and population becomes constantly narrower. So far as such a cycle can be expected, giant India and little Puerto Rico are far along in the stage of population explosion. Mexico and Samoa seem to be in early stages, with the greatest burst yet to come. The population rate in Japan is still rising but the rate of increase is slacking off rapidly, due to several probable factors: rapid urbanization, Western ideas, and a conscious, effective birth control program. It is significant that Japan is the one nation of Asia that is not underdeveloped or agrarian. Finally, some countries the longest industrialized and urbanized, such as France and England, actually have a stable or declining population.

A growing population can mean greater opportunities but it can also mean more problems. It is not the concern here to take part in the great debate about solutions or to succumb to the wilder fears about "overpopulation" but rather to point to some of the consequences of such growth. Growing numbers in the agrarian countries mean more crowded villages. This means more flocks and herds on the pastures and more intensive cultivation on already tired, eroded soil. Cultivable land becomes scarcer as it is subdivided among the heirs in each generation.

A particular problem for the change agent arises from the fact that people with little land but many mouths to feed cannot afford to take chances to experiment with new crops or techniques. This means that more and more children have to leave rural areas to look for jobs in crowded cities where there are not enough jobs for those already there. It means increased poverty at a time when these nations need money for capital investment.

Naturally, population pressures result in more building, expanding, and filling up. People who were once strung along rivers and spread across plains or valleys will be huddled into shacks and compounds that spring up along railroads, mines, and the loading platforms of great plantations. The common areas and protective sanitary open spaces around villages will be eliminated. The West had its day of slum-building and is fighting its way out, particularly to eliminate the remaining minority "ghettos." The agrarian nations in transition toward commercial, industrial societies are just entering their periods of great expansion when such conditions occur.

It is hoped that these countries can profit by the experience of the West so they can avoid the ugly features that have marred the urbanization and industrialization that occurred in Europe and America. And certainly one of the principal needs is to keep the population expansion within limits. It is hopeful, therefore, to note that the nations of the non-Western world with the densest populations—India, Pakistan, Puerto Rico, Egypt—have set up government bureaus and administrative machinery to cope with the problem of family planning, primarily to limit the number of births. Their success so far has not been very great, principally it seems because communication techniques have been poor. But limiting births can be done, as the case of Japan illustrates so graphically.

9
American Cultural Values

Misinterpretation

In order to understand how ideas are transferred from one culture to another it is very important to know the role and characteristics of the change agents involved. Several of the cases in this manual indicate that a failure was due to the change agent's misinterpretation of the motives and needs of the hoped-for borrowers of the innovations. Such misinterpretations may result from the change agent's failure to learn enough about the receiving culture; but they may also rest on false suppositions, derived from assuming that conditions taken for granted in the home culture also exist in the other culture.

All men, in agrarian or industrial societies, have much in common in the solution of their problems. A peasant farmer in India and a commercial farmer in Texas are both pragmatic and must be shown that an improvement is genuine before they will adopt it, and a Lao farmer tries to get help from the supernatural in producing rain just as the American turns to prayer when a close family member is seriously ill. Nevertheless, it still does not follow that all the basic assumptions of people with different cultures are the same. Despite similarities, the unlikenesses are significant enough to block communication and thus impede change. If the change agent expects the people of the recipient culture to have precisely the same motivations or behaviors as are common in his culture, he is seriously risking failure of understanding.

The worst part of most such misapprehension of cultural realities is that it is unintentional. The individual does what is "natural" or what makes "common sense." He may not realize that his "natural" tendencies to action are inevitably limited by his own cultural experience, including his unconscious assumptions. To examine the cultural as well as individual premises of one's own actions is a difficult process. If one always stayed with people of the same background, this examination would never be necessary and most people would probably be better off without doing it. However, if one is to deal with people of another culture, or simply to understand them at a distance, knowing one's own cultural assumptions is of the first importance. Thus, hybrid corn grown by Spanish-American farmers in Arizona was superior in terms of the Anglo-American economy and the change agent assumed the value of corn was the same. However, these Spanish-Americans valued it primarily for its taste and texture as a human food rather than as feed for animals. The United States administrators of Palau assumed that if individuals participated in an American system of electing public officials, democracy would be absorbed into the culture. However, the islanders interpreted leadership and social control differently, and manipulated their way around the "democratic" idea. In both cases the problems arose principally because of the cultural misperception of the planners who were putting mistaken reliance on "natural" and "common sense" assumptions which were relevant to the American scene but inadequate in contacts with people of another culture.

Culture creates unconscious blinders for all mankind. Other people do not act "naturally," that is, in accordance with a universal value system. Thus the American or other change agent must be given some opportunity of knowing himself as a product of American and Western culture. This means principally that he look analytically at his own assumptions and values. He should have some idea what influences his decisions and actions in introducing new ideas and what his reactions will be to difficulties among the people with whom he will be working. In short, he needs to know how being an American and a Westerner may help or hinder him in his mission.

American Cultural Values

In the age of cultural pluralism, what is meant by "American culture"? Is not the United States several streams of culture flowing side by side? There is probably more acceptance of this idea today than at any time since the founding of the country. And yet, there is still a national core, usually characterized as that of the middle class, having its origins in Western European culture. The language is English, the legal system derives from English common law, the political system of democratic elections comes from France and England, the technology is solidly from Europe, and even more subtle social values, such as egalitarianism (though modified), seem to be European derived. Thus, it seems justifiable to characterize the middle class value system of the United States, as derived originally from Europe but modified to suit local conditions, as the core of American culture.

All people born and raised in this country will have been conditioned by this national culture, although obviously the middle class will be most strongly marked. And though it is not implied here that there are no differences in other subcultural streams, it does mean that irrespective of region, national origin, race, class, and sex, there are points of likeness that will occur more frequently than among groups of people in other countries.

Where does this American character come from? As mentioned above, it seems to come from a European base that has been subsequently modified to meet local conditions. The values derived from life on the frontier, the great open spaces, the virgin wealth, and the once seemingly limitless resources of a "new world" appear to have affected ideas of freedom. Individualism seems to have been fostered by a commitment to "progress" which in turn was derived from expansion over three hundred years. Much of the religious and ethical tradition is believed to have come from Calvinist (Puritan) doctrine, particularly an emphasis on individual responsibility and the positive work ethic. Anglo-Saxon civil rights, the rule of law, and representative institutions were inherited from the English background; ideas of egalitarian democracy and a secular spirit spring from the French and American Revolutions. The period of slavery and its aftermath, and the European immigration of three centuries, have affected the American character strongly.

American Culture

Is it possible to provide a thumbnail sketch of the most obvious characteristics of this system? Most social scientists would probably agree to the following:

The number of people in America is considerable, compared to other countries, and they are located primarily in the cities and towns of a large area of diverse natural environments, still with considerable mineral and soil wealth and still not intensively exploited. There is an exceedingly elaborate technology and a wealth of manufactured goods that is now the greatest in the world.

Although the country has a strong agrarian tradition in which farming is still regarded as a family occupation, and although farming produces an extraordinary yield of foodstuffs and fibers, the nation has become urbanized and dominated by the cities. The farming population consists of less than 10 percent of the total, and agriculture has become so mechanized it can now be considered as merely another form of industry. Daily living is characteristically urban, regulated by the clock and calendar rather than by the seasons or degree of daylight. The great majority of individuals are employees, living on salaries paid by large, complex, impersonal institutions. Money is the denominator of exchange, even property having a value only in terms of its monetary worth. The necessities of life are purchased rather than produced for subsistence.

Because of the high standard of living and high level of technology, people have long lives. The birth rate is low but the death rate is among the lowest in the world. Thus, although there is a continuing expansion of population, it is much less rapid than in most of the agrarian nations.

Americans exhibit a wide range of wealth, property, education, manners, and tastes. However, despite diversities of origin, tradition, and economic level, there is a surprising conformity in language, diet, hygiene, dress, basic skills, land use, community settlement, recreation, and other activities. The people share a rather small range of moral, political, economic, and social attitudes, being divided in opinion chiefly by their denominational

American Cultural Values

and occupational interests. Within the past decade there seems also to have been a separation of opinion based on age. There are some regional variations but these are far less than the tribal or ethnic pluralisms found in the new nations of South Asia and Africa. The narrow opinion range throughout the country seems to be primarily a product of the relatively efficient mass education system which blankets the country and the wide spread of mass communication, from which all people get the same messages.

There are status differences, based mainly on occupation, education, and financial worth. Achievement is valued more than inheritance in determining an individual's position. Although in theory all persons have equal opportunities, certain limitations exist, particularly those based on ethnic background and sex. A Negro may be appointed as a member of the Cabinet, but it is improbable that he would be elected as President at the present time. There are now Negro mayors, but there are still no Negro governors. Women also are prevented from serving in certain positions or occupations. Despite these limitations, most people move about freely; they change jobs and move up and down in status with considerable frequency.

The basic American kinship unit, though evidently weakening, is still the nuclear family of husband, wife, and children. Newly married couples set up their own small households and move several times in a lifespan. The family rarely has continuing geographical roots. Most couples have few children. Marital relationships are fluid and not particularly stable, with divorce quite common. Old people and unmarried adults usually live apart from their kin. Instead of strong kinship ties, people tend to rely on an enormous number of voluntary associations of common interest—parent-teachers' association, womens' clubs, social fraternities, church clubs, recreational teams, political clubs, and many others.

The general level of education is high, with literacy normal but not universal. From the age of five to eighteen the child usually is in an academic institution, learning the culturally approved goals of good health, character, and citizenship. Also, he learns basic and standard skills rather than any hereditary specialization—reading, writing, arithmetic, typing, liberal arts, driving cars, basic mechanics, housekeeping. Specialization comes later in the professional training that ordinarily takes place in college. More and more young people are extending their education through four years in college, although this is not yet legally required.

The moral tone of the country is heavily Calvinist Protestant but there are many other sects of Christianity, besides other religions and cults. Religious beliefs and practices are concerned almost as much with general morality as with man's search for the afterlife or his worship of deities. Family relations, sexual customs, man's relationship to other men, and civic responsibility are all concerns of religion. A puritanic morality has become generalized and secularized, part of the total culture rather than that of any single religious sect. Formal religion is compartmentalized, as are many other aspects of American life. A high percentage of the Protestants who form the bulk of the population attend church infrequently, and religious ideas are seldom consciously mixed with secular ones. The church serves a strong social function, being the center of many clubs and groups. Religion can hardly be considered a particularly unifying institution of American life. The spirit of the country is secular and rationalistic. Most people are not antireligious but merely indifferent.

Material Well-Being

The rich resources of America, along with the extraordinary growth of its industrial economy, have brought a widespread wealth of material goods such as the world has not seen before. There has been a wholesale development and diffusion of the marvels of modern comfort—swift and pleasant transportation, central heating, air conditioning, instant hot and cold water, electricity, and laborsaving devices of endless variety. The high value placed on such comforts has caused industries to be geared to produce ever greater quantities and improved versions. Americans seem to feel that they have a "right" to such amenities.

Associated with this attitude toward comfort (which has itself resulted in elaborate waste disposal facilities), and an advanced state of medical knowledge, Americans have come to regard cleanliness as an absolute virtue. A most familiar slogan is, "Cleanliness is next to godliness," and although this is not heard as often as it once was, the word "dirty" is still one of the chief epithets in the language, as in "dirty old man," "dirty hippie," "dirty business," "dirty deal," etc.

Achievement and success are measured primarily by the quantity of material goods one possesses, both because these are abundant and because they indicate how much money an individual earns. This material evidence of personal worth is modified by the credit system; but still, credit purchases will carry an individual only so far, after which credit agencies will refuse to advance more without evidence of fundamental wealth.

Since there is little display value in the size of one's paycheck or bank account, the average individual buys prestige articles that others can see: expensive clothing or furniture, a fine car, a swimming pool, an expensive home, or one of the endless variety of devices that may have other functions but can also readily be seen by visitors—power mowers, barbecue paraphernalia, television, and stereophonic systems. A person's status is affected to a secondary degree by his level of education, type of occupation, and social behavior; but even these qualities seem to be significant only in terms of how much income they help him to obtain. Thus, a college professor who has earned his Ph.D. will have less status in the general community than a business executive or film actor who has no college education but commands a much larger salary.

People other than middle class Americans also value comfort and the saving of human labor, and one of the motivations to change everywhere is to perform traditional tasks more easily. However, many peoples of the world have found themselves unable to acquire so many laborsaving devices and have thus concentrated on the satisfaction of other needs; and it should be recognized that many of the spiritual or esthetic goals they pursue will outlast most of the machine-made devices treasured in America. But, their choices have been limited by their comparative poverty. Comfort in such circumstances has not been so highly valued; and in fact, Americans have been accused by this token of being excessively materialistic.

Twofold Judgments

A special characteristic of Western thinking, fully reflected in American ways, is that of making twofold judgments based on principle. The structure of the Indo-European languages seem to foster this kind of thinking and the action that follows. A situation or action is assigned to a category held high, thus providing a justification for positive effort, or to one held low, with justification for rejection, avoidance, or other negative action. Twofold judgments seem to be the rule in Western and American life: moral-immoral, legal-illegal, right-wrong, sin-virtue, success-failure, clean-dirty, civilized-primitive, practical-impractical, introvert-extrovert, secular-religious, Christian-pagan. This kind of polarized thinking tends to put the world of values into absolutes, and its arbitrary nature is indicated by the fact that modern science no longer uses opposite categories, in almost all instances preferring to use the concept of a range with degrees of difference separating the poles.

Judgment in terms of principle is very old and pervasive as a means of organizing thought in Western and American life. It may derive from Judeo-Christian ideas. In any event, it is deeply rooted in the religions that have come from this base as well as in the philosophy of the West. Its special quality should be recognized. More is involved than merely thinking in opposites. Other peoples have invented dual ways of thinking: the Chinese Yin-and-Yang, the Zoroastrian dual (though equal) forces of good and evil, male and female principles, and the Hindu concept of the forces of destruction and regeneration as different aspects of the same power. However, other peoples do not usually rank one as superior and thus to be embraced on principle as a guide to conduct.

This kind of thinking seems to force Americans into positions of exclusiveness. If one position is accepted, the other must be rejected. There is little possibility of keeping opposite or even parallel ideas in one's thinking pattern. This is not the case in other cultures. In Buddhism and Hinduism disparate local beliefs exist alongside beliefs that are derived from the main theology. No one questions the fact that in Japan people may worship in a Buddhist temple as well as in a Shinto shrine; or that in the

American Cultural Values

southern form of Buddhism, in Laos and Thailand, people propitiate the local spirits ("phi") as well as observe the ritual forms of Buddhism. This is quite different from the Christian attitude in which all that is believed to be supernatural but is not Christian is classified as superstition or paganism.

The average Westerner, and especially the American, bases his personal life and community affairs on principles of right and wrong rather than on sanctions of shame, dishonor, ridicule, or horror of impropriety. The whole legal system is established on the assumption that rational people can decide if things have been "wrong." The American is forced by his culture to categorize his conduct in universal, impersonal terms. "The law is the law" and "right is right," regardless of other considerations.

Moralizing

One of the most basic of the twofold decisions Americans make is to classify actions as good or bad. Whether in the conduct of foreign affairs or bringing up children or dealing in the marketplace, Americans tend to moralize. Judging people and actions as absolutely right or wrong may have been a source of considerable strength in American history but it has also created pitfalls, particularly in the way it has influenced Americans in their relationship with other peoples. The attitude has frequently led Americans to indignation and even to warfare about the behavior of other peoples, Vietnam providing the most obvious recent example.

Every people has its own code of proper conduct. This is such an important part of any culture that some effort to understand it must be made. But this aspect of a cultural system is probably the most difficult to learn. And the greatest difficulties will occur if the outsider assumes that other people's basis of judgment is the same as his, or even that proper conduct will be based on moral rather than other kinds of principles.

In many other cultures, rank or esteem, the dignity of a person, the honor of an individual, compassion for an unfortunate, or loyalty to a kinsman or co-religionist may be the basis for judgment as to proper conduct. Most forms of sexual behavior may not be considered subject to moral considerations. The American, as an heir to the Western tradition, is familiar and comfortable with a code of conduct derived from absolute principles (mostly religious) and supported by a code of law enforced by central authorities. This entire code is supposed to be impersonal, and to a considerable extent it is. The morality tale of the honest, law-abiding policeman or judge who punishes his own law-breaking son probably does occur more frequently in America than in societies where kinship considerations are given more weight.

One other feature of this kind of thinking that can lead to considerable personal and public problems is that the American tends to overreact to the discovery that the ideal behavior he was taught to expect from parents, public servants, spouses, and other adults is not always present in real life. Some individuals react by becoming "tough" and "cynical" and "wise" to the corruption of the world. Others, particularly exemplified by the youth of the past decade, organize to eliminate by whatever means are available the "failures" of the older generation. This kind of thinking encourages the individual to believe that whatever differs from the ideal version of high moral excellence is of the utmost depravity. It tends to direct the individual to see corruption and evil everywhere. And while such moralistic indignation may serve the culture well in some instances (as in the fight against pollution), it can also have negative consequences, particularly when the moralizer is trying to work with people of another culture.

Work and Play

Another kind of twofold judgment that Americans tend to maintain is based on a qualitative distinction between work and play. To most persons brought up in the present-day American environment of farming, business, or industry, work is what they do regularly, purposefully, and even grimly, whether they enjoy it or not. It is a necessity, and for the middle aged, a duty. A man is judged by his work. When strangers meet and attempt to establish cordial relationships, one of the first topics of discussion is the kind of work each does. It is a primary role classifier. Work is a serious, adult business, and a man is supposed to "get ahead" or "make a contribution" to community or mankind through his work.

Play is different. It is fun, an outlet from work, without serious purpose except possibly to make subsequent work more efficient. It is a lesser category, a later topic of conversation after one's occupation is identified. And although some persons may "enjoy their work," this is a matter of luck and by no means something that everyone can count on since all jobs contain some "dirty work," tedium, and tasks that one completes just by pushing on. Work and play are considered to be different worlds; there is a time and place for each, but when it is time for work, then lighter pursuits should be put aside. There is a newer emphasis in contemporary America on pleasure-seeking as a primary goal in life, but so far this seems to be an attitude espoused by a minority only, the young who have rejected the former goals of society and the retired old who have already completed their years of work.

The American habit of associating work with high or necessary purpose and grim effort and play with frivolity or pleasure seems to have a positive function in the American cultural context, but it may be quite out of place in another culture. For many peoples the times of most important work may also be times of festivity or ceremony. Work and play may be interwoven. A threshing floor may be a dancing arena, and building a new house or netting a school of fish may provide the occasion for a whole community to sing and joke together. Preparing the proper songs or dishes will be as "practical" an activity as cutting thatch or caring for nets.

The combination of work and play is not completely foreign to Americans, although urban industrial society does not seem favorable for it. The American frontier, and even Midwest farming communities until thirty or forty years ago, combined the two in their husking bees, house-raising and threshing parties. In the early decades of this century, before wheat combines and farms of large acreage dominated agriculture in the Midwest, farmers made the social and work rounds for several weeks in midsummer. Not only did they work together, but they also feasted, socialized, and even managed a considerable amount of courting. It was a point of pride for each farmer's wife to have the largest quantities of elaborate food available for the men when they came in from the fields. The unmarried girls made a particular effort to be there to search out the bachelors. It was a gay time as well as a time of hard work. It should also be pointed out that song and work has been well represented in the American past in the vast repertory of work songs that were once sung by occupational groups.

Basically, the nonindustrial societies have patterns of work and play that are closer to those known to preindustrial Americans; work and play are intermixed rather than distinct forms of activity.

Time Is Money

Closely related to the American distinction between work and play is a special attitude toward time. Whenever Americans interact with people in nonindustrial countries, both quickly become aware that their outlook in regard to time is different. In many such countries the local people actually make a distinction in the spoken language, referring to *hora Americana* versus *hora Mexicana* or *mong Amelikan* versus *mong Lao*. When referring to the American version, they mean that it is exact, that people are punctual, activities are scheduled, time is apportioned for separate activities, and the measure is the mechanical clock; their own time lacks this precision.

Probably misunderstandings with people of other cultures occur most frequently in relation to work. For Americans, "time is money." Work is paid for in money and one should balance his work against time or through regular periods for a fixed salary. A person works for a stated number of dollars per hour and eight or ten hours per day for 40 or 48 hours a week. Work beyond the normal is "overtime." Play or leisure time is before or after work time. An employer literally buys the time of his workers along with their skills, and schedules and assigns work to be balanced against the gain he will obtain. In this way of thinking, time can be turned into money, both for the employer and employee, and work turned out faster than planned can release extra time for more work and more gain.

Equating work with time, using the least amount of time to produce the largest amount of work, expecting that time paid for will be marked by sustained effort, budgeting of man hours in relation to the cost of the end product—these are central features of the American industrial economy that have contributed a great deal to its productiveness. And although Americans may complain about the necessity of routine and the tyranny of the clock during working hours, they are thoroughly accustomed to such strictures. The activities of leisure—eating, sleeping, playing, courting—must take place during "time off." No wonder time to them is scarce and worth saving.

Such a precise concept of time is usually foreign to peoples of nonindustrial cultures. In most agrarian societies, especially in the villages, time is geared to seasonal requirements and the amount of daylight available. Many routines reflect, not hourly or daily repetitions based on wage labor, but the needs of individual and social life, the cycles of crops, fluctuations in daily temperature, and the round of ceremonial observances. The cities of these countries have all adopted the Western concept of time to some degree, although it is frequently noted that the rural pattern is still maintained in modified form in the urban context. Individuals simply do not keep hours or appointments precisely and are surprised when they learn that an American is irritated by a missed appointment.

Effort and Optimism

Americans are an active people. They believe that problems should be identified and effort should be expended to solve them. Effort is good in itself, and with proper effort one can be optimistic about success. The fact that some problems may be insoluble is very difficult for an American to accept. The high value connected with effort often causes Americans to cite the principle that "It is better to do something than to just stand around." This thinking is based on the concept that the universe is mechanistic (it can be understood in terms of causes and effects), man is his own master, and he is perfectible almost without limit (DuBois, 1955: 1233–1234). Thus, with enough effort, man can improve himself and manipulate the part of the universe that is around him.

This national confidence in effort and activity, with an optimism that trying to do something about a problem will almost invariably bring success in solving it, seems to be specifically American. Such an attitude is probably a product of the continual expansion of American culture during the past three hundred years, first along America's frontiers and later in its industrial growth. Obstacles existed only to be overcome, and bad conditions needed only be recognized to be rectified.

Effort and optimism permeate the life of the individual because of his cultural upbringing. Coming from an "open class system," where status is usually achieved rather than inherited, both privilege and authority should be deserved and won.

Effort, achievement, and success are woven through the fabric of American life and culture. Activist, pragmatic values rather than contemplative or mystical ones are the basis of the American character. Serious effort to achieve success is both a personal goal and an ethical imperative. The worthwhile man is the one who "gets results" and "gets ahead." A failure "gets nowhere" or "gets no results," for success is measured by results (although there is a little "credit for trying"). The successful man "tackles a problem," "does something about it," and "succeeds" in the process. A failure is unsuccessful through his own fault. Even if he had "bad breaks" he should have tried again. A failure in life "didn't have the guts" to "make a go of it" and "put himself ahead."

This is a very severe code. No one is certain how widespread it is among Americans but it is probably recognizable to most. It indicates a culture in which effort is rewarded, competition is enforced, and individual achievement is paramount. Unfortunately, the code raises serious problems. One of the most important is that it calls all those in high positions successes and all those in low ones "failures" even though everyone knows the majority must be in lower positions. A code of this sort by its very nature creates much frustration in all those who have not been able to achieve high positions.

This traditional optimism of the American personality has been tempered to a certain degree in recent years, though primarily in the kind of goals sought rather than whether they can be achieved. Concentration on pragmatic effort seems unchanged, and even those Americans who are most disillusioned with the current state of affairs seem convinced that enough effort will produce success—for their new goals, however, rather than the old ones.

American Cultural Values

But it has become clear to everyone that whatever effort is expended, some situations are beyond the American's ability to control. Problems once thought to be simple are now seen to have a complexity not previously recognized. A weaker enemy cannot simply be bombed into submission with more and more explosives. Industrial production cannot be guided by the profit motive alone if one wants to breathe clean air and to swim in clean water. The inner city of an industrial nation cannot survive if it is abandoned by the well-to-do who move to the suburbs. These are some of the problems that have arisen because of a simplistic view of manipulation of the environment, both human and natural. Some pundits now feel they are beyond human correction, but although the optimism of the average man has probably been tempered in recent decades, his method of overcoming these obstacles is unchanged—simply put in greater effort.

The American overseas is prone to evaluate people and situations according to this code. When he observes that those in authority have achieved their position by means other than their own effort, he may become bewildered, angered, or cynical. He may quickly make an activist judgment and try to remedy the situation, using his own code. Or he may shift (usually unconsciously) from the notion of work as task-oriented, which many peoples share in their own fashion, to an emphasis on busy work, on hurrying and pressuring, on encouraging activity for its own sake.

To peoples in other parts of the world, a history of failure in recent times has been as compelling as the technological and economic achievements of America. Their experiences may have taught them to value passivity, acceptance, and evasion rather than effort and optimism. This will not be because they have no interest in getting things done but because of their history of reversals. They lack the confidence of the American.

Before taking action, other peoples may therefore make many preparations which the American, so concerned with technical efficiency, will consider unnecessary. These may consist in extensive consultation with others to build up a consensus, giving favors to win personal loyalties, trying to adjust proposed plans to religious and other traditional beliefs, and considering all alternatives, including the real possibility of not risking action at all. American demands for bustle and effort, for getting down to business, may not only be interpreted as nagging, pushing, and ill-mannered, but sometimes as downright frightening, especially when a wrong judgment could lead to personal disaster. After an initial failure, the American determination to "try again" or "try harder the next time" may seem particularly foolhardy. Merely to intensify one's effort and to try again on a bigger scale when resources are limited may appear as the most reckless compounding of original folly.

And as is not unusual, other peoples frequently do judge American behavior correctly. The American passion to exert greater effort in the face of continuing difficulties has not always produced the hoped-for success. In Vietnam, for example, although an admittedly much weaker enemy clearly and early indicated that they would fight differently than in previous wars, the military heads of the United States went ahead with conventional bombing and ground maneuvers for almost ten years without ever altering their procedures significantly except to intensify them. At the end of this decade, the enemy seemed hardly any weaker than at the beginning. And it must be admitted that such a procedure is only possible for America because it has unprecedented wealth and industrial production.

The effort to which Americans normally commit themselves is expected to be direct and efficient. Americans want to "get down to business" and confine themselves to the problem or proposal specified. Misunderstandings have consequently occurred because other peoples, particularly Latins, have tended to be less direct. They indulge more in rhetorical speech during conferences and discussions, refusing to confine themselves rigidly to the agenda at hand. All this indicates more concern with social values than is usual in the American manner of conducting affairs. Perhaps the impersonal, technological approach leads to more production but the social verities have their place also, and they are still significant in many parts of the world.

American assumptions about effort and optimism include a faith in progress and a constant view toward the future. Practically all life is arranged to fulfill the needs of children and of the generations to follow. There is a pervasive accent on youthfulness; the values exemplified in commercial advertising and entertainment almost always emphasize the young, and the old are not commonly sought out for their experience. Adults attempt to hold back middle and old age. In general, elderly people are bypassed, either left in old folks' homes or in isolated retirement, in both cases removed from practical affairs. An ironic aspect of the situation in the 1960s was the rejection by a considerable part of American youth of this idealized "youth culture." "You can't trust anyone over thirty," they say.

An accent on youthfulness is particularly American, although it seems to be shared to a lesser degree by other achievement-oriented industrial societies. In the agrarian nations, or wherever tradition is important, people tend to equate age with experience. The old are treated with deference and the oldest male is usually the chief decision-maker of the basic kin unit.

Other cultures have had their periods of success, but it appears rare for progress to be a central value throughout the entire existence of a culture. It is only since World War II that American faith in the future has been modified significantly, with the realization that there are many undesirable consequences if technological progress is allowed to take place with few controls. But despite recent reversals, the general American attitude is still that the future should contain bigger and better successes, if not on this planet, then on others. This attitude also implies that the new and modern are better than the old and traditional. Technological and economic life must progress. No one—not even the strongest dissidents of the left or the right—expects to keep America as it is today or to return it to what it was yesterday.

Man and Nature

The greater effort that normally marks the American's response to obstacles may sometimes seem shallow, irreverent, or premature to people in other cultures. Some obstacles deserve respect and there are limitations to what man can do, even if he is the cleverest manipulator of the environment to have appeared so far. The new ecological approach is an indication that the American is becoming aware of some limitations on his capacities, but whether this will deflect his value system in a basic way remains to be seen. Up to now, American man has attempted to conquer nature. It has been something to overcome, to improve, to tear down and rebuild in a better way. He has tried to "break the soil," to "harness" the natural resources, to treat the natural environment like a domestic animal. He has divided the plants and animals into categories of useful and harmful. Harmful plants are weeds and harmful animals are "varmints"—the first to be uprooted or poisoned and the second to be trapped, shot, or poisoned. American farmers and ranchers have been notorious for killing predators. The only kind of hawks they knew until recently were "chicken hawks" which were shot any time they appeared and their carcasses hung in long festoons on wire fences. Coyotes and bobcats are still trapped and hunted without compunction by Westerners, who can get bounties of a few dollars for the feet and ears of one of these animals. And although on occasion hawks and coyotes may kill a few chickens or sheep, they primarily live on mice, rats, rabbits and other small animals whose populations must be kept in balance by such predators. Even a weed is merely a "plant growing out of place" from man's point of view.

It must be admitted that many of the achievements of Americans are due to this conquering attitude toward nature. The enormous agricultural productivity is one such achievement, although credit must also go to the fact that there were large expanses of very fertile land available. But it must also be admitted that the American has paid and is continuing to pay high prices for these agricultural successes. Natural resources, particularly forests, water, and the air, have been squandered and despoiled over large areas. Nature's balance has often been upset. Such "wonder" insecticides as DDT are now under strong attack by conservationists as destroying many "useful" insects and birds, as well as for their effect on human health.

This conquering attitude toward nature appears to rest on at least three assumptions: that the universe is mechanistic, that man is its master, and that man is qualitatively different from all other forms of life. Specifically, American and Western man credits himself with a special inner consciousness, a soul, for which he does

American Cultural Values

not give other creatures credit. In most of the non-Western world man is merely considered as one form of life, different only in degree from the others. The Western biologist also shares this view, which is the primary reason that traditional Western culture came into conflict with biological views in the nineteenth and twentieth centuries. In the so-called animistic religions, all living creatures are believed to have something corresponding to a soul, with no sharp dividing line between man and the other animals. Spirits are even attributed to plants and inanimate objects, such as soil, rocks, mountains, and rivers. In the Hindu and Buddhist world the belief in a cycle of rebirths strongly affirms man's kinship to nonhuman forms. In the cycle of existences man can become an insect, a mammal, another type of man, or even a form of deity. The validity of such beliefs is far less important than the fact that man's attitude toward nature is influenced by them (and after all, there is no more empirical basis for Christian beliefs than for Buddhism or Hinduism). Basically, most people, (except Westerners) consider man and nature as one, and they more often work with nature than simply attempting to conquer it.

During long periods of trial and error, peoples of all cultures have worked out adaptations to their natural environments. These adaptations may lack much by Western standards but they do enable the inhabitants to survive, sometimes in quite difficult circumstances. Such peoples through experience have evolved systems of conservation, methods of stretching and restoring their slim resources, and elaborate accommodations to climate, vegetation, and terrain. Some such adaptations now embedded in tradition and religion are the Middle Eastern desert-derived pattern of Islamic ritual hygiene, austerity, and almsgiving; preindustrial Japanese frugalities in house structure, farming, and woodworking; and Southeast Asian village economies in the measured use of rice, bamboo, and fish. These and similar adaptations to natural environments are high developments in the balanced utilization of limited resources.

When, with a facile confidence that nature can be tamed by ever costlier mechanical devices, Americans and other Westerners attempt to brush aside the experience of centuries, it is perhaps temporarily exciting to the local people. However, they are not apt to be reassured if they have information about the realities of the environment that is ignored by the rushing, pushing, self-assured newcomers, particularly since the local solutions sometimes outlast the glamorous innovations of the specialists. For example, a well-drilling project in Laos was based on a system that had been worked out in Florida where the water table is high the year around. The specialist drilled wells in one large area of Laos during the rainy season and found water almost every time, at a relatively high level. However, all these wells went dry during the dry season, since in Southeast Asia the water level drops markedly during this period. Most Lao probably knew this and would have revealed it if asked.

In environments that seem adverse (such as the rainy tropics, the arctic, or the desert), experience has shown that Western man's goods and machines rot, rust, freeze, or grit up all too quickly, requiring huge and costly effort merely to keep them going. This is not surprising since this machinery was developed primarily for use in a temperate zone where precipitation is spread more or less evenly throughout the year.

A graphic example of the lack of adaptability of Western machines has been observed during the military struggles in Southeast Asia in recent years. Tanks and other mechanized equipment were developed with the solid land forms of America and Europe in mind. However, their use has been drastically curtailed in the rice paddies of Vietnam and Laos. The mobile foot soldier, unencumbered with heavy gear, can slip through the soggy fields and marshes in constant readiness to fight while the tank or halftrack is bogged down in mud. The insurgent forces in Laos and Vietnam have made their greatest drives just before the heavy rains set in, knowing that the mechanized forces with American equipment will be mostly immobilized until the land dries again.

Equality of Men

The tendency to moralize has been operative in supporting another important trait of American culture, egalitarianism. Americans believe all people should have equal opportunities for achievement. This is more of a moral imperative than an actual fact of American life and has always been so. From the earliest times there have been some groups of people who were treated as inferior, and great differences of wealth, education, influence, opportunity, and privilege exist in the United States. Nevertheless, the experiences that Americans underwent along the frontiers and through the process of immigration did represent a huge historical experiment in social leveling. The legal and institutional heritage prescribes equal rights, condemns special privileges, and demands fair representation for every citizen. The latest efforts to obtain equal treatment for minority groups have been spearheaded by legal resolutions (Supreme Court decisions) and other re-emphases of the egalitarian nature of the society. Inequality, unless a product of achievement or lack of it, is considered to be wrong, bad, or "unfair."

There are, of course, ethnic minorities which have not been assimilated into the major society and which are treated unequally. The main disadvantaged groups now are of African, Mexican, and Amerindian ancestry. Although it is currently fashionable to regard this difference of treatment as based on race, other explanations are just as plausible. None of these groups really constitute a race and people with basically very similar appearances and genetic background (such as those of Italian, Spanish, Chinese, or Japanese ancestry) face much less discrimination. But these latter groups have attempted to adopt the Euro-American cultural pattern while Mexican-American and Amerindians have tended to maintain certain distinctive cultural patterns. The case of the Afro-American is probably unique, in that these people constitute the only group whose ancestors were held in slavery by the majority.

It is probable that the American attitude toward equality of treatment really means "within the major value system"; that is, people are, or should be, treated equally if they accept the basic beliefs and behaviors of the social majority. In this sense, the American idea is similar to that of the Muslims, who have always taught that all men are equal under Allah; discrimination by race or any other criterion has been rare so long as one was dealing with acceptors of the faith, and within the ranks of believers the only significant feelings of superiority have been based on supposed relationships with the Prophet. People on a direct line of descent from Mohammed are considered higher than those on a more remote line.

There has been one other form of unequal treatment in American society, that between males and females. Although female liberation movements are fashionable now, the fact is that the American female is already in a position of more nearly equal treatment than in most other nations, and certainly those outside the West. In practice, women are barred from the highest positions and are discriminated against in certain professions. But there are few educational limitations and they can enter freely into economic affairs. Even marriage is considered to be a kind of partnership, an unusual arrangement among the vast range of cultures of the world.

Despite the remaining evidences of unequal treatment toward the unassimilated ethnic minorities and women, the basic American value judgment of equality among men (and women) has not changed. Open patterns of subordination, deference, and acceptance of underprivilege call forth sympathies for the "underdog" and American activist values call for efforts to do something about such matters. This impulse tempts Americans overseas to interfere directly in the life ways of other peoples. The American does not have the patience to deal with persons whose authority seems neither justified nor deserved, or to wait for the oridinary man who will act only when he has received the go-ahead from the figures of prestige or respect in his culture.

Another consequence of American egalitarianism is a preference for simple manners and direct, informal treatment of other persons. This can work to the American's advantage if kept within limits; but where people differ in rank and prestige, offense can be given if all are treated in a breezy, "kidding," impersonal manner. It is much better to try to acquire some of the local usages of long titles, elaborate forms of address and language, and manners of courtesy and deference, than to try to accustom other peoples to American ways. American "kidding" and humor are very special products of an egalitarian culture and generally work best at home.

American Cultural Values

Since all Americans are supposed to be equal in rights, and since "success" is a primary goal that can only be measured by achievement, a high value must be assigned to individuality. This accent on individual worth seems to be largely a heritage of frontier days and later economic expansion when there were plenty of opportunities for the individual to achieve according to his abilites. However, with population expansion and the filling up of the country, individuality has had to be limited to some extent. It is now known that the ravages of the natural environment are largely due to unchecked drives by industrialists toward individual achievement.

Although individual equality has been stressed throughout American history, the goals and ways of achieving success have been limited. The successful man was one who was better than everyone else but in a way similar to theirs; one might have more and better things than another, but they should be the same kinds of things. And with the full development of urban, corporate life, this similarity of goals seems to have evolved into personal conformity. The organization man has superceded the rugged individualist. Thus, individual self-sufficiency has steadily decreased. One indication of this development is a growing demand for security. And since Americans have abandoned the kinship system for this purpose, they now try to protect themselves with impersonal group insurance which they hope will cover all contingencies. In their efforts to attract new employees, corporations now advertise insurance benefits as much as the challenge of the work and the salary, and these "fringe benefits" are just as often the main concern of prospective employees. Americans buy insurance for the smallest items in their lives, even insuring household appliances against breakdown. Government too becomes more and more a giant insurance corporation, to its direct employees and to the citizenry in general.

Humanitarianism

The American trait of coming to the aid of unfortunates is widespread and well known. It expresses itself in impersonal generosity which is activated by calls for help when unpredicted events of unfortunate or disastrous effect occur. Earthquakes, floods, famines, and epidemics are only a few of the kinds of events that strike a responsive chord in American society. At the end of both world wars American generosity was primarily responsible for getting European nations back on their feet. Not only are they generous, but Americans also show a tremendous amount of efficiency at such times, often more than in "normal" times.

A dramatic illustration of this competence was witnessed in the aftermath of a battle in Vientiane, Laos, at which time the capitol was badly damaged. American diplomatic and assistance efforts in the preceding years had not been particularly impressive. In fact, the battle occurred principally because American diplomatic and military bureaus had come to the point of backing two opposing ideological factions of Laotians, supplying both groups with weapons. U.S. assistance efforts had been bogged down by a lack of cultural understanding of the Lao and by administrative problems in the aid mission itself. But after the capitol had been heavily damaged by shelling, the American International Cooperation Administration, as well as other American groups in the city, went into action in a manner that was truly impressive. Although many areas had been flattened and an unknown number of people killed, within two to three weeks the city was on its feet again. Besides providing needed goods, the American officials thought nothing of working day and night, and their organizational ability was much more clearly demonstrated than in their inept efforts at military diplomacy which led to the battle. In three to four months, there was hardly a sign that the battle had taken place.

American humanitarianism is a characteristic that can hardly be criticized. It is of a special type, however, and contains one possible basis of misunderstanding in that it is usually highly organized and impersonal. For many other peoples humanitarianism is personal. They consequently do not share with everyone; they cannot. But through personal and kinship obligations, by religious almsgiving, and in other traditional ways, they give what they can. The American must not blind himself to the existence of these other patterns and also must perceive that other peoples are just not as rich as he is. The American tendency can hardly be praised if it is merely converted into a standard of negative judgment against other peoples' ways.

American Cultural Values

An American tends to condemn begging and the systems that support it, presumably because it involves personalized asking and giving. But it is worthwhile to look into the realities of such a system, as for instance that of *baksheesh,* the Middle Eastern begging tradition. The halt, lame, and blind line up with outstretched palm at the mosque or church door. The American is likely to condemn the cruelty of such a system, but in fact these people are being taken care of by their community according to traditional rules. Every member of the Islamic faithful is expected to give 10 percent of his income (*zaka*) in direct alms to the unfortunates who personally ask for it. This particular pattern of generosity is one that has been worked into the communal life of the society, in keeping with its meager resources. The difference between this system and the Community Chest is mainly one of organization and personalization.

10

Field Procedures

The Need

The change agent working in another culture stands in a middle position. In a sense he must be a cultural interpreter, understanding not only something of the culture where he is working but also having a fair insight into his own cultural assumptions. Moreover, he must fulfill this need without being a full-time social scientist. His job in fact is much more difficult than that of the research scientist, who is required only to study and analyze the local system. The change agent must do this but he also has to introduce certain foreign innovations into the other system. It cannot be emphasized too often that people are much more willing simply to give information about themselves than to change their habits, the first of which is all the researcher requires but the second of which is needed by the change agent.

The change agent cannot be expected to carry out a complete study of the society where he is working, if for no other reason than that he also is responsible for his technical specialty and administrative duties. However, he should certainly be able to obtain insights, any of which could prove useful. He can get such information through study of existing published social science material and through his own observations in the field, facilitated by some knowledge of anthropological field methods. It is hoped that this final chapter will contribute in some small measure to the latter method of information collection.

Field Procedures

Although the usual change agent will not have the time, desire, or background to devote to full-time research, he will have some spare time when he gets to his field post, as well as some opportunities for mixing with the local people. This will occur unless he elects to go only to the houses and compounds of his fellow countrymen or cultural group. Unfortunately, the latter choice is made much too often, primarily to avoid the unpleasantries of culture shock, but social scientists believe it is self-defeating in the long run. Not only does it cut off the contacts that are useful in promoting change, it also cuts off the sources of vital local information. Despite the difficulties, the change agent is advised to take advantage of all reasonable cultural contacts with the local group.

Culture Shock

The first few weeks, and sometimes even months, spent in a new cultural context are among the most critical for the change agent as well as for the field researcher. This is a period when the outsider is still a visitor, inundated by a wealth of new sounds, sights, smells, and noises which can either pique his curiosity or set up strong revulsions. If the newcomer acquires an accepting attitude at this time, he has won a major battle.

It is natural for this initial period to be disturbing. The cues and expectations which the individual had become thoroughly accustomed to in his own system are suddenly taken away, to be replaced by others which can be quite different. The events of life are no longer very predictable. But the person so afflicted should know that this experience, known as culture shock, has happened to countless people throughout history, all those who have moved from one system to another for varying lengths of time. Tourists, merchants, diplomats, immigrants, social scientists, and technical specialists have gone through it successfully. Of course, there are those who did not manage it with success. Perhaps if they had known better what to expect, more people would have adapted adequately. The anthropologist believes that adaptation to a new cultural context can be the source of much inspiration and discovery. But the initial period is often critical.

Some persons seem to have more tolerance and less anxiety than others when faced with new and unusual situations. They may have had more exposure to cultural differences in earlier years. A variety of cultural environments in childhood—travel, learning another language, even studying other ways through books—are some of the experiences that can help to develop the adaptability that will build cultural bridges. But no one is a perfect cultural chameleon unless he has rejected his own cultural background completely, a very unusual occurrence. Thus, nearly every prolonged contact with another cultural system will cause some shock and require some readjustment. A description of such an experience by one of the authors will exemplify the reaction:

> My first field trip in a foreign land was to India where I went to make a study of factory workers in a large city. I made initial contacts with faculty members of the local university and all seemed to be going well. A school teacher of the area was recommended for taking me to the large factory city about fifty miles from the university town. He located a room for me and I moved in.
> My place was on the second floor of a tenement building on a narrow, dark street. At this time it seemed like something out of the Casbah or *Arabian Nights*. There was a Hindu temple on the street below where throughout the day I could watch the worshippers ring a gong, pour water on the phallic stone of the diety, Shiva, and squat to one side for reciting prayers. Also, I could frequently hear the chant of Brahmin priests. The temple floor was wet and dirty from the spilled water and countless bare feet of the worshippers. On occasion, cows would wander into the altar area to eat the flowers left by the faithful. When I would look inside, I would be aware of the room's lack of cleanliness and that it was inhabited by many mice.
> To venture outside took considerable courage since the people of the neighborhood stared at me, often it appeared in an unfriendly manner. It seemed to me that they would have paid no more attention to a Martian. I soon found out that the Europeans and Americans of the city never ventured into this quarter, learning that they stayed in their own compounds or in better districts. I had studied and could speak some Hindi, but at this time I was too shy to use it any more than absolutely necessary. And even at those times, the local people seemed to have difficulty understanding me. Becoming more and more nervous with my surroundings, I decided to go to a

Field Procedures

nearby village where I had learned there were workers who commuted to the city.

Again the school teacher made arrangements, finding a place in a relatively clean government guest house. There were no other guests, although there was an English-speaking government official living across the road who was willing to serve as an interpreter for the time being. He obtained a temporary servant for me from the nearby village, a man who had probably never worked for a foreigner before.

My next self-assigned task was to start interviewing the village people to find out about factory work, but I was very shy and kept postponing the inevitable. By this time I could speak Hindi well enough to send the servant to the market for some tea and a few edibles. The man did as he was told, although he misunderstood several details. When he returned he prepared tea. The only furniture in the room was a table and two chairs, which the servant arranged for the tea. When I reached for some sugar, which was in a paper bag just as it had been purchased, I found it crawling with ants. I spent some time picking out the insects before putting the sugar into my tea, and instructed the servant to put the remainder in a better place.

I drank my tea in a state of nervous tension, mainly because the servant squatted just in front of the table and watched my every move as if I had two heads. I wanted desperately to be alone but was not sure I could explain this properly without hurting the man's feelings. After all, I knew he was from the village where I wanted to do my study. Ultimately he went away on his own but when he had gone I found the bag of sugar on the other chair with a veritable convoy of ants traveling to and fro, each carrying a tiny crystal of sugar. The sight of these ants and my inability to handle what should have been a simple problem was very irritating.

When evening fell I was upset by the many unfamiliar sounds coming from the nearby village and the surrounding countryside. The bird calls were unfamiliar and there was a constant yapping which I later learned was from jackals. I slept fitfully and when morning came I was so unsettled by the unfamiliarity of everything that I ran out to catch the first train to the city. I returned to the university town to join my wife and son without even bidding my host goodbye.

However, after several days I did come back to the scene of my trials and slowly adjusted myself. I stayed then for a year, the time I had originally planned, until most of what had been unfamiliar and frightening became understandable and not unpleasant. I learned to move about freely, both within the industrial city and in the nearby villages and I also learned to use my Hindi tolerably well. [Niehoff: field observation]

Looking back at this experience, the individual events that led up to the shock do not seem so terrible, but it must be admitted that the author has had considerable other field experience since and has learned to adjust much easier. Also, it is probable that the individual events do not cause the shock so much as does the whole series together. There are too many unfamiliar things occurring during one time period. Then, too, the author might have been more sensitive to such influences than most others would be.

The majority of overseas workers will not experience culture shock so severely, primarily because they are not expected to live in as intimate association with local people as is expected of the cultural anthropologist. Moreover, they usually have more assistance to help in adjustment than does the individual scholar. Change agents are normally part of large organizations which help take care of many of their physical needs and act as a buffer between them and the local communities. Nevertheless, since it is necessary to learn something about the local cultural system, it is also necessary to participate to some degree; and since such persons will have had less orientation to other cultural ways than a social scientist, it is to be expected that cultural differences will have more effect.

Perhaps the simplest manifestation of culture shock is to try to avoid everything about the other people. Also, the visitor may raise his voice to a shout when he finds the foreigners unable to understanding simple English or his version of the local language. At its strongest, culture shock can reduce one to numb fatigue or constant anger against the foreigners. One anthropologist defines the symptoms manifested by Americans as "excessive preoccupation with drinking water, food, and dishes, fear of physical contact with servants, great concern over minor pains and skin eruptions, a hand-washing complex, fits of anger over delays and other minor frustrations, a fixed idea that people are cheating you, delay and

Field Procedures

outright refusal to learn the language of the country, an absent-minded, far-away stare (sometimes called the tropical stare), a feeling of helplessness, a desire for the company of people of one's own nationality, and a terrible longing to be back home—to be able to have a good cup of coffee and a piece of apple pie, to walk into that corner drugstore, to visit one's relatives, and, in general, to talk to people who really make sense" (Foster, 1962: 187–188).

When and if such a reaction occurs, it is important to recognize it for what it is—a temporary attitude that will pass as soon as the outsider becomes more familiar with local customs. This will occur if, in this early period, the newcomer purposefully pushes ahead and bends all efforts to understand the other system. The new ways will become familiar and even comfortable only by coming back to them again and again, seeking understanding without applying the values of one's own culture. Such a technique is suited to American activist values. If this is not done, there is a real danger that the outsider will reject the local system as inexplicable and turn to his fellow countrymen and familiar activities. Once this happens, understanding will probably never occur.

Although it is true that the most difficult period is practically always at the initial stage of a change agent's stay in a new country or culture, he will have to learn and adjust to new ways continually, and should have less difficulty as time passes. It will come as somewhat of a surprise for him to realize after a while that he is accepting new forms of behavior with very little pain. Also, although the first tour in an unfamiliar culture will normally produce the most severe form of culture shock, this kind of reaction will reoccur at later times when the individual encounters other cultural systems, although with less severity.

Rapport

The change agent, just as the social scientist, must win some degree of acceptance by the community or group where he hopes to institute change. He must gain the confidence of the local people at least to the extent that they will talk with him freely and sincerely about the real conditions of their lives. Such rapport is a must before any work which requires the voluntary cooperation of the local people on any change project can begin. The more theoretical social and psychological sciences as well as the more practical disciplines, such as medicine, psychiatry, and education, agree in stressing the importance of rapport between the investigator and his subject. Without it, the respondent is much more likely to provide only stereotyped or expected answers.

Basically, the investigator should not find rapport hard to establish if he displays a genuine interest in the culture of the people he is studying. Men respond to inquiry concerning their lives more easily than is supposed by nonsocial scientists, just so long as they do not fear unpleasant repercussions for divulging information. There is probably no subject that an individual finds more interesting than himself, which includes his beliefs and behavior. Secondarily, he is interested in his neighbor. The combination of self and neighbors constitutes the human element of society and culture. Added to the natural desire of people to talk about themselves, the sincerely interested outsider has a definite advantage simply because he is usually an educated and important person in the eyes of the local people. In the past, most Westerners in the agrarian nations of Asia, Africa, and Latin America were either uninterested in the customs of the local people or had an initial negative bias. The local people were considered barbaric or backward in advance. Casual tourists, besides making such negative prejudgments, would not usually have enough cultural background to question local people intelligently. Thus, to meet outsiders who are interested in the local cultural systems for the purpose of learning rather than criticizing is an experience few village or even educated non-Western people can resist.

There are certain basic precautions which the outsider should observe to gain the minimal confidence essential. The specific ways of winning rapport can be as varied as are the cultural forms. However, in general, one must put the people of the other culture at ease. When making acquaintances with some people, open tactics, such as those the American is comfortable with, may be successful; with others, these manners may be so strange as to be misunderstood or even appear downright offensive. Thus, back

Field Procedures

slapping, or "kidding around," or a casual invitation to "make yourself at home, we're always informal," may be as unfathomable to another people as are Japanese hissing (a sign of politeness), German stiff bowing, or the Latin *abrazo* (mutual embracing) to Anglo-Americans.

Probably in general, it is best to act with reserve until one is fairly familiar with local patterns of interaction. If one finds after a while that local people act with informality, American customs can fit in easily and nothing will be lost; but if their behavior is highly formal it will probably never be wise to act in the American way. To foster rapport does not imply converting others to one's cultural ways, but rather responding to their cues, learning some of their values, and making some adjustment to their culture. This does not mean to ape them indiscriminately, but at least to follow their lead in matters important to them. It adds up to an honesty of approach which is worth spelling out:

1. Explain truthfully but as simply as possible the purpose in asking for and accumulating knowledge about the local culture. Enquiries may be suspect at first, but people are flattered by genuine queries from respected strangers. If nothing happens that suggests hidden intentions, their suspicions will fall away and they will accept the fact that none are present. A lie or false pose will almost always become apparent fairly quickly and will damage the investigator's reputation as well as that of others who might follow.
2. Begin with subjects which have the least potential threat, and proceed to new ones only with the consent of the local people. Also, enter new places for observation only with local consent or preferably by invitation. Secret observation or interrogation with disguised intentions too closely resembles spying. The change agent interested in a local culture has neither the rights nor duties of a detective or lawyer. Anything sacred or dangerous in their beliefs is best discussed openly and at their initiative. In general, it is not necessary to attempt secret techniques if one can eliminate the fear of repercussion. This seems to be the only consistent block to release of information.
3. Respect local values, conventions, taboos, and prejudices even when it is not possible to go along with all of them. Ignorance of local customs will usually be forgiven, but contempt will not.

By asking for guidance, one not only learns local customs but shows his good faith to his hosts.
4. Maintain confidences. Information given privately, especially if it can be harmful for the informant if disclosed, must not be disclosed to others. Social scientists have often followed through with this policy by trying to keep their informants and the places they have studied anonymous.
5. Refrain from making moral, esthetic, or other judgments about the culture or persons from whom the information is coming. This is not easy; but if learning is the prime consideration, it is essential. Any condemnation or even high praise of information or its source is not only irrelevant in a learning situation but is likely to estrange the informant or bias the responses. Some reactions of surprise, incredulity, or disdain are involuntary and almost unavoidable in cross-cultural contacts. But training and concentration can compensate for many such automatic responses. The good investigator of another way of life is like a good diplomat in this respect. He keeps a poker face and finds a way to indicate his interest and friendly intentions without committing himself by overt praise or criticism. A continual display of one's immediate reactions is not only naive; it is a sure way to close off further contact or to bias the responses of persons from another culture.
6. Avoid expressing nostalgia, vainglory or invidious comparisons between one's own culture and the local one. Field research is not a debate. If the purpose is to build rapport and obtain information, it does nothing but harm to prove the inferiority of the local cultural ways. If informants want factual information about the researcher's way of life (and many will), it should be given to them honestly, in relatively simple terms. There is much curiosity about Western and American life.
7. Come acceptably vouched for and try to stay clear of too close identification with any social level or faction. It has been a common experience in social science that the best results are obtained if the field worker follows the lines of personal relationship, descends a hierarchy gradually, and when working with a low-ranking person, to have at least seen those of higher authority or prestige. To work through the hierarchy is to pay deference to the scale of values held by the community. There are lines of relationship that unite all levels and factions of a culture. The efficient field worker will find and follow them without identifying closely with any.

Field Procedures

The rules above from social science research for winning and holding rapport may appear very stern. However, valid information comes only through careful diplomacy. Basically, the field worker needs to have a genuine respect for the persons from whom he is learning. But the change agent, as well as the social scientist, must always keep in mind that the subjects are human beings who have the capacity and will distort information unless they are treated with tact and consideration, and perceive no threat from the outsider.

Participant Observation

Although direct questioning can produce a certain amount of information, anthropologists have found that studies based only on spoken statements are incomplete at best and inaccurate at worst. The primary reason this is so is that people do not always do what they say they do. Every culture has its ideals and concepts of what is proper and improper. When individuals are questioned directly about what is done, they tend to describe the ideal pattern or else tell the questioner what they think he wants to be told. If they can visualize any personal harm or benefit from releasing information, individuals will tend to unconsciously distort the information or tell downright falsities. Language is by no means merely a medium for describing events in the real world. In fact, it can be just as easily considered as a medium for influencing others. Thus, it is natural for distortion to creep into statements.

For instance, in village India one might inquire as to the occupations of Brahmins and Chamars. The answer might well be that Brahmins are priests and Chamars are leather-workers. Yet investigation in a particular village would usually show that the majority of both Brahmins and Chamars are farmers. A few of the Brahmins would know how to conduct certain ceremonies and would do so in their spare time; but their main economic support would come from the cultivation of their fields. A very few of the Chamars would pick up dead cows and process the hides, but the great majority would have given up this occupation for farming.

One of the authors noticed that many rum shops were operated by East Indians in Trinidad. Knowing that the use of alcohol is against Islamic law, he asked if local Muslims ever operated such shops or drank rum. The response was negative, in keeping with Islamic strictures. Later investigation showed that many of the Muslims drank rum and some even operated rum shops. When confronted with this information, other Muslims explained that such people were not good and that things had been different in the old days (Niehoff: field observation). Individuals invariably have an explanation for such differences in behavior. One anthropologist wrote a methodology of village field research which he entitled "Behind Many Masks." During his village stay, many things were not told to him or were distorted behind the social masks people were wearing. Some of the most vital information was only learned at the very end of his study, when the threat of consequences was practically removed (Berreman, 1962).

In other words, the behavioral culture often differs from the verbal one. Anthropology distinguishes between the *real* and *ideal* of culture. And the fact is that people tend to pay lip service to their moral code (the *ideal*), often with complete faith, long after they have ceased conforming to it. What this means to the field worker is that he cannot rely completely on what people say, even when they are trying to be sincere. The way he corrects this deficiency is to also observe what they do.

There is still another disadvantage to complete reliance on verbal information: that much which would be significant for understanding is not brought out by direct questioning. The questioner often does not know what specifically to ask; and the informant, who takes most of his own culture for granted, neglects to mention many small details and even fairly large incidents of cultural significance. One of the authors collected many accounts about local spirits from his Lao assistant. Most of the stories were about spirits that had bothered people far out in the remote villages and as if they had happened long before. One day the author saw a man standing rigidly in the town market place, his hair dirty and dishevelled and his clothes in rags. The merchants were throwing him scraps of raw meat. It was an inexplicable sight in terms of the author's understanding of the culture up to that time, so he asked his assistant who willingly said that the man

Field Procedures

was possessed by a tiger spirit and had been around town for several weeks. It had not occurred to the Lao assistant that the author would be interested in a contemporary tiger man living in town (Niehoff: field observation).

Participation in a local culture has another real advantage. Probably the best way of convincing local people that one is interested in their way of life is to seek their help in learning some of their ceremonial and social customs. Many peoples of the agrarian nations think (not completely without justification) that Westerners look down on their religious and social practices. Before the era of national independence, perhaps most Westerners overseas did feel superior morally to the local cultures, and took few pains to hide the fact. Although political conditions have changed, some of this old national ethnocentrism still persists. Consequently, a change agent can gain much good will by letting the local people know that he would like to attend some of their religious ceremonies, wedding, fiestas, and other communal activities. At first, they may be a little surprised and not quite sure he is serious; but given a little encouragement, they will make every effort to include him in future gatherings. Genuine interest, including participation when possible, will please the local people greatly. In all but the most conservative cultures, the newcomer will be swamped with invitations to attend local affairs. If they are convinced of his sincerity, the local people will explain with great patience what a given ceremony means and he will learn much, as well as build up confidence to a degree that is difficult by merely asking people what they do.

Although it was a pleasure to interact with the East Indians of Trinidad, one of the authors and his wife literally had to find an escape from some of the visits and requests for attendance to local affairs. Once they became aware of the pair's interests, the men appeared night after night to tell stories and to take the husband out to visit spirit places, and the women would come in the very early morning and during the day to discuss family gossip with the wife and to report on medicinal plants. After some months of constant attention, the pair set aside at least one afternoon a week during which they would go to an unknown beach where none of the local people could find them (Niehoff: field observation).

A final advantage to be derived from participation is that new interests will be developed in the overseas tour. The recreational facilities are usually inferior to those in the home country despite the amenities provided in the foreigners' compound. The Western technician who attempts to follow only customary pastimes may therefore have quite a bit of time on his hands. But if he can open the gate to the culture of the people with whom he is living, he will find new interest in his work and leisure. A true cross-cultural experience is of great value in enriching the personality of twentieth-century man. Although Peace Corps volunteers often have bitter comments to make of their tours, and social scientists who have studied their experiences also have criticisms, they are generally agreed that the experience of living and working in another culture was very valuable. It is quite possible that providing several thousand or hundred thousand young people from an urban industrial culture with a true cross-cultural opportunity will ultimately be the greatest contribution of the Peace Corps program.

Most Americans or other Westerners should maintain a continuity with their own culture while overseas. Nevertheless, anthropologists feel that they would be missing many unique opportunities if they spent all their free time with American colleagues, playing poker, going to parties or American movies. Participation in the local culture is therefore a very valuable way to add a new dimension to the overseas experience, as well as being an ideal way to obtain most useful information.

Using the Local Language

It is clear that a change agent's work is made easier if he can use the native language directly. Conversing in the local idiom will make more knowledge available, decrease the possibility of misunderstandings, and help to establish rapport with local people. However, adequate comprehension or fluency is not acquired without effort by most people. It means much time studying; and with the other responsibilities of the usual change agent, such time is not always available.

Any foreign language can be learned by anyone of normal in-

Field Procedures

telligence, although the rate may vary with different people. In the plural societies of Asia and Africa, people consistently learn one another's languages, sometimes each person learning as many as four or five. This is done without formal study, by merely imitating the speech of one's neighbors over a period of months or years. However, these people are living in the cultural milieu where the languages are spoken. Learning can come through formal training also, as is indicated by the experience of the smaller European countries, such as Denmark, Switzerland, and Holland. Children are taught two or three foreign languages through their school years, and when they are adults they can handle this many.

The foreign specialist normally will not have studied the language of the agrarian nation where he is working, except possibly just before coming on his tour and that usually will have been a very brief period. Even if he has been fortunate enough to have received basic groundwork in the local language, he will not have achieved fluency or anything approaching it when he arrives at his post. He may quickly find an interpreter because he wants to get on with his work. Then, as his responsibilities increase, he will find that he has less and less time to devote to language study; and with the interpreter available, he will find that he is devoting less and less time to speaking the language himself. If this happens, it will be unlikely that he will learn the local idiom.

Missionaries invariably learn the language of their area, and frequently more than one. They normally go through a formal study period first. However, as soon as they arrive at their posts, they deliberately throw themselves into situations where they must speak the local language—with no interpreter. In Southeast Asia it was a common practice for Protestant missionaries to spend three to six months living in a villager's house where no English-speaking person was available. Admittedly this entails fairly deep cultural immersion, but it is one way of learning a language as well as much of the culture of a people. After this period, the American missionaries could get along comfortably, if not with complete fluency, in the language. It is worth noting that the villager's household is better for this purpose than is that of the city bureaucrat or merchant, for the simple reason that the villager will rarely know or be in the process of learning English or any other European language. When this latter is the case, the local people can spend all the time available in practicing their English.

Most foreign specialists are not expected to go through such an intensive language learning experience; but if they want to speak at all, they will need to spend a fair amount of time actually conversing, and without the help of an interpreter. Even a simple ability in a local language will help, if for nothing more than to establish a good bond of understanding with the local people.

But irrespective of what social scientists may believe and preach, it is clear that many, and probably most, change agents depend on interpreters for their work and will continue to do so. Consequently, some consideration of interpreter choice must be made. Just because an individual speaks good English and seems to know the local language well is not enough. This person can serve as a bridge or a wall. If he has no sympathy with the problems or culture of the local people, he will be particularly harmful for establishing rapport. This has happened frequently when Americans or Europeans have hired persons from a third culture or nation, simply because they spoke the language of the specialist better than the natives. However, such "third nationals" frequently have a condescending attitude toward the local culture, being much more anxious to impress their employer than the people they are supposed to interpret.

The change agent should do all possible to assure himself that the interpreter knows the local language well, which is surprisingly enough not always the case. The interpreter who does not know the language well will tend to fill in gaps of what he did not hear by his own ideas. Thus, the change agent must be adamant in instructing the interpreter to translate the words of the informants fully and literally. Choosing or summarizing what is important is a task for the change agent.

Field Procedures

There are several general requirements for field study. First, even before gathering specific data, the change agent, like the social scientist, needs to decide what is representative or typical.

Field Procedures 247

He will have to generalize from the information he gathers and thus he needs to do some sampling. He can do this by seeing a variety of situations before he begins his detailed study, to find out what village or community arrangement is most "typical," what combination of religious or ethnic elements are most often found together, and what are the most consistently occurring survival problems. Without some such rough sampling, he cannot expect to apply findings from one area to those of another. He will be spending all his time doing unique studies. Then there is the problem of establishing rapport, which has already been discussed.

The third step is the necessity of deciding from whom he will get his information. The anthropologist uses native informants, who are the real actors of the culture. He goes step by step through the ramifications of each custom as it comes up. For instance, if he wants to learn about the local patterns of family life and kinship, he systematically goes through the names of all the personal relatives known by the informant. He obtains this information in the local language. He gets what general relationships the informant is able to put into words, but more importantly he collects anecdotes about real-life incidents of family group members. Although the researcher may get some general statements of given customs from his informants, he cannot expect this. Analysis and generalization is his responsibility. He cannot ask the informant if age is a determining principle for assigning status position. Rather, he must decide, on the basis of how young men greet their fathers and uncles, who keeps the family money, and what happens to a person when he gets beyond his active years. Most people take their own culture so much for granted that they are unable to analyze it. Furthermore, they are not trained in social science.

Native, local informants are best precisely because they are not self-designated generalizers. They describe the local situation concretely and are either unable, or have no reason, to gloss it over, pretty it up, distort or disguise it in the interest of theory or pseudo-systematics. For the same reason, a learned informant can be unreliable, not because he knows less (although often he will not be in direct touch with real village or local community conditions), but because he predigests the information. Thus, he can be as much of a barrier as a poor interpreter can be. He passes the information through a sieve of theory or evaluation that inevitably distorts it, which is especially harmful in the beginning. Later the questioner may be able to see what was untrue, but at the start he must take most information at face value. Direct questioning may be taxing, time-consuming, and perplexing at first. However, consulting experts or relying entirely on written sources is not enough. It can be maintained that social science has progressed almost in direct proportion to the degree that inquiry has been pushed to the man at the grass roots level.

The field methods that have been described so far are based primarily on anthropological research. Since the anthropologist is concerned with all customs and behavior, he tries to achieve a fairly broad coverage. On the other hand, although the change agent can probably put to good use most information he personally elicits, he will not usually have the time, nor perhaps interest, to study everything. But even if he limits his research to behavior related to his own specialty—education, agriculture, animal husbandry—the same field methods are applicable.

The anthropological field worker at first takes cultural inventories. Confronted with an unfamiliar culture, he must act as an explorer. He draws up a catalog of everything worth noting that distinguishes the particular culture from others—tools, furniture, house types, clothing, domesticated plants, medicines, foodstuffs, and all the behavior which goes with these things. He will also collect information about ritual objects, songs, legends, and supernatural beliefs. The social scientist wants to be able to identify these things in the native language and to understand what function they serve to help satisfy life needs. Other ways of looking at the data should provide answers as to how an item got into the culture, its possible connection with myth or legend, whether it is communally or individually owned, how it is inherited, and so on endlessly.

The change agent may not be interested enough or have sufficient time to make such a complete survey, but he can at least try to get such information as concerns his specialty. Even narrowed down this much, such research may prove to be a complex under-

Field Procedures 249

taking, primarily because of the interrelatedness of customs. For example, agricultural practices often involve religious beliefs and are also affected by such behaviors as social relations, food preferences, and trade practices. A newcomer may not at first understand enough of the intricate web of interconnections, nor command enough of the language to follow native descriptions. Nevertheless, patient and systematic work with knowledgeable informants and refusal to apply one's own values will produce many surprising insights.

Anthropologists have found it essential to take regular and extensive notes regarding their cultural findings. This is particularly important at the start of research, before one is adapted too much to the local way of life. The differences in sights, sounds, customs, and things will be very apparent the first few weeks and months. Later, many differences will hardly be noticed. The quantity of notes will decrease as time passes. However, one should continue to take them throughout the entire period of one's stay; for although the quantity may decrease later, the quality should improve, and the most important insights will come later. Most anthropologists make it a rule to write some notes every day, for the amount of knowledge desirable is almost limitless. Even in one's own culture there are enormous areas of activity of which any individual is either unaware or knows about only in a very general way.

Whether one takes notes in the presence of the informants or writes them down later will depend on attitudes of that culture and the relationship of the local people to the researcher. If they are suspicious of an outsider's motives, note-taking can put them on edge and either make them reluctant to continue talking or cause them to deliberately distort the facts. Needless to say, using a tape recorder is even more unnerving when people are suspicious of the researcher's intentions. On the other hand, if the local people understand why the interrogator is taking notes, (as they should) and are in sympathy with his aims, note-taking will not bother them at all. Anthropologists have found that certain peoples, who have been completely neglected in previous times, are so interested in having their cultures described and preserved in writing that they want the information written down. In general, it is people who have been studied excessively and who have been treated badly by outsiders who are reluctant to give information openly. As an overall policy, until the researcher knows more about the local people, it is probably best to write notes after interviews. With a little practice, considerable detail can be remembered. And although it cannot be claimed that complete accuracy will result with this technique, it is felt to be more desirable than having large amounts of distortion in the information or having the source cut off completely.

Whatever the amount of research done on the culture, it can be divided into several phases. The usual change agent can try to familiarize himself as much as possible with the culture through written sources, then conduct as much of a field survey as possible, to be followed by more intensive work on cultural aspects directly related to his specialty. While his change project is underway he should keep checking the cultural problems which arise in response to the innovation. Finally, it is to be hoped that every change agent will be interested in making an evaluation, both of what happened to his particular innovation, and what happened to the culture as a result of its acceptance. Such case studies of successes and failures are of great value in making wiser decisions in the future. Then perhaps some day a memory will be developed in the field of technical assistance.

Recommended Reading

Those who are interested in further study of this approach to the change process, especially in the village world, can consult the following works by the authors of this book:

Arensberg, Conrad. "Upgrading Peasant Agriculture," *Journal of World Business*. New York: Columbia University, January-February 1967.

Niehoff, Arthur. *Planned Change in Agrarian Countries*. Alexandria, Virginia: Human Resources Office, 1969.

———. *A Casebook of Social Change*. Chicago: Aldine · Atherton, 1966.

Niehoff, Arthur, Everett Rogers, and Robert Solo, eds. "Promoting Change in the Community" in *The Transfer of Technology to Developing Countries*. East Lansing: Michigan State University (in press).

Niehoff, Arthur, and Charnel Anderson. "The Process of Cross Cultural Innovation" in *International Development Review*. Washington, D.C.: June 1964.

References

Ablett, R. N. "Community Development in the Former Somaliland Protectorate," *Corona*. London: April 1961.
Adams, John B. "Culture and Conflict in an Egyptian Village," in *American Anthropologist*, vol. 59, No. 2: 1957.
Adams, Richard N. "A Study of Labor Preference in Peru," in *Human Organization*, vol. 10, No. 3: 1951.
———. "A Nutritional Research Program in Guatemala," in Benjamin D. Paul, ed., *Health, Culture and Community*. New York: Russell Sage Foundation, 1955.
Aguilera, Donna, Marlene Farrell, and J. Messick. *Crises Intervention: Theory and Methodology*. Los Angeles: C. V. Mosby Co., 1970.
"Akowonjo Village Poultry Improvement Scheme," *Community Development Bulletin*. London: September 1951, pp. 78–79.
Alers-Montalvo, M. "Cultural Change in a Costa Rican Village," *Human Organization*, vol. 15. Ithaca, N.Y.: Winter 1957, pp. 3–5.
Andrews, Stanley. *Technical Assistance Case Reports*. Washington, D.C.: International Cooperation Administration, 1960.
Benedict, Ruth. *Patterns of Culture*. New York: Mentor Books, 1946.
Berremen, Gerald D. "Behind Many Masks." Monograph 4. Ithaca, N.Y.: Society for Applied Anthropology, 1962.
Bogue, Robert, and Aziz Habashy. *Health Education in Three Villages in Egypt*. New York: World Health Organization, 1952.
Carr, D. E. B. "Adult Literacy in Buganda," *Corona*. London: April 1952, pp. 144–48.
Carstairs, G. Morris. "Medicine and Faith in Rural Rajasthan," in Benjamin D. Paul, ed., *Health, Culture and Community*. New York: Russell Sage Foundation, 1955.

Cassel, John. "A South African Health Program," in Benjamin D. Paul, ed., *Health, Culture and Community*. New York: Russell Sage Foundation, 1955.

Castillo, Hernan, Teresa Castillo, and Arcenio, Revilla. "Accopata: The Reluctant Recipient of Technological Change." Monograph. Ithaca, N.Y.: Human Organization, 1963.

Christian, H. L. "The La Plaine 3-F Campaign," *Community Development Bulletin*. London: December 1953, pp. 20–22.

Cohen, Ronald. "The Success That Failed, An Experiment in Culture Change in Africa," in *Anthropologica*, vol. 3, No. 1, 1961.

Coutts, Philip. "Five Dams: A Community Development Project in Uganda," *Corona*. London: August 1953.

Covar, Prospero. *The Masagana/Margate System of Planting Rice: A Study of an Agricultural Innovation*. Quezon City: Community Development Research Council, University of the Philippines, 1960.

Cowper, Lawrence T. "Rural Health Education," *Community Development Bulletin*. London: March 1958, pp. 26–29.

Dobyns, Henry F. "Experiment in Conservation," in Edward H. Spicer, ed., *Human Problems in Technological Change*. New York: Russell Sage Foundation, 1952.

Dube, S. C. *India's Changing Villages*. London: Routledge and Kegan Paul, Ltd., 1958.

DuBois, Cora. "The Dominant Value Profile in American Culture," in *American Anthropologist*, vol. 57, No. 6, Pt. 1: 1955.

Einseidel, Luz A. *Success and Failure in Selected Community Development Projects in Batangas*. Quezon City: Community Development Research Council, University of the Philippines, 1960.

Erasmus, Charles J. *Man Takes Control*. Minneapolis: University of Minnesota Press, 1961.

"Everybody's Uncle," *Maryknoll*. June 1959, pp. 20–24.

Evans, A. J. "The Ila VD Campaign," in *The Rhodes-Livingstone Journal*, Capetown, South Africa, No. 9, 1950.

Foster, George M. *Traditional Cultures and the Impact of Technological Change*. New York: Harper and Bros., 1962.

Fraser, T. M. "Sociocultural Parameters in Directed Change," in *Human Organization*. Ithaca, N.Y.: Spring 1963, pp. 96–98.

Freidl, Ernestine. "The Role of Kinship in the Transmission of National Culture of Rural Villages in Mainland Greece," in *American Anthropologist*, vol. 61, No. 1: 1959.

Gillin, John P. "Some Signposts for Policy," in *Social Change in Latin America Today*. New York: Harper and Bros., 1960.

Hayden, Howard. "Community Development in Moturiki, Fiji," *Oversea Education*. London: January 1953, pp. 2–12.

Holmberg, Allen R. "Changing Community Attitudes and Values in Peru: A Case Study in Guided Change," in Richard N. Adams, ed.,

References

Social Change in Latin America Today. New York: Random House, 1960.

Hunt, Chester L. "Cultural Barriers to Point Four," in Lyle W. Shannon, ed., *Underdeveloped Areas.* New York: Harper and Bros., 1957.

"The Hunters." Cambridge: Contemporary Films, Peabody Museum, Harvard University. 16 mm film.

Junod, Violaine. "Entokosweri: Managing a Community Service in an Urban African Area," in *Human Organization.* Ithaca, N.Y.: Spring 1964, pp. 28–35.

Khan, Anwaruzzaman. *Introduction of Tractors in a Subsistence Farm Economy.* Comilla, East Pakistan: Academy for Rural Development, Nazeria Press, 1962.

The Koror Community Center. Technical Paper No. 46. Noumea, New Caledonia: South Pacific Commission, August 1953.

Laufer, Leopold. *Israel and the Developing Countries.* New York: The Twentieth Century Fund, 1967.

Lewis, Oscar. "Medicine and Politics in a Mexican Village," in Benjamin D. Paul, ed., *Health, Culture and Community.* New York: Russell Sage Foundation, 1955.

Link, Eugene P. and Sushila Mehta. *Victories in the Villages—India.* Plattsburgh: New York State University College, 1964. Mimeographed.

Linton, Ralph. *The Study of Man.* New York: Appleton-Century-Crofts, 1936.

Lizitsky, Gene. *Four Ways of Being Human.* New York: Viking Press, 1956.

Mahony, Frank. "Report on a Study of the Pilot Project in Range Management Near Afmadei," in *Community Development Review.* Washington, D.C.: June 1961, pp. 34–39.

Mason, H. "Progress in Pare," *Oversea Education.* London: July 1952.

Matthiessen, Peter. *Under the Mountain Wall.* New York: Ballantine Books, 1962.

Mayer, Albert. *Pilot Project, India.* Berkeley and Los Angeles: University of California Press, 1958.

McClelland, David C. *The Achieving Society.* Princeton, N.J.: Van Nostrand, 1961.

Mead, Margaret. *New Lives for Old.* New York: Wm. Morrow and Co., 1956.

———. *Cultural Patterns and Technical Change.* New York: Mentor Books, 1961.

Millard, I. S. "The Village Schoolmaster as Community Development Leader," in *Mass Education Bulletin.* London: June 1950, pp. 42–45.

"Miss Goodall and the Wild Chimpanzees." Berkeley: University of California, n.d. 16 mm film.

Montgomery, John. *Cases in Vietnamese Administration.* Saigon: Michigan State University—Vietnamese Advisory Group, 1959.
Mtawali, C. W. "A Health Campaign in Tanganyika Territory," in *Community Development Bulletin.* London: June 1951, pp. 54–56.
O'Dea, Thomas F. "Changing Attitudes Toward Economic Cooperation," in *Community Development Review.* Washington, D. C.: March 1958, p. 48–52.
Orata, Pedro T. "Community Education in Rural Philippines," in *Oversea Education.* London: April 1954.
Palmer, J. E. S. "Self-Help to Irrigation," in *Community Development Bulletin.* London: March 1962, pp. 44–45.
Philips, Jane. "The Hookworm Campaign in Ceylon," in Howard M. Teaf, Jr. and Peter G. Franck, eds., *Hands Across Frontiers.* Ithaca, N.Y.: Cornell University Press, 1955.
"Protein Advisory Group," in *United Nations.* Geneva: Food and Agricultural Organization/World Health Organization, 1970.
Roberts, Lydia J. *The Dona Elena Project.* Rio Piedras, Puerto Rico: University of Puerto Rico, Department of Home Economics, 1963.
Schweitzer, Albert. *The Forest Hospital at Nambarene.* New York: Henry Holt, 1931.
Sharp, Lauriston. "Steel Axes for Stone Age Australians," in Edward H. Spicer, ed., *Human Problems in Technological Change,* New York: Russell Sage Foundation, 1952.
Siloe, The Process of Community Development. Bogota: Centro Interamericana de Vivienda y Planeamiento, 1958.
Shamsudeen, A. N. "Lessons From a Set-Back," in *Oversea Education.* London: July 1956, pp. 60–61.
Singh, Rudra Datt. "The Village Level: An Introduction of Green Manuring in Rural India," in Edward H. Spicer, ed., *Human Problems in Technological Change.* New York: Russell Sage Foundation, 1952.
Smith, Bruce L. "Communications Research on Non-Industrial Countries," in Lyle W. Shannon, ed., *Underdeveloped Areas.* New York: Harper and Bros., 1957.
Spicer, E. H. "Sheepmen and Technicians," in E. H. Spicer, ed., *Human Problems in Technological Change,* New York: Russell Sage Foundation, 1952.
Stein, Morris I. "They Volunteered for Peace." New York: New York University, 1964. Mimeographed.
Summary Report for a Rural Cooperative—San Jose de Naranjo, Costa Rica. Washington, D.C.: Pan American Union, 1957.
Textor, Robert B. "Notes on Indonesian Villagers' Participation in Programs to Modernize Rural Life," Indonesia, 1954. Mimeographed.

References

"The Turan Agricultural Project," in *Community Development Bulletin*. London: American Friends Service Committee, 1956.

Useem, John. "Democracy in Progress," in Edward H. Spicer, ed., *Human Problems in Technological Change*. New York: Russell Sage Foundation, 1952.

Uzoma, R. I. "Adult Literacy Work at Akriba in the Delta of the Niger," in *Oversea Education*. London: July 1948, pp. 737–41.

Wagley, Charles. *Cultural Hints for U.S. Personnel Going to Latin America*. Washington, D.C.: Department of State, Foreign Service Institute, 1952.

Wellin, Edward. "Water Boiling in a Peruvian Town," in Benjamin D. Paul, ed., *Health, Culture and Community*, New York: Russell Sage Foundation, 1955.

Yao Darko, Charles. "The Story of Nkwabeng Water Supply," in *Advance*. Ghana Department of Social Welfare and Community Development. January 1962, pp. 69–71.

Index

Ablett, 98, 137, 170
Aboriginals, Australian, 42, 65
Achievement, 213, 220
Adams, R. N., 130
Adaptation, 8, 30
Administrators, 137
Africa, 26, 64, 85, 105, 144, 179, 187
Afro-Americans, 24, 29
Age, 104
Aggression, 13
Agricultural extension, 93
Agriculture, 139, 151, 153, 168, 173, 196
Aguilera, 169
AID, 86
Airplanes, 72, 189
Alcohol, 193
Alers-montalvo, M., 139, 155
Americans, 39, 56, 146, 163
Ancestry, 147
Andrews, S., 97, 122
Animal husbandry, 113
Anthropology, 9, 10, 248
Archeology, 182
Arctic, 30
Arizona, 33
Australopithecus, 26

Bananas, 120
Behavior, 12, 16

Beliefs, 17, 156
Benedict, R., 57
Berreman, 242
Bible, 65
Biological drives, 12
Birth rate, 204
"Black," 19, 23
Blood type, 22
Boats, 72
Bogue, R. and A. Habashy, 141
Brahmin, 140
Breast feeding, 126
Buddhism, 5, 55, 84, 87, 163, 172, 187, 214
Buganda, 174
Burials, 58
Bushman, 32

Cambodia, 84
Capitalism, 47
Captives, 18
Cargo cults, 69
Carr, D. E. B., 174
Carstairs, G. M., 133
Cassel, J., 64, 85, 134, 157
Caste, 51, 145, 152
Castillo, H., 145, 151
Cattle, 64, 85
Central authority, 148, 185
Ceylon, 101

259

Change: cultural, 203; forced, 3, 80; genetic, 15; language, 38; urban, 81; voluntary, 4, 80; *see also* Change agents
Change agents, 1, 5, 7, 83, 106, 113, 131, 232, 248
Children's games, 60
Chimpanzees, 17
China, 75, 77
Christianity, 3, 22, 76, 80, 90, 132, 149, 171
City, 124, 174, 190
Classes, 50, 146
Cleanliness, 212
Clothing, 192
Coffee, 86
Cohen, R., 88
Colonization, 22, 176, 190
Colombia, 55, 101, 124, 138
Comfort, 212
Common sense, 208
Communication, 15, 84, 88, 89, 115, 196; feedback, 89, 91, 97, 98, 100; intergroup, 98; interpersonal, 96; symbolic, 17
Communism, 80
Community development, 83, 87, 101, 103, 110, 144, 166
Competition, 122, 201
Congo, 144
Conspicuous giving, 45
Continuity, 66, 170
Conservation, 164
Consumption, 154
Convenience, 121
Cooperatives, 139, 154, 159, 173
Corn, 77, 93
Cornell, 171
Costa Rica, 122, 139, 155
Coutts, P., 116
Covar, P., 105
Cowper, L. T., 99, 116, 138
Cultural competition, 67, 69, 70; conservatism, 66; history, 25, 35; integration, 65
Culture, 5, 7, 16, 29, 30, 31, 203, 241; shock, 233
Customs, 5, 60, 61, 103

Dani, 60
Democracy, 3
Demonstration, 93, 131
Developed countries, 33, 35
Dialects, 87
Diffusion, 2, 71, 78
Discrimination, 62
Distribution, 153
Dobyns, H. F., 164
Dominica, 149
Dube, S. C., 90, 153
DuBois, C., 219

Ecology, 63, 224
Economics, 44, 119, 149, 195, 198
Ecuador, 120, 121, 158
Education, 121, 194, 211
Educator, 138
Effort, 219, 222
Egalitarianism, 62, 143, 226
Egypt, 8, 141
Einseidel, L. A., 153, 169
Electricity, 122
Enculturation, 18, 52, 61, 67
End, the, 250
English, 37, 245
Environment, 21, 31, 221, 225
Epidemic, 170
Erasmus, C. J., 56, 120, 121, 124, 136, 158
Eskimo, 32, 39
Etawah, 140
Ethnics, 146, 227
Ethnocentrism, 66, 75, 143, 180
Euro-Americans, 13, 25, 33, 53, 64, 78, 125, 202
Europe, 1, 34
Evans, A. J., 129
Evolution, physical, 14

Factionalism, 127
Farmer, 53
Fatalism, 117, 158

Index

Feasts, 46
Felt need, 115
Females, 228
Fetish, 142
Field techniques, 239–40, 246
Fiesta, 47
Fiji, 166
Finances, 83
Firearms, 2, 41, 43, 76
Flexibility, 167
Food habits, 193
Foster, G. M., 150, 182, 237
Fraser, T. M., 6, 134, 146, 152, 155
Freidl, E., 125
Friends, American, 146, 172
Frontier, 217
Function, 61, 62

Generalization, 39
Generosity, 124
German, 24
Ghana, 141
Ghosts, 57
Gillin, J. P., 140
Goodall, Miss, 17
Gossip, 99, 100
Greece, 125
Greetings, 16
Guam, 99, 116, 138
Guatemala, 129
Guidelines for change, 174

Hair form, 20
Hayden, H., 166
Headman, 141
Health, 114, 157, 168
Holmberg, A. R., 94, 172
Horse, 73
Houses, 30, 124
Humanitarianism, 229
Hunt, C. L., 184
Hunting and gathering, 44, 51
Hybrid corn, 41
Image, 102
Imitation, 125
Independence, 182

Individuality, 229
India, 6, 8, 28, 37, 58, 90, 96, 103, 114, 116, 127, 134, 140, 144, 146, 148, 151, 152, 153, 155, 157, 159, 168, 170, 185, 193, 197, 234, 241
Indians, American, 2, 12, 18, 26, 61, 68, 72, 77, 108, 119, 164
Industrialization, 1, 206
Industry, 70, 112, 198, 205
Informants, 247
Innovations, 3, 134, 135
Instability, 117
Intelligence tests, 25
Interpreters, 246
Inventions, 26, 36, 72
Irrigation, 52, 90, 118, 145, 155
Islam, 227, 231
Israel, 151, 168, 173

Jamaica, 139
Japan, 24, 35, 75, 77
Jordan, 97, 128
Junod, 105

Khan, A., 154, 155, 159
Kinship, 46, 48, 143, 183, 197, 211

Labor, 162
Land tenure, 153
Language, 36, 39, 86, 186, 192, 244
Laos, 5, 55, 86, 117, 121, 129, 141, 163, 165, 172, 187, 188, 201, 226, 230, 242
Latin America, 29
Latrines, 6, 144
Laufer, L., 168
Leaders: civic, 141; religious, 106
Leadership, 136
Learning, 17
Lewis, O., 145, 148
Life stages, 60
Linguistics, 37
Link, E. P., and S. Mehta, 103, 127, 140, 144, 157
Linton, R., 78
Literacy, 121, 173, 191

Lizitsky, G., 42

Machines, 226
Mahony, F., 49, 85, 97, 147
Maintenance, 172
Manus, 202
Maori, 41
Markets, 153
Marriage, 48, 58
Maryknoll, 107
Mason, H., 174
Mass media, 91
Matthiesen, P., 60, 68
Mayer, A., 96, 114, 115, 117, 140, 151, 159
McClelland, D. C., 117
Mead, M., 57, 202
Medicine, 121, 133
Medicine man, 157
Melting pot, 19, 190
Mental ability, 24
Mexico, 145, 148, 150
Middle class, 125, 191
Middle East, 187
Military, 188
Millard, I. S., 139
Minorities, 147, 162, 188
Misperceptions, 92
Missionaries, 80, 245
Modernization, 69
Monsoon, 55
Montgomery, J., 154
Morality, 212, 215
Mtawali, C. W., 92

Nationalism, 180
Nation-state, 49, 79
Nature, 224
Navahos, 57, 61, 108
Nazis, 23
Negroes, 19, 21
Needs, 111
New Guinea, 68, 69
Niehoff, field observations, 87, 93, 104, 121, 129, 136, 141, 165, 236, 242, 243

Nigeria, 56, 88, 90, 120
Nomads, 75, 108
Novelty, 129

O'Dea, T. F., 155, 159
Officials, 136
Orata, P. T., 152

Pacific, 35
Pakistan, 155, 159, 168
Palau, 127, 146
Palmer, J. E. S., 122
Papago, 164
Participant observation, 241
Participation, 161
Peace Corps, 88, 138, 176, 244
Peasants, 44, 46, 80, 117, 194
Penicillin, 56, 120
Personal achievement, 59
Personal characteristics, 102
Peru, 89, 94, 107, 126, 145, 150, 155
Peyote, 77
Philippines, 105, 152, 153, 169
Phillips, J., 101
Plants, 72
Play, 217
Plural societies, 185, 189, 190, 245
Point Four, 55
Politics, 148
Pollution, 6, 33, 63
Population, 179, 203
Power structure, 51
Prayer, 54
Predictability, 107
Prestige, 123
Principle, 215
Profit motive, 46, 119
Progress, 222
Proprietors, 152
Psychology, 9
Pueblo, 58, 74
Puerto Rico, 153

Race, 20, 23, 27, 29
Rapport, 87, 237
Rat control, 116

Index

Rationality, 43, 134, 154, 156
Religion, 139, 184, 198, 212
Reward-punishment, 45, 128
Rhodesia, 129
Rituals, 47, 53, 55, 243
Roads, 153
Roberts, L. J., 153
Roles, 103
Rumors, 100

Schools, 188
Schedules, 151
Schweitzer, A., 144
Shamsudeen, A. N., 168
Science, 54, 70
Sexuality, 13, 14
Siloe, 101
Singh, R. D., 169
Skin color, 21, 22
Slavery, 23
Smallpox, 140
Social change, 76; control, 52; organization, 3, 48, 142; reform, 43; recognition, 14
Socialism, 47
Sociology, 9
Somalia, 49, 97, 137, 147, 170
Soul, 224
Southeast Asia, 28, 32, 53, 74
Soviet Union, 79
Special interest, 49
Specialization, 105
Speciation, 19
Spicer, E. H., 109
Status, 211, 213, 220
Stein, M. I., 138
Subsistence, 45
Success, 220
Supernatural, 52, 57, 156
Survey, 101, 111

Tanzania, 92, 173
Taxes, 79
Technicians, 162
Technology, 40, 70
Territory, 48

Texas, 93
Textor, R. B., 121
Thailand, 117, 122
Theology, 57
Time, 169, 217
Tool making, 15; tradition, 40
Training, 10
Transportation, 189
Transvestites, 62
Troubleshooting, 98
Tribes, 186
Trinidad, 27, 58, 242, 243
Tropics, 34
Tuberculosis, 157
Turkey, 75

Uganda, 116, 128
Underdeveloped, 176
United States, 60, 62, 185
Useem, J., 146

Vaccination, 140
Values, 56, 208, 227
Vegetables, 155
Venereal disease, 92, 129
Vicos, 94, 155, 159, 171
Vietnam, 154, 188, 222, 226
Villages, 7, 54, 66, 67, 90, 195, 219

Wagley, C., 57
Warfare, 13, 60
Water boiling, 89, 126, 158
Wellin, E., 89, 126
Wells, 5, 116, 122, 141, 163, 172
Western, 52, 59, 63, 132
Westernization, 8, 178, 179, 180
"White," 19, 20
Women, 104, 143
Work, 34, 150, 151, 216, 218
Writing, 37, 38, 74

Yao, C., 142
Yaws, 55, 56
Youth, 104, 223

Zulu, 64, 134, 157

LIBRARY OF DAVIDSON COLLEGE